António Vieira

António Vieira

Six Sermons

Edited and Translated by

MÓNICA LEAL DA SILVA

LIAM MATTHEW BROCKEY

OXFORD
UNIVERSITY PRESS

OXFORD
UNIVERSITY PRESS

Oxford University Press is a department of the University of Oxford. It furthers
the University's objective of excellence in research, scholarship, and education
by publishing worldwide. Oxford is a registered trade mark of Oxford University
Press in the UK and certain other countries.

Published in the United States of America by Oxford University Press
198 Madison Avenue, New York, NY 10016, United States of America.

© Oxford University Press 2018

First issued as an Oxford University Press paperback, 2019

Library of Congress Cataloging-in-Publication Data
Names: Vieira, Antonio, 1608-1697, author. | Silva, Monica Leal da, 1967-
editor.
Title: Antonio Vieira : six sermons / translated and edited by Monica Leal
da Silva and Liam Matthew Brockey.
Description: New York : Oxford University Press, 2018. | Includes index.
Identifiers: LCCN 2017042783 (print) | LCCN 2018004820 (ebook) |
ISBN 9780190858575 (ebook) | ISBN 9780190858582 (ebook) |
ISBN 9780190858568 (hardcover) | ISBN 9780190066666 (paperback)
Subjects: LCSH: Catholic Church—Sermons. | Sermons, Portuguese.
Classification: LCC BX1756.V6 (ebook) | LCC BX1756.V6 S5313 2018 (print) |
DDC 252/.02—dc23

For Beatriz and Leonor

Contents

Acknowledgments

OUR MOST HEARTFELT thanks go to Jurgis Elisonas, whose careful reading accompanied us from our first drafts. Noël Golvers, another perennial friend, helped us with our Latin, something for which we are very grateful. We would also like to thank Thomas Cohen, Stuart Schwartz, Ana Maria Valdez, and Herman Prins Salomon for their prompt responses to our questions about António Vieira and for their valuable insights. A special recognition is also due to the librarians and archivists who have undertaken the difficult task of digitalizing books and creating searchable databases. Without these powerful tools, our work would have taken much more time than it did. In particular, we are grateful to Dra. Cristina Pinto Basto, Dra. Fátima Gomes, and the rest of the staff of the Biblioteca da Ajuda in Lisbon, as well as the librarians at the Biblioteca Nacional de Portugal. We are also grateful for the professionalism of the production team at Oxford University Press in New York and Newgen KnowledgeWorks in Chennai, and in particular our production coordinator and copyeditors, whose competence and erudition helped make this a far better book. Finally, we owe a debt of gratitude to family and friends in America and overseas whose continual encouragement helped sustain our spirits over the years required to achieve our goal. This book is dedicated to our daughters, Beatriz and Leonor, who we hope will read these sermons in the original Portuguese.

About the Editors/Translators

Mónica Leal da Silva was born in Lisbon, Portugal, and educated at the University of Lisbon. She has taught Portuguese language and literature at the elementary, secondary, and university levels for over twenty years. Since immigrating to the United States, she has taught at Princeton University and Michigan State University. Mónica Silva is the author of three acclaimed works of children's literature, as well as works of cultural criticism, published in Portugal. She also has made translations of historical scholarship in the United States and the United Kingdom. In addition to teaching and writing, Mónica Silva has contributed to published forums on social and educational issues.

Liam Matthew Brockey is an historian of early modern Europe, and a specialist in the history of Roman Catholicism and the Society of Jesus. Educated at the University of Notre Dame and Brown University, he has written extensively on Jesuit missions in China, Japan, and India, as well as on the Portuguese Empire. He is the author of two monographs, *Journey to the East: The Jesuit Mission to China, 1579–1724* and *The Visitor: André Palmeiro and the Jesuits in Asia*, and many scholarly articles. Liam Matthew Brockey has recently served as president of the American Catholic Historical Association and was elected to the Academia Portuguesa da História.

VERA EFFIGIES CELEBERRIMI,
P. ANTONII VIEYRA,
è Societ. Jesu, Lusitanicorum Regum Concionatoris, et Concionatorum Principis;
quem dedit Lusitania mundo Ulyssipo Lusitaniæ, Societati Brasilia Obijt Bahiæ
Prope nonagenarius Die 18 July Ann. 1697. Quiesoit in regio Collegij Bahy:
ensis templo, ubi sepultus frequentissimo urbis concursu, æterno orbis desiderio
Arnoldo VanWesterhout Sculp. Rom. Sup. perm.

Engraving of António Vieira by Arnold van Westerhout, Rome, first quarter of the
eighteenth century. Biblioteca Nacional de Portugal, shelfmark E-4341-P.

Introduction

ANTÓNIO VIEIRA IS the most celebrated seventeenth-century author in Portuguese. In his day, Vieira's combination of moral courage and eloquence made him a towering figure across early modern Europe and around the Atlantic world. In a golden age of oratory, he was one of its most skilled practitioners. In a time of imperial rivalries, he took a hand in struggles on a global scale. And in an era of spiritual and political crisis, he spoke with a singular, tirelessly critical voice.

Vieira first gained renown in colonial pulpits, as a young Jesuit in Brazil. He enjoyed even greater success upon his return to his native Portugal, playing the role of royal confidant and court preacher. His field of action, however, was not limited to Lisbon: Vieira traveled throughout northern Europe and to the papal curia in Rome as the diplomatic envoy of João IV, the king of Portugal. Then, after a decade in the highest circles of power, he crossed the Atlantic once again to work as a missionary in the Amazon. Whether in Europe or Brazil, he employed his forceful rhetoric against the corruptions of his day. He was fearless in the face of powerful adversaries, repeatedly confronting the viciousness of the Inquisition and the consuming greed of colonial society. Words were his weapons. Vieira spoke like the biblical prophets he so admired, chastising some, consoling others, seeking to be a pastor for all who heard him. Those who listened could not help but stand in awe of his eloquence, even if some saw it as more of a reason to persecute him.

Vieira's life spanned nearly the whole of the seventeenth century, from the age of Bellarmine until that of Bossuet. The Europe of his birth in 1608 was still dominated by Spain, with Portugal ruled from Madrid by the scions of the house of Habsburg. By the time of his death in 1697, however, Louis XIV of France was the master of the continent, and Portugal had regained its independence. This political reconfiguration was the outcome of decades of war and social upheaval, and Vieira witnessed much of it from privileged positions at Europe's courts. In Lisbon, Paris, Rome, or The Hague, he had a clear view of the great shifts that took place during his lifetime. But unlike other continental observers who trained their gaze on Europe alone, Vieira was a man of a new age, although one keenly conscious of his heritage. His horizons stretched around the world. At his birth and in his youth, in the early 1600s, Portugal still possessed a globe-spanning empire. Over the course of his life, the vast Portuguese overseas domains in Asia, Africa, and South America contracted in the face of challenges by Dutch, English, and French rivals. The tribulations of empire were therefore never far from his mind, and they distinctly tinged Vieira's prophetic vision.

António Vieira belonged to both the Old World and the New. He therefore invites comparison not only with his peers in early modern Europe but also with the famed preachers of the Atlantic World whose sermons and tracts are the foundational texts of American history. Like his counterparts in the colonies to the north, such as Roger Williams, Richard Mather, or John Cotton, Vieira made pastoral work in Brazil synonymous with political action. But unlike these men, whose influence stretched mainly between colony and metropole, Vieira's presence was felt wherever his words were read or heard around the Catholic world, whether in Castilian at Mexico City, where Sor Juana Inés de la Cruz read him; in Italian at Rome, where Queen Christina of Sweden heard him preach; or in Portuguese in Beijing, where his Jesuit missionary brethren received copies of his printed sermons.

For all of Vieira's importance in his day, his works were not translated into English then, and even though his importance in the cultures of Portugal and Brazil has only grown since, he remains largely unknown to readers of English. He enjoyed considerable fame in late seventeenth-century Europe, but not even the fact that Catherine of Braganza, the Catholic daughter of Vieira's patron King João IV, was the royal consort of the English sovereign sufficed to make him known across the Channel. In the intervening centuries, few attempts have been made to translate his texts into English.

This book is an endeavor to make Vieira's justly celebrated discourses available in English, even if the six texts translated here represent only a small selection from the twelve volumes of his sermons. It shall, moreover, be noted that his collected works consist of more than just sacred oratory; they also comprise theological writings and political tracts, as well as hundreds of letters.[1] The sermons translated here will serve as an introduction to Vieira's thought and style as communicated from pulpits in Portugal and Brazil. The texts were written over the span of half a century, from the early 1640s until the early 1690s, that is, from his youth in Bahia, to his mature years in Lisbon and São Luís de Maranhão, to his old age once again in Bahia. In these sermons, Vieira addresses a range of themes related to the spiritual and moral aspects of life in the seventeenth-century Atlantic world: colonial wars, the creation of a plantation society, the unjust treatment of indigenous peoples and African slaves, the corrupt practices of imperial administrators, the role of missionaries and the difficulties of conversion, and the faults of contemporary preachers who failed to stir their audiences to piety, charity, and justice. These were the burning questions that fired Vieira's rhetoric, the ones that made him such a controversial figure in his day, and all of them emerge clearly in the selection of sermons found here.

ANTÓNIO VIEIRA WAS born in Lisbon on February 6, 1608, into a family of minor officials.[2] Little would have been known about his ancestry had the Inquisition not sought to examine his family tree in the 1660s for traces of Jewish or Muslim blood. The investigation revealed that his paternal grandfather, who later became a clerk, had been in the service of a provincial nobleman, as had his paternal grandmother, a *mulata* of African or Indian origin. Vieira's father, Cristóvão Vieira Ravasco, became a clerk in the municipal courts of Lisbon after a stint as a soldier, and his mother, Maria de Azevedo, was employed as a baker by a Franciscan community.

---

1. An edition of Vieira's complete works, accompanied by scholarly analyses, has appeared recently. See António Vieira, *Obra Completa*, ed. Pedro Calafate and José Eduardo Franco, 4 vols. in 30 bks. (Lisbon: Círculo de Leitores, 2013–2014).

2. The following sketch of Vieira's life derives from early modern and modern biographies. The first account of his life was written by his fellow Jesuit André de Barros (1675–1754) nearly half a century after Vieira's death. The first comprehensive modern biography was that of João Lúcio de Azevedo, published almost a century ago, a text which retains its value despite its age. More recently, J. J. van den Besselaar and Ronaldo Vainfas have written more condensed analyses of Vieira's life and times. In English, the biographical sketches by Charles Boxer and Thomas Cohen are essential. See Barros, *Vida do Apostolico Padre Antonio Vieyra* (Lisbon: Officina Sylviana, 1746); Azevedo, *História de António Vieira*, 2 vols. (Lisbon: Livraria Clássica, 1918–1921); Van den Besselaar, *Antônio Vieira: O Homem, A Obra, As Ideias* (Lisbon: Ministério da Educação e Ciência, 1981); Vainfas, *Antônio Vieira: Jesuíta do Rei* (São Paulo: Companhia das Letras, 2011); Boxer, *A Great Luso-Brazilian Figure: Padre Antonio Vieira, S.J., 1608–1697* (London: Hispanic and Luso-Brazilian Councils, 1957); and Cohen, *The Fire of Tongues: António Vieira and the Missionary Church in Brazil and Portugal* (Stanford, Calif.: Stanford University Press, 1998).

His maternal grandfather had served in the royal armory in Lisbon, and this position helped secure the family's later status, since Vieira's father gained a place in royal administration as part of his wife's dowry. And so Cristóvão Vieira Ravasco left for Brazil in 1609 as one of the first clerks of the newly erected colonial high court, bringing the whole family to settle in Salvador da Bahia five years later. There, Vieira's mother bore another son and two daughters, all of whom spent their lives in Brazil. Longevity was a family trait. His father reportedly died at the age of ninety-eight, while his mother lived until she was at least eighty.[3]

Little is known about the future preacher's youth. At the end of his life, Vieira wrote down some recollections that give a hazy picture of the time before he entered the Society of Jesus. In addition to the education he received from his mother, he studied at the Jesuit college in Bahia. There he would have followed the typical academic program used in Jesuit schools throughout Europe and in the Spanish and Portuguese overseas colonies: years of Latin grammar, reinforced by compositions and declamations, gradually turning toward the study of rhetoric based on the writings of authors such as Cicero and Quintilian. According to his first biographer, a fellow Jesuit in the early eighteenth century, Vieira had great difficulty memorizing his lessons and writing. Convinced that his mediocre ability required intervention, Vieira prayed daily that the Virgin would lift the clouds that seemed to impede his thoughts until one day he felt an *estalo*, a smack, which resulted in instant illumination and a dramatic change in his academic success. After that moment, Vieira recalled, his newfound eloquence gained him the respect of his fellow students and of his Jesuit teachers, who began to consider him as a candidate for their order.[4]

In 1623, when he turned fifteen, António Vieira joined the Society of Jesus. This was not an unusual choice for talented, pious students who studied in Jesuit schools. His biographers, however, have long noted that he joined without alerting his parents, who might not have given their consent, since he was their eldest son. Vieira's years as a novice can hardly be described as a time of meditative retreat from the world. Halfway through

---

3. Vainfas, *Vieira*, pp. 22–23. For a general overview of colonial Brazilian history, see Stuart B. Schwartz, *Early Brazil: A Documentary History to 1700*, trans. Stuart B. Schwartz and Clive Willis (Cambridge: Cambridge University Press, 2010), and Leslie Bethell, ed., *Colonial Brazil* (Cambridge: Cambridge University Press, 1997).

4. The famous *estalo* was first described by Barros. See his *Vida*, p. 8.

his initial two-year probation period, Dutch forces besieged and captured Salvador da Bahia, forcing the population, Jesuits included, to flee the city. A joint Portuguese-Spanish fleet brought an army which successfully reclaimed Bahia in May of 1625, just before Vieira finished his novice training. The experience of living in the Brazilian countryside inspired him to devote himself to teaching doctrine to Indians and African slaves, and so he set to studying their languages, but his superiors did not agree to divert him from the standard academic track. Rather, they assigned Vieira to teach Latin, intending for him to resume his studies after some time spent as a teacher, as was common for young Jesuits. It was also common for junior members of the Society to compose the annual reports that Jesuit custom mandated to be sent to the order's superiors in Rome. In 1626, Vieira was assigned the task of composing the account of the Jesuits' activities during the siege of Bahia, an invaluable eyewitness account of this important event and the oldest of his writings that have survived to the present.[5]

António Vieira's formal education was concluded in the early 1630s as he proceeded through the Society's philosophy and theology courses. Like his confreres who reached advanced studies, he read deeply in Aristotle's works and then in Aquinas's *Summa Theologica*. Upon reaching the midpoint of his theology studies in 1634, he was ordained a priest. When he had finished reading speculative theology, by the late 1630s, it was time for him to be assigned a specific ministry.[6] In recognition of his academic competence and maturity, Vieira's superiors charged him with teaching part of the theology course in Salvador. It was in this same period that he began to gain fame in the pulpit. The oldest sermon in his collected works dates from 1633, but his first major sermon was the congratulatory discourse he gave after a Dutch attack on Bahia was repulsed in 1638. Taking to the pulpit again in 1640 at the moment of another colonial crisis, he cemented his early renown with the first sermon included here. The strain of repeated attacks against the city of Salvador accounted for

---

5. Details of Vieira's early years within the Society of Jesus are found in the modern biographical sketch by Serafim Leite, the author of the most comprehensive history of the Brazilian Jesuits. See his *História da Companhia de Jesus no Brasil*, 10 vols. (Rio de Janeiro: Instituto Nacional do Livro, 1938–1950), vol. 4, pp. 3–8. The annual letter mentioned here, in Vieira's Portuguese translation of his Latin original, can be found in his *Cartas*, ed. João Lúcio de Azevedo, 3 vols. (Lisbon: Imprensa Nacional, 1970), vol. 1, pp. 3–70.

6. Further details about Jesuit education in colonial Brazil are found in Leite, *História*, vol. 7, pp. 141–189.

the depth of feeling that Vieira expressed as he addressed God and his fellow colonists.[7]

The early flourishing of Vieira's oratory came at a crucial moment. Not only did the Dutch fleet abandon its siege of Bahia in 1640, but a palace coup later that year returned a Portuguese king to the throne in Lisbon after sixty years of Castilian rule. Owing to his youth and intellectual vigor, as well as to the reputation of the Society of Jesus in Lisbon, Vieira earned a place as one of the three men sent to Portugal to proclaim Brazilian loyalty to João IV. Once in Lisbon, Vieira developed a personal friendship with the new king and queen that would endure for years. At the monarchs' request, he remained in Portugal for the next decade to serve as royal adviser, confessor, and preacher. So from the other side of the Atlantic came a new, forceful voice, which would be heard not just among colonial administrators but at the royal court and by the king himself. Vieira had a meteoric rise. His demonstrations of oratorical skill on the most important national stage earned him recognition and the support of influential political allies. This combination of alliances and patronage turned the gifted preacher into a powerful figure.

THE PRINCIPAL ELEMENTS of António Vieira's thought began to emerge during his time in Portugal in the 1640s. There are two that predominate in his sermons and other writings, one pastoral and the other prophetic. They reinforce each other and at times are difficult to separate. The pastoral element had its roots in his training as a Jesuit but also stemmed from a deep-seated conviction of the possibility for all to experience conversion and merit salvation. The prophetic one is a unique vision, with messianic overtones, of a divine plan for the Portuguese Empire. The combination of these two impulses spurred Vieira's writing and actions, aimed at reforming contemporary society and elucidating God's will. Although he would only begin to put his theories to paper two decades later, the germ of his broader vision was already present in the early years of his first stay in Portugal.[8]

---

7. On Dutch attacks on Bahia, see C. R. Boxer, *Salvador de Sá and the Struggle for Brazil and Angola, 1602–1686* (London: Athlone, 1952), pp. 40–68, and C. R. Boxer, *The Dutch in Brazil* (Oxford: Clarendon, 1957), pp. 19–27, 85–98. More broadly, the presence of the Dutch in Brazil has been recently re-evaluated in a volume of essays entitled *The Legacy of Dutch Brazil*, ed. Michiel van Groesen (Cambridge: Cambridge University Press, 2014).

8. Vieira's contribution to the spiritual context of the Portuguese Restoration is discussed in Van den Besselaar, *Vieira*, pp. 16–35, and João Francisco Marques, *A Paranética Portuguesa e a Dominação Filipina*, 2nd ed. (Lisbon: Imprensa Nacional, 2010), pp. 375–393.

The acclamation of King João IV in 1640 was, for Vieira, the first step in the realization of a providential plan for Portugal and its empire. But he was very aware that the new king was in a weak position: Not only did Philip IV of Spain not concede defeat to the Portuguese subjects who had risen in revolt, the papacy did not recognize the new king's legitimacy, and the Dutch did not slow their assaults on the Portuguese colonial empire. To fight battles against Castile on the Iberian Peninsula, to wage a diplomatic war against the Habsburgs in the courts of Europe, and to engage the Dutch on the high seas around the globe was a trio of challenges that demanded more resources than João IV could muster. Vieira, a man of astute political vision, was not blind to this, and he repeatedly suggested changes to royal policy that would shore up the new regime. Among his ideas was one that clearly reveals the twin guiding principles of Vieira's thought: João IV had to put an end to the harassment of Portuguese New Christians by the Inquisition.

The term "New Christians" refers to individuals of Jewish ancestry who, by the seventeenth century, had suffered more than a hundred years of institutionalized discrimination and outright persecution for suspicion of heresy. New Christians were numerous among the Portuguese mercantile elite, and the Inquisition's aggressive moves drove many of them into exile. Seeing their commercial savvy as crucial to the success of the Portuguese Restoration, Vieira urged the king to bar the Inquisition from targeting New Christian merchants. The pastoral perspective also made Vieira reject the idea, then widespread among Portuguese clergy and laity, that New Christians had contaminated blood and were therefore a permanent threat to the "Old Christian" community. Indeed, he would later denounce any essential distinction between Christians. In the 1640s, Vieira took his notions a step beyond the embrace of New Christians. He further proposed that the king accept the return of Portuguese Jews, taking the presence of Jewish communities in Italy and Rome itself, where they lived under papal authority, as reason for dismissing the objections of Inquisitors and other critics. There is no understating the bold nature of such proposals: the Holy Office of the Inquisition, in addition to many other lay and clerical voices, including those of many Jesuits, had not only sustained a climate of virulent anti-Jewish rhetoric but fomented violent persecutions against Jews and New Christians in Portugal for decades.[9]

---

9. On Vieira's proposals, as well as the issue of New Christians more generally, see António José Saraiva, *The Marrano Factory: The Portuguese Inquisition and its New Christians,*

The prophetic side of Vieira's thought was formed through his long study of sacred scripture, especially the books of the Old Testament, and his understanding of Portuguese history.[10] He concluded that God had chosen the Portuguese to bring about the unification of the world under the standard of Christ. This divine mission had been confirmed, in his view, by the voyages of discovery that began in the early 1400s and the articulation of the empire in the succeeding decades. This expansion, which had revealed the true dimensions of the world, had finally permitted the gospel to be preached around the globe. The efforts of his Jesuit brethren to spread Christianity in Asia, Africa, and the Americas had played no small role in this endeavor, from the journeys of Francis Xavier in the 1540s to the missions of Vieira's time, but their work was far from finished. Confident that there was a guiding force behind history, he probed the prophetic works of the Bible to grasp the various ways in which God had made His plan known to men. Vieira's search for insight took him deep into ancient and modern commentaries, as well as to patristic writings. Interestingly, he sought living Jewish authorities on the Hebrew texts that he considered most crucial. For instance, while serving on the king's behalf in negotiations to end Dutch hostilities against the Portuguese colonies between 1646 and 1648, Vieira met with the principal rabbis of Amsterdam. His later prophetic writings bear the marks of these encounters, and with Menasseh ben Israel in particular.

Vieira's travels on behalf of King João's diplomatic and economic interests took him not only to the Netherlands but also to France and England in the late 1640s. Service to the Braganza monarchy, however, was not his sole motive: he was acting on his own convictions when he sought to preserve Portugal's newfound independence. To this end, Vieira attempted to convince New Christian merchants living in exile in northern Europe to make loans to the crown.[11] He also sought marital alliances for the heirs

1536–1765, trans. and rev. H. P. Salomon and I. S. D. Sassoon (Leiden: Brill, 2001), esp. pp. 192–217.

10. A useful overview of the prophetic themes in Vieira's work, as well as a sampling of his prophetic writings, is found in J. J. van den Besselaar, Antônio Vieira: Profecia e Polêmica (Rio de Janeiro: EdUERJ, 2002). An analysis in English is found in Cohen, Fire of Tongues, pp. 119–191, and Maria Ana Travassos Valdez, Historical Interpretations of the "Fifth Empire": Dynamics of Periodization from Daniel to António Vieira (Leiden: Brill, 2010), esp. pp. 223–314.

11. Scholars have long maintained that Vieira was instrumental in ensuring that New Christian investors would provide capital for the General Brazil Company, chartered by King João IV in 1649, by insisting that the crown protect investors from prosecution by the Inquisition. This

to the Portuguese throne, in particular a French wife for the king's old-est son. Judging it to be nearly impossible for the Portuguese to confront both Spain and the United Provinces, Vieira went so far as to suggest that the king sell or cede Pernambuco, the part of northeastern Brazil that the Dutch had occupied since 1630, as the price for peace with that tenacious adversary.[12] Such strong words on political matters made him a formidable figure at court but also gained him many detractors. Not only was his sug-gestion that Portugal abandon part of its empire taken as a treasonous betrayal in some court circles, the Inquisition resented his proposals to check its power. Indeed, many of Vieira's fellow Jesuits did not appreci-ate his fight with such a feared rival, especially since they supported the Inquisition's work of persecution. Moreover, Vieira had chosen an impoli-tic side in an internal debate about the Jesuits' Province of Portugal, which he favored splitting into two. So controversial were his interventions that the Jesuit curia in Rome sent orders to dismiss him from the Society. King João IV blocked the Portuguese provincial officer from delivering this blow and instead chose to send Vieira on a diplomatic mission to Rome in early 1650. Unsuccessful in Italy, where Spanish interests reigned, Vieira retreated to Lisbon. There, in light of his recent difficulties, he decided in 1652 to become a missionary. The king offered to nominate Vieira for a bishopric, but he rejected the idea, since it would have obliged him to leave the Society of Jesus. He preferred instead to return to Brazil.[13]

Rather than go back to Bahia, however, Vieira chose the Amazon as his mission field. His ambition was to reanimate the Jesuit endeavor in Maranhão, an area along the far northern coast of Brazil. That mission had faltered in the previous decade, when his colleagues were expelled by mutinous colonists or lost in shipwrecks. While this territory is an integral part of Brazil today, in 1650 it was a distant frontier, one sepa-rated from the region of Salvador da Bahia by great distance and difficult

---

interpretation has recently been revised considerably, insisting that the presence of English merchant capital, as well as Old Christian mercantile interests, played more important roles in this royal project, Vieira's overtures to New Christian merchants notwithstanding. For a brief discussion in English, see Leonor Freire Costa, "Merchant Groups in the 17th-century Brazilian Sugar Trade: Reappraising Old Topics with New Research Insights," *E-Journal of Portuguese History* 2.1 (Summer 2004): pp. 1–11.

12. The complex negotiations between the Portuguese and the Dutch over Pernambuco, with special attention to Vieira's proposal, are analyzed in detail by Evaldo Cabral de Mello in *O Negócio do Brasil: Portugal, os Países Baixos e o Nordeste, 1641–1669*, 2nd ed. (Rio de Janeiro: Topbooks, 1998), pp. 53–118.

13. Leite, *História da Companhia de Jesus*, vol. 4, pp. 12–32.

sailing conditions. Moreover, from 1630 until 1654, Dutch occupiers held Pernambuco, a large region between the colonial capital and Maranhão. The Dutch colonial presence, though it was about to end by the time of Vieira's return, effectively split Portuguese Brazil in two. So if it was a true missionary challenge that he sought when he sailed to São Luís de Maranhão in 1653, Vieira was not to be disappointed. He was headed for a distant, unruly fringe of the Portuguese Empire where recent Jesuit memory was marked by all manner of mortal reverses.

At issue in many of the Jesuits' struggles in Maranhão was the enslavement of indigenous peoples, a practice that Vieira would fight with even more vigor than his predecessors. Unlike in the area of Bahia, where slaves imported from Africa had replaced indigenous ones over the course of the preceding century, landowners in Maranhão relied upon forced labor by Amazonian Indians. Repeated royal decrees had attempted to ban Indian slavery, but none could remain in force when confronted with the determined resistance of the settler population. Alleging the impossibility of paying for Indian labor and citing the barbaric ways of the indigenous peoples, colonists argued for the right to own slaves captured in just wars, or to ransom those who faced death by cannibalism from even wilder savages. Fully aware of the specious nature of these arguments, mission superior Vieira, like his predecessors, sought to insert himself and his confreres between the indigenous peoples and the settlers. The Jesuits' goal was therefore to protect the Indians from the depredations of the colonists by denouncing unjust enslavement, all the while ensuring that indigenous peoples were evangelized.[14]

The Jesuit party arrived in mission territory at São Luís de Maranhão in early 1653 and found themselves almost immediately embroiled in controversy over the question of Indian slavery. A new royal order to free all indigenous slaves had been emitted coincident with the Jesuits' arrival, something the settlers promptly blamed on them. Vieira and his colleagues attempted to avoid an immediate confrontation on the issue and as a result were not expelled right away. At length, however, he could not keep silent about the injustices that he witnessed in the colony. It was in the pulpits of São Luís that he offered some of his most moving sermons, denouncing colonial vices and hypocrisy with memorable verve.

---

14. António Vieira's role in the debates over Indian slavery in the Amazon is discussed in detail in John Hemming, *Red Gold: The Conquest of the Brazilian Indians* (Cambridge, Mass.: Harvard University Press, 1978), pp. 312–344.

The Sermon of Saint Anthony, translated in the present volume, shows Vieira at his most original, reproaching his audience in the Brazilian wilderness through an allegory of fish in Atlantic waters. Facing resistance so rebellious that it succeeded in having the crown withdraw its total ban on Indian enslavement, Vieira returned to Lisbon in 1654 to seek new laws to facilitate his efforts.[15]

Vieira was confident of a warm embrace at court, despite the resistance he had felt in Maranhão. He sought and received provisions from the king to mitigate settler maltreatment of the Indians, especially the enslavement that resulted from illegal capture and trade. Vieira's recent challenges in the mission field are discussed in the Lenten sermons that he preached during his stay in Lisbon in 1655, two of which are included here. Now that he was an outsider to the politics and factionalism that had nearly brought about his ruin six years earlier, he spared no one with his thundering oratory. In both his Sexagesima Sermon and the Sermon of the Good Thief, Vieira took aim at the temporal and spiritual administrators of the Portuguese Empire.[16] In the first of these sermons, which he preached in the royal chapel, he celebrated the missionary vocation and pilloried the ineffectiveness of preachers whose empty words produced no spiritual benefits. In the second, he exposed the ways in which imperial officials gained illicit rewards from their posts and showed how the complicity of kings in their officials' crimes would lead to their mutual damnation.

After delivering his rhetorical blows, Vieira headed back to the Amazon to spend the next decade fighting settlers on the question of Indian slavery. From his base at São Luís de Maranhão, he traveled about Maranhão and Pará, the expansive territory near the mouth of the Amazon River. His work was initially aided by the presence of a strong royal governor, André Vidal de Negreiros, who actively investigated the purported justice of the so-called just wars that had produced many of the settlers' captive laborers. But relations between the Jesuits and the settlers became tense after this official's departure, especially as the missionaries sought to administer the Indians according to the terms of the royal edicts secured by Vieira. Without the strong arm of royal government to assist in their efforts to minister to the indigenous inhabitants of a vast region, the Jesuits were no match for the settlers.

---

15. On Vieira's sermons about Brazil and those given in pulpits there, see Cohen, *Fire of Tongues*, pp. 50–118.

16. The political context of Vieira's 1655 Lenten sermons is examined ibid., pp. 66–93.

Vieira and his brethren, however, did not remain barricaded in a colonial cloister during these conflicts. They headed out on expeditions up the region's rivers in search of new groups to proselytize. In addition to supervising his subordinates' journeys as superior in Maranhão, Vieira was appointed inspector of the missions in that district in 1658. This task obliged him to visit the *aldeias*, indigenous villages, to which the Jesuits ministered, and to draw up a set of rules for missionary life and pastoral care.[17] But in the silence of the Amazonian forests Vieira's thoughts strayed far beyond strictly missionary concerns. There he contemplated the broader question of God's plans for the Portuguese Empire and began to set his ideas down in writing. Picking up the prophetic threads left behind by the poet Gonçalo Annes Bandarra in the early sixteenth century, Vieira elaborated a new vision of the role of Portugal and its monarchs in the creation of the Fifth Empire to which the Book of Daniel alludes. Vieira also drew on the millenarian strands of Portuguese thought which held that King Sebastião had not perished in battle in Morocco in 1578 and that he would one day return to claim his rightful throne. Seeing that João IV had indeed restored Portuguese independence, Vieira associated him with these prophetic notions and envisioned that the king—even after his death in 1656—would return to complete the work of ushering in the new global, Christian imperial age under the Portuguese royal standard. These ideas, set down in a 1659 letter titled *Esperanças de Portugal*, "Hopes of Portugal," and sent to a few select figures at court, were bound to arouse suspicion. The powerful enemies left behind by Vieira in Lisbon had long dreamed of revenge, and this written proof of his unusual theories would give them the opportunity to exact it.

EVENTS IN MARANHÃO brought about Vieira's return to Portugal before long. Six years of confrontation in the Amazon over the issue of Indian slavery finally reached a breaking point. Once again, the Jesuits faced implacable anger, and once again the colonists had the upper hand. Vieira and his colleagues were imprisoned and put aboard Lisbon-bound ships in 1661. This time, however, instead of resuming his privileged position at court, Vieira found himself facing a changed political scene. The weak young king, Afonso VI, was under the control of a court faction

---

17. The rules that Vieira drew up are analyzed and reproduced in Luiz Felipe Baêta Neves, *Vieira e a Imaginação Social Jesuítica: Maranhão e Grão-Pará no Século XVII* (Rio de Janeiro: Topbooks, 1997), pp. 137–182, 387–400.

that resented Vieira's influence, and the Jesuit's longtime ally, the dowager queen, could do little to protect him. It was at this moment that the Inquisition moved against Vieira, taking his outlandish claims about the resurrection of João IV as evidence of heresy. But realizing that Vieira was a formidable adversary who would be difficult to convict, the inquisitors took additional precautions to isolate him as they prepared their attack. He was sent away from Lisbon, where his admirers and allies were still numerous, to house arrest in Coimbra, and his writings were forwarded to the Roman Inquisition to be evaluated by the pope's own theologians. Roman condemnation of Vieira's ideas seemed to seal his fate, but the Jesuit would prove his tenacity in theological argument. The Holy Office would not come out of this duel on top.[18]

In his defense against the accusation of heresy in the early 1660s, Vieira played for time. Uncharacteristically, his judges permitted him to remain in a Jesuit house near Coimbra while he recovered from several bouts of illness. After recovering his health, he successfully pleaded for a delay during which to produce a written explanation of the eschatological ideas outlined in his 1659 *Esperanças de Portugal*. Deprived of books, Vieira relied on his prodigious memory in preparing his response, recalling a wealth of patristic sources as well as points from medieval and early modern commentaries. A man of millenarian convictions who considered the dawn of a new age to be imminent, he delayed in the hope of divine deliverance. But the inquisitors grew tired of Vieira's stalling and moved him from his house arrest to their jail in the autumn of 1665. Shortly afterward, they leveled charges of heresy, suggesting that his messianic prophecies were a form of Judaizing.[19] His close relations with New Christians and his support for the return of Jews to Portugal only served to confirm the inquisitors' suspicions. In the end, the Inquisition issued a condemnation

---

18. Vieira's confrontation with the Portuguese Inquisition is succinctly reviewed in José Pedro Paiva, "Revisitar o Processo Inquisitorial do Padre António Vieira," *Lusitânia Sacra* 23 (January–June 2011): pp. 151–168. The documents related to his trial have been recently edited by Adma Muhana and Paulo Borges in Vieira, *Obra Completa*, vol. 3, bks. 2, 3, and 4.

19. Recall that Vieira had met with rabbis including Menasseh ben Israel (1604–1657) during his visit to Amsterdam. The parallels between ben Israel's thought and Vieira's are perhaps seen most clearly in the echoes of that author's *Esperança de Israel*, published in Spanish translation at Amsterdam in 1650, and Vieira's *Esperanças de Portugal*. Both texts exist in modern editions. See Menasseh ben Israel, *The Hope of Israel*, trans. Moses Wall, ed. Henry Méchoulan and Gérard Nahon (Oxford: Oxford University Press, 1986), and António Vieira, "Esperanças de Portugal. Quinto império do mundo. Primeira, e Segunda Vida del-Rei Dom João Quarto. Escritas por Gonçaliannes Bandarra" in Vieira, *Obra Completa* ed. Adma Muhana, vol. 3, bk. 4, pp. 63–106.

of Vieira in December 1667, sparing him the capital punishment that it imposed on others convicted of heresy but obliging him to confess his errors. His judges insisted that he hear his sentence twice: once in their court and again in front of his brethren at their college in Coimbra. But instead of seeking to wash their hands of Vieira, the Jesuits stood along-side him in solidarity for the more than two hours that it took to read his condemnation.[20]

The punishments imposed by the inquisitors stipulated that Vieira return to house arrest, that he be deprived of the faculty to preach or debate theological matters, and that he remain in Portugal. But in little over six months, he saw all of these restrictions lifted. The political situation at court had shifted once again, and the palace coup that brought King Pedro II to power saw Vieira's adversaries fall. From condemned prisoner in Coimbra, the sixty-year-old Jesuit returned to grace with the title of royal confessor in Lisbon. His rehabilitation was not complete, however, and he had reason to believe that his good fortune might not last. In order to secure his position, in 1669 Vieira asked for leave to argue at the papal court for the canonization of the Jesuits who had been martyred by Brazilian Indians. Fortunately for him, the situation in Rome was also vastly different from that which he had experienced when he had last been there two decades earlier: not only had Portugal concluded its twenty-eight-year war with Spain, but Pope Clement IX had recognized the Braganza dynasty's claim to the Portuguese throne. A new period of cordiality in Portuguese relations with the papacy had begun after a generation of hostility, and Vieira sought to take advantage of the change. He also intended to turn papal power against the Portuguese Inquisition, to have himself exempted from its jurisdiction at least, and at most to have the tribunal extinguished.

Vieira was warmly received at the Jesuit curia in Rome but was unable to gain an entrée with the ailing Clement IX. He bided his time through the election of Clement X, seeking to perform his duties as procurator for the canonization effort while expanding his circle of allies. Not surprisingly, Vieira won many new friends from the pulpit, and his renown for preaching spread among the city's elite despite the fact that he had only recently begun to learn Italian. In the early 1670s, he was invited into the intellectual circle of Queen Christina, the former ruler of Sweden who had abdicated her throne in 1654 and converted to Catholicism the following year. Vieira preached before the pope, his fellow Jesuits, and also

---

20. Vainfas, *Vieira*, p. 237.

Rome's Portuguese community, winning high praise for his sermons. But the reward he sought came only after five years in Rome when the pope turned to consider the activities of the Portuguese Inquisition. Vieira had intended for Clement X to reform the tribunal, and to that end he wrote denunciatory tracts which accused it of fabricating heretics in order to justify its existence. Ideally, the Jesuit envisioned, the distinction between "Old Christians" and "New Christians" would be abolished and, along with it, any consideration of purity of blood.[21] In all likelihood swayed by Vieira's condemnations, Clement X proclaimed the suspension of the tribunal in Portugal in 1674 and in the following year exempted Vieira forever from the jurisdiction of the Portuguese Inquisition.

With a formidable shield against persecution to arm him, the famed preacher returned to Lisbon. Arriving in late 1675, Vieira was once again received warmly at court, where he took part in meetings of the royal council and assumed the role of elder statesman. He was instrumental in securing yet another royal decree that prohibited Indian slavery and in ensuring the appointment of an official board made up of representatives of religious orders, especially Jesuits, charged with the organization of the mission villages of indigenous peoples in the Amazon region. Vieira also played a role in the establishment of another colonial trading company, one that he hoped would better coordinate investment and agricultural production in Maranhão.[22]

Vieira's most enduring endeavor, one that consumed the final twenty years of his life, was the organization and publication of his considerable corpus of sermons. The superior general of the Society of Jesus and the king of Portugal had both requested that he undertake this daunting task, one that obliged him to revisit the notes he had made over the decades and go over them with a firm editorial hand. To be sure, several of his sermons had been published individually over the years; some had even been translated into Castilian and had circulated widely.[23] In part to eliminate the

---

21. This late period of Vieira's fight against the Inquisition is examined in H. P. Salomon, ed., *Queimar Vieira em estátua: As* Apologias *(1738, 1743) do Senhor Inquisidor António Ribeiro de Abreu em resposta às* Notícias Recônditas *atribuídas ao Pe. António Vieira (1608–1697)* (Lisbon: Universidade de Lisboa, 2014), pp. 21–41.

22. Vieira's final stay in Lisbon is analyzed in Azevedo, *História*, vol. 2, pp. 183–222.

23. This distribution accounts for the texts being read in Mexico City and Beijing. Sor Juana Inés de la Cruz (c. 1651–1695) disputed one of Vieira's theological claims from his *Sermão do Mandato* (c. 1650), causing a public scandal in Mexico City in the early 1690s. See Robert Ricard, "António Vieira et Sor Juana Inés de la Cruz," *Bulletin des Etudes Portugaises et de*

errors found in corrupt versions of his texts and in part to ensure recognition for his ideas by setting them down in print in polished form, Vieira took up the editorial task in the late 1670s. To meet the first goal, he drew up a list of unauthorized editions, which was included in the preface to the first volume, published in 1679. And to meet the second goal, he secured a royal license to bar the printing of other versions of his works in Portugal for a decade.[24] Demand for his printed sermons ran high, and so Vieira continued his efforts until he died, a new volume appearing every year or two even after his death.

António Vieira struck a valedictory tone in the preface to his first volume of sermons, contemplating death as he approached the age of seventy. But the Inquisition returned to Portugal before death came for him. The papal-ordered suspension was lifted in 1681, and the tribunal resumed its habitual persecutions. Weary of his battles with the Holy Office, and wary of its treacherous intents despite his personal exemption from prosecution, Vieira returned to Brazil and retired to Salvador da Bahia. He took up residence in a Jesuit estate on the outskirts of the city, the Quinta do Tanque, preaching occasionally in Salvador. The present volume contains one of these discourses from the end of his life, a sermon given to a slave brotherhood. Much of his time, however, was devoted to writing. In addition to revising his sermons, Vieira resumed his prophetic works. These were projects he had traced in the famous texts that had brought him under attack by the Inquisition. In his final years, Vieira greatly expanded these projects, revealing more fully his understanding of biblical prophecy and Portuguese history, and further demonstrating his skills as an exegete. But unlike his sermons, these writings were not published during his lifetime; it was two decades after his death that his *História do Futuro*, "History of the future," was printed in Lisbon.[25] Vieira's other famous text of this genre,

l'Institut Français au Portugal 12 (1948): pp. 1–34, and Juana Inés de la Cruz, *Selected Writings*, trans. and ed. Pamela Kirk Rappaport (New York: Paulist Press, 2005), pp. 20–24, 219–290. Editions of Vieira's sermons can be found in the catalog of the Jesuits' Beitang library, with evidence of their arrival in Beijing dating to the late seventeenth century. See Noël Golvers, *Portuguese Books and their Readers in the Jesuit Mission of China (17th and 18th centuries)* (Lisbon: CCCM, 2011), pp. 77–79.

24. The list of authorized and unauthorized editions of his sermons is found in the front matter of the first volume, along with the royal privilege which barred rival publications. See António Vieira, *Sermoens* (Lisbon: João da Costa, 1679).

25. The original edition of this work, readily available in digital format, is António Vieira, *Historia do Futuro. Livro Anteprimeyro* (Lisbon: António Pedroso Galrão, 1718). A modern edition is found in Vieira, *Obra Completa*, vol. 3, bk. 1.

the massive synthesis of prophetic writings called the *Clavis Prophetarum*, "Key of the prophets," remained in manuscript for three hundred years.[26]

One should not think that António Vieira's final years in Bahia were idyllic. His return to the colonial capital after many decades spent in Europe and elsewhere in Brazil was a return home and a return to court intrigue. Vieira's relatives in Salvador were part of a political faction; his brother, Bernardo Vieira Ravasco, held an important post in royal administration as secretary of state, and his sister had married one of the high court judges. The return of the celebrated Jesuit preacher and diplomat only served to strengthen the position of the clan within Bahian society. It was perhaps unfortunate for António Vieira that he was drawn into the conflicts between his family and another faction, which was led by a newly appointed governor general. The Jesuit attempted to mediate between his relatives and the governor but was rebuffed, being accused, along with his brother, of complicity in the street violence between the factions which left two men dead in the summer of 1683. Seeing himself and his kin threatened, Vieira availed himself of political remedies from Lisbon. Intervention from highly placed allies in Portugal ensured that the Vieira Ravasco clan would regain its prominence in the end, but only after their enemy in the governor's palace was removed from office.[27]

Beyond these moments of crisis, Vieira kept on corresponding with members of the court until his final days. In order to fulfill a request from the queen of Portugal, Maria Sophia of Neuburg, he prepared a cycle of sermons about Francis Xavier.[28] These texts, one of which is included here,

---

26. Translated and annotated versions of his *Clavis Prophetarum* have only been available since 2000; the most recent edition is António Vieira, *Chave dos Profetas*, trans. António Guimarães Pinto, in Vieira, *Obra Completa*, vol. 3, bks. 5 (Book 1) and 6 (Books 2 and 3). For an analysis of the *Clavis*, see Silvano Peloso, *Antonio Vieira e l'Impero Universale: La Clavis Prophetarum e i Documenti Inquisitoriale* (Viterbo, Italy: Sette Città, 2005); and Valdez, *Historical Interpretations of the "Fifth Empire,"* pp. 32–49, 265–282.

27. This episode is known as the Braço de Prata affair because of the nickname of the governor, Antônio de Sousa Meneses, who had lost his right arm in battle against the Dutch and used a silver limb. Further details about the Vieira Ravasco clan in Bahia and its involvement in the affair are in Stuart B. Schwartz, *Sovereignty and Society in Colonial Brazil: The High Court of Bahia and Its Judges, 1609–1751* (Berkeley: University of California Press, 1973), pp. 275–279. The broader social and cultural context of Bahia in the late seventeenth century is discussed at length in João Adolfo Hansen, *A Sátira e o Engenho: Gregório de Matos e a Bahia do Século XVII,* 2nd ed. (São Paulo: Editora de UNICAMP and Atelié Editorial, 2004), esp. pp. 105–190.

28. The Xavier sermons are found in volume 8 of the editio princeps. See António Vieira, *Xavier Dormindo e Xavier Acordado* (Lisbon: Miguel Deslandes, 1694).

were an extended meditation on Xavier as a missionary and a member of
the Society of Jesus, two of the most salient facets of Vieira's own identity.
It was fitting that the great preacher should carry on speaking until the
end. He persisted even after blindness began to afflict him, dictating his
thoughts to a Jesuit companion. António Vieira died on July 18, 1697, and
was buried in the Jesuit church in Salvador de Bahia. His temporal end
was not, however, the end of his literary production. His writings continued to be published for decades after his death, being received with
great interest not only in Portugal but widely across Catholic Europe and
throughout the Portuguese-speaking world.

DURING HIS LONG life, Vieira gained renown in the pulpits of Brazil and
Europe. This fame endured after his death in the twelve volumes of sermons published between 1679 and 1699, in addition to his other texts and
prophetic writings.[29] In the first instance, the sermons translated in the
present volume were spoken words meant to be heard. Later on, under
Vieira's editorial supervision, they became printed words meant to be
read. Both forms of delivery evoke aspects of the cultural climate of the
Catholic world in the seventeenth century. From the pulpit, the preacher
addressed large audiences who could be moved by changes in tone, dramatic gestures, and changing cadences. In an era that prized a preacher's
ability to elicit emotional responses, such techniques were crucial adjuncts
to eloquence. By contrast, the printed word—even when transcribing an
oral discourse—stood alone on the page. Devotional texts, sermons among
them, served for contemplation as well as for inspiration. But some of
them were, then as now, also prized for their literary merits, that is, for
their structure, their style, their practice of exegesis and their display of
erudition.[30]

---

29. As a result, the scholarly bibliography on Vieira's thought is vast and continually expanding. In conjunction with the three hundredth anniversary of his death, a volume solely
devoted to bibliographic references was published: José Pedro Paiva, ed., *Padre António
Vieira, 1608–1697: Bibliografia* (Lisbon: Biblioteca Nacional, 1999). Images of these works
and of some of Vieira's letters are reproduced in a contemporaneous exhibition catalog: José
Pedro Paiva, ed., *Padre António Vieira, 1608–1697: Catálogo da Exposição, Novembro 1997–
Fevreiro 1998* (Lisbon: Biblioteca Nacional, 1997).

30. The best study of Vieira's sermons within the context of seventeenth-century sacred
oratory is by Margarida Vieira Mendes, *A Oratória Barroca de Vieira*, 2nd ed. (Lisbon:
Caminho, 2003), esp. pp. 33–83. A useful overview can be found in João Francisco Marques,
"Introdução Geral à Paranética," in Vieira, *Obra Completa*, vol. 2, bk. 1, pp. 9–47. The broader
Iberian context of preaching and sermons is considered in Marques, *Paranética Portuguesa*,

.he religious culture of seventeenth-century Europe and its offshoots ?as, sermons were primarily intended to edify. But there is no denying they were also forms of popular entertainment. Sermons of the type sented here were not a weekly occurrence as part of the regular liturgy. .ther, they were given on feast days throughout the year or were commissioned for special occasions. Cycles of sermons by the same preacher could be expected during Advent and Lent, although not all churches provided the stage for such events. In the cities of Catholic Europe, as well as in colonial cities, it was common for preachers from different religious orders to compete for pulpits and for the more desirable places on a seasonal schedule. Municipal councils, devotional brotherhoods, and male and female religious communities typically sought the best preachers to enliven their solemnities and thereby increase their social prestige. In court cities such as Lisbon, the pulpit of the royal chapel was the most prized of all, since displays of oratorical prowess there might bring material benefits to a preacher or his community. In such a climate, it is unsurprising that someone as skilled as Vieira would be invited repeatedly to the most prestigious pulpits. But it would be an error to assume that master orators such as Vieira reserved their talents for elite audiences at court. It is clear that he gave many sermons to his Jesuit brethren, to communities of nuns, to charitable brotherhoods, and even to slaves on Brazilian plantations and Indians in Amazonian mission villages.

The printed sermon enabled the preacher to extend the reach of his words far beyond that of his voice. While the dramatic effects employed in the pulpit are not so easy to detect in print, the literary qualities are clearly seen. As a result, not only was there a large market for printed sermons in early modern Europe, sermons circulated in manuscript. Such texts were short and, indeed, ephemeral; they were typically sold unbound in pamphlet format. The extent of their distribution in the seventeenth century is difficult to surmise, but large numbers survive, suggesting that individual sermons had a wide readership. Evidence from colonial libraries across the Portuguese world, no less than references in correspondence, reveals that even readers in distant colonies and mission stations eagerly sought such texts.

---

pp. 203–297, esp. 276–291; Hilary Dansey Smith, *Preaching in the Spanish Golden Age: A Study of Some Preachers of the Reign of Philip III* (Oxford: Oxford University Press, 1978); and Felix Herrero Salgado, *La Oratoria Sagrada Española de los Siglos XVI y XVII* (Madrid: Fundación Universitaria Española, 1996).

On the page, we see the artistry of Vieira's prose.[31] Reading his sermons demands attention to the cohesion and intricate structure of his arguments. Even though in the Sexagesima Sermon, for example, he wittily criticized his fellow preachers' saturation with baroque clichés, he, too, in his own manner, worked within the stylistic conventions of his era. But his surprising associations between words, ideas, and authors; his love for evocative images and for disturbing paradoxes—all the baroque elements in the sermons were his own or his appropriations from canonical authors. Nothing in Vieira was purely decorative, nothing had been repeated to exhaustion by others before he used it; the clarity of language and its pastoral purpose were never sacrificed.

Vieira's voice was unique, arising from a profound indignation with the manifold injustices of his time and in contrast with the complacency of so many of his contemporaries. He was a man of strong words and indefatigable action, impatient with both moral and literary conformity. Vieira reproached his fellow preachers' worn and sterile rhetoric; he saw them engaged in idle intellectual games, eager to please others with their mastery of the latest fashion, and distracted from their pastoral responsibility. Although Vieira was as comfortable as they were in churches and salons, he also dwelt in the discomforting world outside, attentive to the suffering of the oppressed and the cruelty of their oppressors. His vast erudition allowed him to escape the snare of custom. Vieira's wide and sharp reading informed his understanding of the world, while his moral intelligence influenced the way he understood past authors. He could make daring assertions, confident that they were anchored in tradition; he turned to the past to suggest a break with present habits and a vision of future conversion. Following in the footsteps of Old Testament prophets, Vieira sought to convert the faithful, and not only—or especially—those not baptized or catechized.

---

31. The literary aspects of Vieira's prose have been the subject of scholarly analyses for decades. Insightful overviews, with bibliographic references to further studies, are found in Mendes, *Oratória Barroca*, pp. 87–141, 205–299; Alcir Pécora, *Teatro do Sacramento: A Unidade Teológico-Retórico-Política dos Sermões de António Vieira* (São Paulo: EdUSP, 1994); João Adolfo Hansen, "Maria ou a Eternidade no Tempo," in Vieira, *Obra Completa*, vol. 2, bk. 7, pp. 9–30; Alcir Pécora, João Adolfo Hansen, and Ricardo Ventura, "Sermões Sacramentais de Vieira ou Mistérios da Fé tornados Mistérios da Razão" in Vieira, *Obra Completa*, vol. 2, bk. 6, pp. 9–38; and António José Saraiva, *O Discurso Engenhoso: Ensaios sobre Vieira* (Lisbon: Gradiva, 1996), esp. pp. 7–110. General overviews of baroque culture include José Antonio Maravall, *Culture of the Baroque: Analysis of a Historical Structure*, trans. Terry Cochran (Minneapolis: University of Minnesota Press, 1986), and Christopher D. Johnson, *Hyperboles: The Rhetoric of Excess in Baroque Literature and Thought* (Cambridge, Mass.: Harvard University Press, 2010).

Vieira's pastoral intentions, as well as his rhetorical agility, stem also from his Jesuit training. In his youth, he learned how to debate points of philosophy and theology and spent years analyzing Latin grammar. From Ignatius Loyola's *Spiritual Exercises*, he learned how to appeal to the senses and summon emotions in his listeners, how to evoke a scene with vivid imagery and create the ambience for persuasion. These techniques prescribed by Loyola greatly influenced baroque culture in general and Vieira in particular. The intended dramatic effect of images in this period was the intense desire for imitation or the feeling of revulsion. And in Vieira's preaching, images were conjured, contrasted, and examined in detail, in order to render his arguments less abstract and more vivid, that is, to make them more effective tools for achieving his pastoral goals.

Vieira read as he wrote, deftly bringing together or contrasting a vast array of ancient, medieval, and contemporary sources, subordinating them all to his ends and subsuming them in his voice. His familiarity with disparate authors can be attested by the very mistakes that he made when quoting them or when identifying the provenance of his citations, a sign that he quoted extensively from memory. His sermons reveal his deep knowledge of sacred scripture, its complexity and contradictions. As an interpreter, he confronted the obscurity of the text; as a theologian, he scrutinized the inscrutable mysteries of God. At times we sense his confidence in his approximation to meaning and to God; at others we see him perplexed, surrendering to obscurity and mystery.

THE SIX SERMONS translated in this volume have been presented chronologically, rather than in the order in which they are found in the editions that Vieira himself organized. Arranging them according to date leads the reader to follow the evolution of Vieira's attitudes over time and in response to the different audiences that he addressed from his pulpits. One of the sermons was given during his youth in Brazil, three more were delivered after he began his missionary work in the Amazon, and the last two were composed toward the end of his life.

The two sermons that open this volume speak of a Brazil in crisis. The first, the Sermon for the Success of the Arms of Portugal against Those of Holland, was preached in the late spring of 1640 at a time of despair.[32] As

---

32. A modern critical edition of this sermon exists with only its analytical apparatus in English. See Frits Smulders, ed., *António Vieira's Sermon against the Dutch Arms (1640)* (Frankfurt: Peter Lang, 1996).

he spoke, a Dutch fleet lay in the harbor of Salvador da Bahia, menac-
ing the colonial capital after having laid waste to sugar mills around the
Bay of All Saints. The memory of the occupation of Bahia by the Dutch
in 1624–1625 was still fresh, as was that of their attempt to seize the city
in 1638. A decade before, they had captured Pernambuco, another pros-
perous agricultural region at the northeastern tip of Brazil.[33] In short,
the Dutch posed a grave threat to the survival of Portuguese Brazil. But
whereas Vieira had preached triumphantly when the Portuguese lifted
the siege two years before, his sermon in 1640 gave voice to the anguish
of imminent disaster. This discourse, delivered after two weeks of devotional manifestations and sermons urging repentance had failed to drive
the Dutch away, took an original tack. Rather than speak to his fellow
Brazilians, Vieira addressed God directly. Adopting the plaintive tone of
David and Job, he argued for deliverance in defiant terms that border on
heretical. One eighteenth-century commentator described it as "the most
vehement and extraordinary discourse that has perhaps ever been heard
from any Christian pulpit."[34]

One major theme in Vieira's argument was that of God's consistency.
Reflecting on contemporary affairs in the light of biblical history, he ques-
tioned why God had acted in one way with the ancient Israelites and in
another with the Portuguese, whose empire He had permitted to expand
around the world. Vieira made a central point about the Calvinist Dutch
being the instrument of divine justice. Not content simply to destroy the
Portuguese state in Brazil, Heaven seemed intent on ending religion as
well—since, in Vieira's view, the heretics would vent their impious rage
against Bahia's Catholics and their churches. Here we see the distant
reach of the confessional strife that had roiled Europe since the days of
Luther and Calvin, the bloody religious conflicts that propelled the Thirty
Years War recast in colonial tints. From the beginning Vieira was determined to argue against God with God, culminating in the confrontation
between the justice of God and the mercifulness of God. After drawing
on all possible arguments from scripture, Vieira closed with a final appeal
to the merciful intercession of God's mother, the Blessed Virgin Mary, to

---

33. The naval battles between the Dutch and Portuguese at Bahia in the late 1630s are discussed in Boxer, *Dutch in Brazil*, pp. 85–99.

34. Guillaume Thomas Raynal, *Histoire Philosophique et Politique des Établissemens et du
Commerce des Européens dans les Deux Indes*, 4 vols. (Geneva: Jean-Leonard Pellet, 1780), vol.
2, p. 381.

whom he argued God should defer. But the final battle between good and evil imagined by the preacher was not to occur at Bahia in 1640. Fearing that they lacked the men for capturing the city, the Dutch sailed away, abandoning Salvador shortly after this sermon was preached.[35]

The second sermon in this volume, the Sermon of Saint Anthony, was given during Vieira's return to Brazil as a missionary. By June 1654, when he stepped into the pulpit of the Franciscan church in São Luís de Maranhão to preach about the thirteenth-century friar, he had spent over a year and a half in the Amazon. The months he had passed sojourning in European outposts and traveling to indigenous settlements had enabled him to gauge social mores on this distant edge of the Portuguese Empire. Vieira's judgment was not favorable, and in this sermon he issued a broad indictment of colonial society. In the pulpit he identified himself with Anthony of Lisbon, whose hagiography contained an episode where the preacher, threatened and ignored by those he sought to convert, decided instead to address the fish in a nearby river.[36] Faced with men who would not listen to his challenging words—akin to the unrepentant settlers of Maranhão who ignored Vieira's—the saint found it more fruitful to speak to animals. Similarly, Vieira pretended to take the variety of sea creatures found in Brazilian waters as his audience, judging the behaviors of the colonists by pointing to the characteristics of different species of marine life and apportioning praise or blame as necessary.

Invoking the examples of the virtuous fish found in sacred scripture and the mythical powers of those described in the natural histories of antiquity, the preacher urged his listeners to recognize the moral perils that surrounded them. He then turned to an unsparing critique of colonial mores, railing against the greed that he saw as the motor of injustice. Vieira lamented that fish devoured each other, but admitted that men did far worse: colonial officials oppressed and exploited the poor; creditors and lawyers destroyed honest gains; landowners exhausted laborers in the fields. Taking remoras as an example, he further denounced those members of the retinues of the powerful who clung to their betters in the hopes of profit. Pointing to octopuses, he denounced sanctimonious individuals who, behind an appearance of virtue, were treacherous

---

35. Boxer, *Dutch in Brazil*, p. 99.

36. Anthony of Lisbon is commonly known to English speakers as Anthony of Padua (1195–1231). He was born in Lisbon but gained fame as a Franciscan preacher and theologian at Padua, where he died.

and malevolent. All grasped for something, Vieira contended—some for power, others for wealth, still others for frivolous luxuries, even if they were poor—and all lost sight of the eternal perils that their ambitions brought upon them. These were not kind words, and Vieira left Maranhão secretly a few days after delivering them. His destination was Lisbon, the imperial capital, where he sought new weapons for his battle against colonial sins.

THE SECOND PAIR of sermons was given during Vieira's return to court in 1655. They were the words of a man of action, a missionary who had seen the empire and considered the breadth of the task before him. Conversion was the challenge he addressed, but he did not understand the work of conversion simply as the evangelization of non-Christians. Rather, Vieira perceived it as the moral reform of the world, the pastoral undertaking necessary to fulfill his prophetic vision. His Lisbon sermons therefore aimed to spur others, especially the king, court, and clergy, into action by reminding them of their roles in that expansive project of conversion. In both texts translated here, Vieira spoke of Portugal and its empire, demonstrating his awareness of courtly and colonial realities. His words were designed to unmask the frivolity of contemporary modes in preaching and to correct the myopia of imperial administrators. From Vieira's pastoral and political vantage points, the scale of the challenges confronting the Portuguese Empire was such that inaction was unacceptable. And so the preacher used strong words to shake the metropolitan elite, summoning up the dangerous consequences of the disregard of their moral duties toward the kingdom and its overseas territories.

Vieira picked the ideal time for such a message. The Sexagesima Sermon, preached on the eighth Sunday before Easter that year, came at the beginning of the Lenten season. His venue was the royal chapel, so he was assured of an influential audience, and his tone was one of confrontation, intended to make the message all the more memorable. Taking the parable of the sower as his theme, Vieira asked why the effects of the word of God in biblical times were not replicated in his day. He enumerated the possible reasons, presented caricatures of contemporary preaching styles, and aimed pointed questions at his elite listeners. He denounced the lack of authenticity in his fellow preachers, wittily scorning them for their empty intellectual exercises, and in the process describing the elements of a properly constructed sermon. It is clear that he intended his message to be heard by the priests who would ascend to pulpits that year to give their cycles of Lenten sermons, so that they might avoid perpetuating the errors he mocked. The preachers' job, he concluded, was to leave listeners perturbed rather than amused. Vieira himself suggested that the Sexagesima Sermon could serve as a key to understanding his thoughts on preaching and therefore placed it first in the 1679 edition of his works.[37]

Of the several sermons preached by Vieira in Lisbon during Lent 1655, the Sermon of the Good Thief, given on Good Friday in the church of the Santa Casa da Misericórdia, stands out. The "Holy House of Mercy" was a charitable brotherhood that had originated in Lisbon in 1498 with royal patronage and had branches throughout the Portuguese Empire. Its membership was drawn from the ranks of noblemen as of commoners, and it was considered the most prestigious of all confraternities in the capital city. This church was only a few steps from the royal palace, and its pulpit was second in importance perhaps only to that of the royal chapel. Directing his words at the audience of crown servants gathered there, Vieira condemned corruption and greed in royal and colonial administration.

Contrasting Christ's words to Dismas with His words to Zacchaeus, Vieira examined the differences between poor and rich thieves. In this reflection on justice, he took aim at the wealthy, criticizing especially the ill-gotten gains of royal officials. Vieira considered the roles both of corrupt servants and of the masters who facilitated their schemes, asserting that their vassals' thefts would be the cause of the damnation of kings. His warning was directed specifically at those who profited from their positions in administration overseas, where they enriched themselves at the expense of the colonies in flagrant disregard of law or justice. Knowing well the high price of lax or corrupt governance in the empire, Vieira urged his legally minded audience to see that justice was served at home and overseas. In keeping with his pastoral goals, he considered how the corrupt ways that he had observed overseas could be mended. He declaimed on the need for thieves to make restitution for their thefts and for kings to ensure that their officials repaid what they had taken illicitly from the imperial commonweal. The correctives proposed by him were sure to be painful, as the confrontations he would experience upon his return to the

---

37. Vieira's suggestion is found in the reader's prologue to the first volume of the editio princeps. Insightful discussions of the Sexagesima Sermon are found in Mendes, *Oratoria Barroca*, pp. 145–199, and Saraiva, *Discurso Engenhoso*, pp. 139–152.

Amazon would be, but Vieira considered them the only way to make it possible for both thieves and kings to achieve salvation.

THE FINAL TWO sermons in this volume come from the last years of Vieira's life, after he returned to Bahia in 1681, and belong to sets of texts that he organized while he was in the process of putting together his larger corpus. The first is found in a two-volume series of thirty sermons dedicated to the Blessed Virgin and titled *Maria Rosa Mística*, which Vieira published in fulfillment of a vow "made and repeated during great, life-threatening perils, from which, through her immense goodness and most powerful intercession, he always came out free."[38] Sermon XXVII is the fifth text translated in the present volume, and it may be the most challenging one, since it explicitly addresses captivity, freedom, and Vieira's attitudes to both. It was preached to a devotional confraternity of African slaves and freedmen in the mid-1680s in the region of Bahia. Such groups were common in the early modern period in Brazil, as well as in Portugal, especially in cities.[39] The sermon mentions male and female slaves, as well as slave owners, in the audience, but the confraternity was a male group dedicated to Our Lady of the Rosary. The presence of such a renowned preacher at one of the brotherhood's devotional gatherings lent great solemnity to the event, as did the presence of the consecrated host upon the altar while he preached. To be sure, the printed sermon that is translated in the present volume probably differs from the text that was given orally. The quantity of erudite allusions and Latin passages in it makes that more than likely, as does its place within a devotional volume intended to be read by members of the educated strata of Portuguese society.

The subject of this discourse was African slavery in Brazil, a topic addressed by Vieira only infrequently in his surviving writings. Given the theme's importance, and considering the vigorous protestations that he made against Indian slavery, scholars have long puzzled at the limited number of pronouncements that he made about the enslavement of Africans

---

38. The texts are in two volumes of the editio princeps, published in Lisbon in 1686 and 1688. The citation is found on the frontispiece of both volumes.

39. The confraternities are discussed in A. C. de C. M. Saunders, *A Social History of Black Slaves and Freedmen in Portugal, 1441–1555* (Cambridge: Cambridge University Press, 1982), pp. 149–156; James Sweet, *Recreating Africa: Culture, Kinship, and Religion in the African-Portuguese World, 1441–1770* (Chapel Hill: University of North Carolina Press, 2003), pp. 206–210; Patricia Mulvey, "Black Brothers and Sisters: Membership in the Black Lay Brotherhoods of Colonial Brazil," *Luso-Brazilian Review* 17.2 (Winter 1980): pp. 253–279; and Patricia Mulvey, "Slave Confraternities in Brazil: Their Role in Colonial Society," *The Americas* 39.1 (July 1982): pp. 39–68.

and at the content of his messages to them.[40] This sermon, delivered late in his life, gives no clear answers to such questions, primarily because it reveals the difficulties encountered by Vieira in reconciling his prophetic understanding with his pastoral responsibilities. He began by describing the massive scale of the transatlantic slave trade—quite a few decades before its height in the late eighteenth century—and recounting the horrific cruelties visited upon African slaves in Brazil. Then he compared their sufferings to those of the ancient Israelites, referring to the Egyptian and Babylonian captivities, and considered the place of slaves in Roman society. Slaves, he suggested, had always been part of the world, and their trials had to play some role in God's plans for humanity. Why did Brazil prosper, the preacher asked, if the engine of its riches was inhumane slave labor? Since the American colony was a fundamental part of his understanding of the history of the Portuguese Empire, surely there was some divine purpose behind this manifest, enduring cruelty. Nevertheless, Vieira also perceived God's punishment of the evil of slavery in the losses suffered by the Portuguese throughout the world in his lifetime.

Unable to resolve this dilemma, Vieira took refuge in pastoral consolation. He told his audience of the freedom to be gained through devotion to the Blessed Virgin and dutiful service as prescribed by Saint Paul. He took the further step of elaborating on the promise found in sacred scripture that those who suffered in servitude in this fleeting life would be eternally repaid in the next life by God, who would serve them Himself as a slave. Vieira also compared the slaves' physical sufferings to the austerity of life within a religious order, although he made it clear that any parallels to the restraints of religious life were far surpassed by the rigors experienced daily by slaves. If his language of consolation fails to convince modern readers and even outrages them, his words of condemnation for the slave owners in his audience are unambiguous.

---

40. Vieira's attitudes toward African slavery have provoked charged debates among scholars. See, for example, David G. Sweet, "Black Robes and 'Black Destiny': Jesuit Views of African Slavery in 17th Century Latin America," *Revista de Historia de America* 86 (July–December 1978): pp. 87–133, esp. 101–123; Magno Vilela, "Uma questão de igualdade . . . António Vieira e a escravidão negra na Bahia," *Oceanos* 30/31 (April–September 1997): pp. 37–52; Luiz Felipe de Alencastro, *O Trato dos Viventes: Formação do Brasil no Atlântico Sul* (São Paulo: Companhia das Letras, 2000), esp. pp. 155–187; Luiz Felipe de Alencastro, "Portuguese Missionaries and Early Modern Antislavery and Proslavery Thought," in *Slavery and Anti-Slavery in Spain's Atlantic Empire*, ed. Josep Fradera and Christopher Schmidt-Nowara (New York: Berghahn, 2013), pp. 43–73, esp. 63–66; and Luiz Felipe Baeta Neves, "Os Quatro Ventos do Mundo e as Três Cores de Gente desta Grande República: Da Escravidão Colonial," in his *Vieira e a Imaginação Social Jesuítica*, pp. 227–248.

Asserting that all men were created equal, regardless of the color of their skin, Vieira reminded the masters that their place atop the wheel of fortune was shaky: chance alone had put them there, a reversal of fortune could well put them in their slaves' place. And if their cruelties were not repaid in this world, they certainly would merit punishment in the next. Although Vieira did not act on these convictions to the extent of urging the kings of Portugal to eradicate African slavery as he had done with Indian slavery, his words were nevertheless remarkable for a Catholic preacher in the late seventeenth century. Unlike his contemporaries who abstained from denouncing the slave owners' evil deeds, Vieira heralded their damnation.[41]

The final text translated here comes from a cycle of sermons that Vieira produced in the early 1690s about Francis Xavier, the famed Jesuit missionary saint who left Europe in 1541 to spend his final decade in Asia. It is unclear if the preacher ever delivered these discourses from a pulpit, but they were published in the form of sermons. Vieira had received a request from the queen of Portugal to write a devotional treatise that she might read during a novena to be held in thanksgiving for the saint's intercession for the safe births of three princes. The first three texts in this series were grouped under the title *Xavier Dormindo*, "Xavier asleep," while the twelve sermons from among which the one included here is taken were collectively called *Xavier Acordado*, "Xavier awake." Throughout the whole cycle Vieira considered the significance of Xavier's teachings and miracles, linking them to the spread of the faith which was integral to the author's eschatological vision.

The sermon chosen for this volume was called simply Arm. It concerned the relic of Xavier's right arm, which was sent to Rome in 1614 at the request of Pope Paul V. Xavier had died in early December 1552 on Shangchuan Island off the coast of China, where he fell sick during an ill-starred attempt to enter the Ming Empire. Unwilling to leave the Jesuit's body in such a remote spot, the Portuguese traders who had accompanied him exhumed his corpse after it had spent three months in the ground.

---

41. Vieira's sermon was delivered at nearly the same time that the cruelty of the Atlantic slave trade was being discussed at the Papal Curia in Rome. Those discussions in 1686, brought about by an Afro-Brazilian envoy from Bahia and Capuchin missionaries from West Africa, addressed many of the same themes that Vieira does. Vieira was therefore not exactly a lone voice crying out in the wilderness, but was very nearly that. See Richard Gray, "The Papacy and the Atlantic Slave Trade: Lourenço da Silva, the Capuchins and the Decisions of the Holy Office," *Past and Present* 115 (May 1987): pp. 52–68.

Finding the body intact, they transported it to Malacca, where it was rebur-
ied; soon after, however, Xavier's Jesuit confreres exhumed the incorrupt
body again and brought it to Goa. Witnesses were awed at the miraculous preservation of the corpse, and its Jesuit guardians accepted only
with the greatest reluctance the pope's command—issued sixty years after
its arrival in India—to sever Xavier's arm and send it to Rome. The forearm was sent to the Church of the Gesù, while the humerus was divided
between three Asian colleges of the Society: Macau, Malacca, and Cochin.[42]
In Vieira's interpretation of these events, the distance between Xavier's
severed arm and the rest of his body represented the missionary saint's
globe-spanning embrace.

Arm was a reflection on relics and obedience. It is fitting that both
themes should have preoccupied Vieira at the end of his life. One of his
concerns in publishing his sermons was to ensure that his words would
be heard farther and endure longer, even after his death, just like the relics
of Xavier's flesh and bones ensured the perpetuation of his saintly presence. His confidence in the power of his preaching to bring about virtuous
actions, a theme that runs through all the sermons included in this volume, matched his belief in the wonderworking power of Xavier's relics.
Like Xavier's reach, Vieira's words carried around the world, and just as
Xavier's inaugural missionary journeys laid the grounds for the expansion
of the church in Asia, so Vieira's efforts sought to expand the church in
America. The other theme binding Xavier and Vieira was their common
membership in the Society of Jesus. In this sermon, Vieira considered
the vow of obedience shared by all Jesuits, adducing Xavier's dismember-
ment as an example of how even saints showed deference to the order's
superiors. Having lived for nearly three-quarters of a century as a Jesuit,
accepting the constraints of a religious order despite his irrepressible indi-
viduality, Vieira offered a deeply felt insight into his order's institutional
spirit.

THE TRANSLATIONS IN the present volume are based upon the editio
princeps, that is, the original twelve volumes organized by Vieira himself, published in Lisbon between 1679 and 1699, and readily accessible in

---

42. The story of Xavier's relics and their postmortem travels is analyzed in Liam Matthew
Brockey, "The Cruelest Honor: The Relics of Francis Xavier in Early-Modern Asia," *Catholic
Historical Review* 101.1 (January 2015): pp. 19–42. The body remains in Goa, the forearm in
Rome, and a part of the humerus in Macau. The other two pieces of the humerus were lost
upon the Dutch capture of Malacca in 1641 and Cochin in 1663.

digitized format.[43] Where necessary, we have consulted modern printings of the sermons. In some instances we have relied upon critical editions, but those only exist for some sermons, not all.[44]

The translations found here reproduce all of the marginal notes included in the first editions, most of them references to biblical passages.[45] Vieira typically gave citations from the Latin Vulgate, although he sometimes referred to the Aramaic Targum or the Greek Septuagint, either of these in Latin translation. We have preserved the Latin passages as they are cited in the editio princeps, including their punctuation (even though it is often different from what is seen in modern editions of the Vulgate). It should be noted that the numbering of the Psalms and the Books of Kings differs in the Catholic tradition that Vieira followed from that used in Protestant Bibles or in the Revised Standard Edition. That is one reason why we have rendered his Latin citations from the Vulgate in our footnotes using the Rheims-Challoner translation, a Catholic Bible based on the Douay-Rheims edition published by English Jesuits between 1582 and 1610, and revised by Bishop Richard Challoner in the middle of the eighteenth century. The editio princeps also contains references to the works of the church fathers, Latin and Greek authors, and medieval and early modern biblical commentators and historians as well as marginal notes on these sources. Where possible, dates have been given for medieval and early modern authors mentioned in the notes. We have made an effort to identify the texts and passages to which Vieira referred in his notes, as well as those that he mentioned without specific references. Where possible, we have borrowed translations from modern editions of those works mentioned in Vieira's citations and notes; where not, we have translated the Latin passages ourselves. The capitalization used in the editio princeps

---

43. The six sermons presented here are found in the following volumes of the editio princeps: Sermon for the Success of Portuguese Arms, vol. 3, pp. 467–496; Sermon of Saint Anthony, vol. 2, pp. 309–345; Sexagesima Sermon, vol. 1, col. 1–86 (here the columns are numerated, not the pages); Sermon of the Good Thief, vol. 3, pp. 317–354; Sermon XXVII of *Maria Rosa Mística*, vol. 10, pp. 391–429; and Ninth Sermon, Arm, of *Xavier Acordado*, vol. 8, pp. 351–388. They can be consulted online at https://www.bbm.usp.br.

44. In addition to the critical edition of the Sermon for the Success of Portuguese Arms found in Smulders, *António Vieira's Sermon*, critical editions for the Sexagesima Sermon and the Sermon of Saint Anthony are found in António Vieira, *Sermões*, ed. Arnaldo do Espírito Santo, 2 vols. (Lisbon: Imprensa Nacional, 2008-2010), vol. 1, pp. 21–62 (Sexagesima); and vol. 2, pp. 419–464 (Saint Anthony).

45. Modern reprintings occasionally contain explanatory notes or essays, but most often they simply reproduce the references found in the margins of the editio princeps without indicating other modern or early modern editions of the works cited.

has been preserved, although the original punctuation has been slightly modified for clarity.

In our English rendering of his sermons, we have sought to remain faithful to Vieira's syntax and style. Our English does not always lend itself, however, to the structures and rhythms of his Portuguese. In some instances, therefore, we had to sacrifice fidelity in order to achieve clarity. On occasion, we have consulted the few translations that do exist of Vieira's sermons. Of the six presented in this volume, only the Sermon of Saint Anthony has previously been published in English translation in its entirety.[46] Parts of Sermon XXVII of *Maria Rosa Mística*, addressed to the slave confraternity in Bahia, have been translated in two different editions.[47] Here this sermon is rendered in full. Only a few paragraphs of the Sexagesima Sermon have been published in translation, while the other three sermons found here have never before been translated into English.[48] With this initial corpus of sermons we hope to introduce readers to António Vieira's beautiful prose, to his insights and his wit, and to his vivid descriptions of the world in which he lived.

---

46. António Vieira, *The Sermon of Saint Anthony to the Fish and Other Texts*, trans. Gregory Rabassa (Dartmouth, Mass.: Center for Portuguese Studies and Culture, 2009). This edition also contains a translation of the 1645 Maundy Thursday Sermon which was preached in the Royal Chapel. In addition to the present volume, this is the only set of complete English translations of any of Vieira's sermons.

47. Robert Conrad, ed. and trans., *Children of God's Fire: A Documentary History of Black Slavery in Brazil* (Princeton, N.J.: Princeton University Press, 1983), pp. 163–174, and Kenneth Mills, William Taylor, and Sandra Lauderdale Graham, eds., *Colonial Latin America: A Documentary History* (Wilmington, Del.: Scholarly Resources, 2002), pp. 218–233.

48. These passages from the Sexagesima Sermon can be found in a survey of preaching by Edwin Paxton Hood, *The Throne of Eloquence: Great Preachers, Ancient and Modern* (London: Hodder & Stoughton, 1885), pp. 113. The same volume also includes a few passages from the Sermon of Saint Anthony, pp. 54–57. There are also short passages from the Sexagesima Sermon translated in Cohen, *Fire of Tongues*, pp. 66–73, passim.

SERMAM

PELO BOM SUCCESSO DAS ARMAS

DE PORTUGAL

Contra as de Hollanda.

Na Igreja de N. S. da Ajuda da Cidade da Bahia.

Com o Santiſſimo Sacramento expoſto. Sendo eſte
o ultimo de quinze dias, nos quaes em todas as
Igrejas da meſma Cidade ſe tinhaõ feito ſuc-
ceſſivamente as meſmas deprecaçoens.
Anno de 1640.

---

*Exurge; quare obdormis, Domine? Exurge, & ne repellas in
finem. Quare faciem tuam avertis, obliviſceris inopiæ noſtræ, & tribulationis noſtræ? Exurge, Domine, adjuva nos
& redime nos propter nomen tuum.* Pſal. 43.

§. I.

570 Om eſtas palavras
piedoſamente re-
ſolutas, mais pro-
teſtando, que oran-
do, dá fim o Profeta Rey ao
Tom. 3.

Pſalmo quarenta & tres. Pſalmo, que deſde o principio
até o fim naõ parece ſenaõ
cortado para os tempos, &
occaſiaõ preſente. O Dou-
tor maximo Saõ Jeronymo,
& depois delle os outros
Gg   Ex-

Frontispiece of the Sermon for the Success of the Arms of Portugal against Those of Holland in António Vieira's *Sermoens . . . Terceira Parte* (Lisbon: Miguel Deslandes, 1683). Biblioteca da Ajuda, Lisbon, shelfmark B-XX-17.

I

Sermon for the Success of the Arms of Portugal against Those of Holland

Preached at the Church of Nossa Senhora da Ajuda in the City of Bahia

With the Most Holy Sacrament exposed. This being the last of fifteen days in which the same pleas were made successively in all this city's Churches.

The Year of 1640.

Exurge, quare obdormis, Domine? Exurge, & ne repellas in finem. Quare faciem tuam avertis, oblivisceris inopiæ nostræ, & tribulationis nostræ? Exurge, Domine, adjuva nos & redime nos propter nomen tuum.

PSALM 43[1]

I

With these piously resolute words, protesting more than praying, the Prophet King ends Psalm Forty-Three. It is a Psalm that, from the beginning to the end, seems nothing short of cut out for the present times and occasion. The *Doctor Maximus* Saint Jerome and after him the other Expositors say that it refers to any Kingdom or Catholic Province destroyed and devastated by enemies of the Faith.[2] But among all the world's Kingdoms, it fits none better than our Kingdom of Portugal; and among all the Provinces of Portugal, it applies to none more precisely than to the

---

1. Psalm 43:23–24, 26, "Arise, why sleepest thou, O Lord? arise, and cast us not off to the end. Why turnest thou thy face away? and forgettest our want and our trouble? . . . Arise, O Lord, help us and redeem us for thy name's sake."

2. Vieira's reference to Jerome and the "other Expositors" likely comes from the list of authors in the voluminous biblical commentaries of his fellow Jesuit, Jean de Lorin (1559–1634). See Lorin, *Commentariorum in librum Psalmorum*, 3 vols. (Lyon: Horace Cardon, 1612–1616), vol. 1, p. 855. See also Frits Smulders, *António Vieira's Sermon against the Dutch Arms (1640)* (Frankfurt: Peter Lang, 1996), p. 234.

wretched Province of Brazil. Let us read the whole Psalm, and in all of its clauses we will see the parts of our fortune portrayed: What we were, and what we are.

Deus auribus nostris audivimus, Patres nostri annuntiaverunt nobis, opus, quod operatus es in diebus eorum, & in diebus antiquis.[3] We have heard (so begins the Prophet) from our parents, we have read in our histories, and our elders have even seen, in part, with their eyes, the wonderful works, the feats, the victories, the conquests that, through the Portuguese in times past, Your Omnipotence has wrought, Lord. *Manus tua gentes disperdit, & plantasti eos: afflixisti populos, & expulisti eos:*[4] Your hand was the one that defeated and subjected so many barbarian, bellicose, and indomitable nations, and the one that deprived them of rule over their own lands, in order to plant the Portuguese in them, as it did, with such well-grounded roots, and to spread and extend them, as it did, to all parts of the world: in Africa, in Asia, in America. *Nec enim in gladio suo possederunt terram, & brachium eorum non salvavit eos, sed dextera tua, & brachium tuum, & illuminatio vultus tui; quoniam complacuisti in eis:*[5] Because the strength of their arm or of their sword was not the strength that subjected the lands of which they took possession, and the peoples and Kings that they made into vassals; rather, it was the virtue of Your omnipotent right hand, and the light and the supreme authority of Your assent with which You showed pleasure with them, and made use of them. Here ends the account or memory of glories past, after which the Prophet moves on to present times and misfortunes.

Nunc autem repulisti, & confudisti nos, & non egredieris Deus in virtutibus nostris:[6] Now, however, Lord, we see all this so changed that it already seems as if You have altogether left us and cast us away from You, because You no longer go before our banners, nor do You command our armies as before. *Avertisti nos retrorsum post inimicos nostros, & qui oderunt nos, diripiebant*

---

3. Psalm 43:2, "We have heard, O God, with our ears: our fathers have declared to us, The work thou hast wrought in their days, and in the days of old."

4. Psalm 43:3, "Thy hand destroyed the Gentiles, and thou plantedst them: thou didst afflict the people and cast them out."

5. Psalm 43:4, "For they got not the possession of the land by their own sword: neither did their own arm save them. But thy right hand and thy arm, and the light of thy countenance: because thou wast pleased with them."

6. Psalm 43:10, "But now thou hast cast us off, and put us to shame: and thou, O God, wilt not go out with our armies."

sibi:[7] You make us, who were so accustomed to winning and triumphing, turn our backs to our enemies, not out of weakness but by way of punishment (since our enemies are the lash of Your justice, it is right that we offer our backs to them).[8] What had once been the spoils of our valor is now lost and has become the prey of their greed. *Dedisti nos tanquam oves escarum, & in gentibus dispersisti nos:*[9] The old, the women, the children, who have no strength or weapons with which to defend themselves, die like innocent lambs at the hands of heretical cruelty; and those who can escape death, exiling themselves to foreign lands, lose their homes and their homeland.[10] *Posuisti nos opprobrium vicinis nostris, subsanationem, & dirisum his, qui sunt in circuitu nostro:*[11] It would not be so much to regret if, after estates and lives were lost, at least honor had been saved; but this, too, is gradually being lost. And the name Portuguese, so celebrated in the Annals of Fame, is now being affronted by the insolent Heretic with his victories, and is now being despised by the Heathen who besieges us, having once so venerated and feared it.

In such an appropriate manner David describes our misfortunes in this Psalm, contrasting what we are today to what we were while it pleased God, so that pain will grow amidst the present experience in opposition to the memory of the past. Here comes to mind what the tongue is not permitted to say; and there is no lack of people who will tacitly argue that the cause of such a remarkable reversal was the change in the Monarchy. It would not be so (they say) if a Dom Manuel or a Dom João the Third lived, or if the fate of a Dom Sebastião had not buried the line of Portuguese

---

7. Psalm 43:11, "Thou hast made us turn our back to our enemies: and they that hated us plundered for themselves."

8. The word *costas* in Vieira's text can mean both the backs of the Portuguese and the shores of Brazil against which the Dutch had brought their naval prowess to bear since the mid-1620s, as António Sérgio and Hernâni Cidade remind us in their edition of the sermon. The Dutch conquered and held the region of Pernambuco in northeastern Brazil, principally along the seacoast, from 1630—ten years before this sermon was given—until 1654. See António Vieira, *Obras Escolhidas*, 2nd ed., ed. Sérgio and Cidade, 12 vols. (Lisbon: Sá da Costa, 1996), vol. 10, p. 45.

9. Psalm 43:12, "Thou hast given us up like sheep to be eaten: thou hast scattered us among the nations."

10. Vieira here refers to the Portuguese colonists who were displaced from Pernambuco in Northeastern Brazil. See Smulders, *Antonio Vieira's Sermon*, p. 246.

11. Psalm 43:14, "Thou hast made us a reproach to our neighbors, a scoff and derision to them that are round about us."

Kings alongside him.[12] But the same Prophet in the same Psalm disabuses us of this false figment: *Tu es ipse Rex meus, & Deus meus, qui mandas salutes Jacob*.[13] The Kingdom of Portugal, as God Himself declared to us upon its foundation, is His Kingdom and not ours: *Volo enim in te, & in semine tuo Imperium mihi stabilire*.[14] And since God is the King—*Tu es ipse Rex meus, & Deus meus*—and this King is the one who rules and governs—*Qui mandas salutes Jacob*—He who does not change is the one who causes these reversals, and not the Kings who changed. So, in view of this certain and flawless truth, our Prophet was a little hesitant in the consideration of so many calamities until, to remedy them, God, who enlightened him, inspired him to give the most high counsel in the words that I took as my Theme: *Exurge, quare obdormis, Domine? Exurge, & ne repellas in finem. Quare faciem tuam avertis, obliviscenris inopiæ nostræ, & tribulationis nostræ? Exurge, Domine, adjuva nos, & redime nos propter nomen tuum.* David does not preach to the people, he does not exhort or reproach them, he does not inveigh against them, though it would be amply deserved; rather, taken captive by a new and extraordinary spirit, he not only turns to God but, piously emboldened, turns against Him. Just as Martha said to Christ, *Domine, non est tibi curæ?*[15] so David expresses his bewilderment reverently to God, nearly charging Him with neglect. He complains of the inattentions of His mercifulness and providence, which amounts to considering God asleep: *Exurge, quare obdormis Domine?* He repeats to Him that He should awaken and not allow the damage to be complete, something that would be unworthy of His mercy: *Exurge, & ne repellas in finem.* He asks Him the reason why He shifts His gaze and averts His face from us—*Quare faciem tuam avertis?*—and why He forgets our misery and ignores our tribulations—*Obliviscenris inopiæ nostræ, & tribulationis nostræ?* And he does not simply ask the reason for what God does and

---

12. Vieira refers to the death of King Sebastião at the Battle of Alcácer-Quibir in Morocco in 1578, the event which heralded the conquest of Portugal by Philip II of Spain. The rule of that monarch's grandson, Philip IV, in Portugal would continue until December 1640, half a year after this sermon was preached.

13. Psalm 43:5, "Thou art thyself my king and my God, who commandest the saving of Jacob."

14. "I will establish to myself an Empire in Thee, and in thy Seed." Early modern Portuguese chronicles reported this declaration made by God to Afonso Henriques (1109–1185), the first king of Portugal, before the Battle of Ourique in 1139. Translated in John Colbatch, *An Account of the Court of Portugal, Under the Reign of the present King, Dom Pedro II* (London: Thomas Bennet, 1700), p. 156.

15. Luke 10:40, "Lord, hast thou no care?"

permits; rather, he asks insistently once and again: *Quare obdormis? Quare oblivisceris?* Finally, after these questions for which he thinks God has no answer, and after these arguments with which he presumes to have convinced Him, he protests before the Tribunal of His justice and mercy that He has the obligation to rescue, help, and liberate us right away: *Exurge Domine, adjuva nos, & redime nos.* And to further oblige the Lord, he does not protest for our own good and remedy, but on behalf of His honor and glory: *Propter nomen tuum.*

This is, all-powerful and all-merciful God, this is the stratagem that he who so conformed to Your heart used to win Your mercy. And this I, too, will use today since the state in which we see ourselves is identical and not merely similar. I shall not preach today to the People, I shall not speak to men; my words, or my voices, will ascend higher, my whole Sermon will be directed to Your Divine breast. This is the last of fifteen continuous days in which all the Churches of this Metropolis have brought their pleas before that same throne of your patent Majesty. And, since this is the final day, it is fitting that on this day we reach for the final and only remedy. Throughout all these days the Evangelical Orators tired themselves in vain preaching penitence to men; and since they have not converted, I want, Lord, to convert You. I come so convinced of Your mercifulness, my God, that, even though we are the sinners, today You shall be the one who repents.

What I come to ask, or protest, Lord, is that you help us and liberate us: *Adjuva nos, & redime nos.* Both of these petitions are in conformity to the place and the time. In a time of such oppression and captivity, what should we ask with greater urgency than for You to liberate us, *Redime nos?* And, at the home of *Nossa Senhora da Ajuda*, what should we hope for with greater confidence but that You help us, *Adjuva nos?*[16] I shall not beg by begging, but by protesting and arguing, for this is the license and liberty of one who asks not for a favor but for justice. If this cause had been ours alone, and I had come to implore a remedy for us alone, I would be asking for a favor and for mercifulness. But since the cause, Lord, is Yours more than ours, and since I come to plead on behalf of Your honor and glory, and for the credit of Your name—*Propter nomen tuum*—it stands to reason that I ask only for reason, it is just that I ask only for justice. Upon

---

16. *Nossa Senhora da Ajuda* is a particularly Portuguese devotion. It translates to "Our Lady of Help," but this invocation is different from other Catholic devotions such as "Our Lady of Perpetual Help."

this assumption I shall challenge You, I shall argue with You; and I so trust Your reason and Your benevolence that I shall convince You, too. If I come to complain of You and to denounce the delays of Your justice, or the inattentions of Your mercifulness—*Quare obdormis? Quare oblivisce-ris?*—it will not be the first time that You will have suffered such excesses from one who advocates Your cause. It is also You, Lord, who shall bear the costs of this whole suit, because Your very Grace shall give me the reasons with which I shall challenge You, the effectiveness with which I shall press You, and all the weapons with which I shall win You over. And if the merits of the cause are not enough for this, they will be supplemented by those of the Most Holy Virgin, in whose help I trust above all. *Ave Maria.*

II

Exurge, quare obdormis, Domine? To want to argue with God and to convince Him by reasoning seems not only a difficult matter but a manifestly impossible endeavor, and moreover a daring temerity. *O Homo, tu quis es, qui respondeas Deo? Nunquid dicit figmentum ei, qui se finxit: Quid me fecisti sic?*:[17] Insolent man (says Saint Paul), bold man, who are you that you dare quarrel with God? Does the clay on the wheel and between the hands of the artisan perchance challenge his reasons and ask him: Why do you do this to me? Well, if you are clay, mortal man, if the hands of God have formed you out of the vile matter of the earth, how can you say to that God, *Quare? Quare?* How dare you argue with Divine Wisdom? How can you ask His Providence for the reason for what He does or does not do to you, *Quare obdormis? Quare faciem tuam avertis?* Venerate His permissions, revere and adore His mysterious judgments, shrug your shoulders with humility at His sovereign decrees, and you will do what Faith teaches you, and what you owe as His creation.[18] So we do, so we confess, and so we protest before Your infinite Majesty, immense God, incomprehensible goodness: *Justus es Domine, & rectum judicium tuum.*[19] Even if we cannot understand Your works, even if we cannot grasp Your counsels, You are

---

17. Romans 9:20, "O man, who art thou that repliest against God? Shall the thing formed say to him that formed it: Why hast thou made me thus?" The imperfections in the Latin passages found in the edition princeps have been preserved here.

18. "Shrug your shoulders," *encolhe os ombros*, does not express indifference but only bewilderment and acceptance of what is not understood.

19. Psalm 118:137, "Thou art just, O Lord: And thy judgment is right."

always Just, You are always Holy, You are always infinite goodness; and even at the full rigor of Your justice, Your punishment never reaches the severity that our guilt warrants.

If the reasons and arguments of our cause were to be founded on their own merits, it would be a great temerity, indeed a manifest impiety, to want to challenge You. But we, Lord, as Your Prophet Daniel protested, *Neque enim in justificationibus nostris prosternimus preces ante faciem tuam, sed in miserationibus tuis multis.*[20] The pleas and the reasons for them that we humbly bring before Your divine gaze, the appeals or embargoes that we lodge against the execution and continuation of the punishments that we suffer, are in no way founded on the presumption of our justice, rather all of them rest on the bounty of Your mercifulness: *In miserationibus tuis multis.* We do argue, yes, but against You with You; we do appeal, but against God with God—against the just God with the merciful God. And since all the arrows shall come from Your breast, they will hardly be able to offend Your goodness. But, when pain is great, it always drags along emotion, and the accuracy of words is a discredit to that pain. And so that the righteous feeling of present ills will not surpass the sacred limits of one who speaks before God and with God, in all that I dare say I shall follow in the solid footsteps of those who, in similar occasions, guided by Your very spirit, have prayed for and implored Your mercy.

When the People of Israel in the desert committed that most serious sin of idolatry by adoring the gold of their jewels in the crude image of a Calf, God revealed the matter to Moses, who was with Him, and added, irate and determined, that this time He would put an end once and for all to such an ungrateful people, and that He would devastate and consume them all, leaving no trace of their generation: *Dimitte me, ut irascatur furor meus contra eos, & deleam eos.*[21] Yet the heart of the good Moses could not bear to hear of the destruction and devastation of his People. He takes the field, he opposes the Divine wrath, and begins to reason thus: *Cur Domine irascitur furor tuus contra Populum tuum?*[22] Why, Lord, is Your wrath so inflamed against Your People? For what reason, Moses? You still seek a more justified reason from God? He has just told you that the People

---

20. Daniel 9:18, "For it is not for our justifications that we present our prayers before thy face, but for the multitude of thy tender mercies."

21. Exodus 32:10, "Let me alone, that my wrath may be kindled against them, and that I may destroy them."

22. Exodus 32:11, "Why, O Lord, is thy indignation kindled against thy people?"

are worshipping idols; that they are adoring a crude animal; that they are denying Divinity to God Himself and attributing it to a mute Statue that their hands have just made, crediting it with the freedom and triumph with which they were released from captivity in Egypt. And, after all this, you still ask God the reason why He is vexed, *Cur irascitur furor tuus?* Yes, and with very prudent zeal. Because even though on the part of the People there were great reasons why they should be punished, on the part of God the reason for not punishing them was greater: *Ne quæso*—Moses gives the reason—*ne quæso dicant Ægyptii, Callidè eduxit eos, ut interficeret in montibus, & delèret è terra.*[23] Watch out, Lord, lest the Egyptians tarnish Your being or, at least, Your truth and goodness. They will say that, cunningly and in bad faith, You have brought us to this desert just to take all our lives here and bury us. And with this opinion spread and agreed among them, how degraded will Your holy name be, after You left it so well respected and exalted in Egypt with so many and such prodigious wonders of Your power? It is therefore convenient, in order to preserve Your credit, to disguise the punishment and not, through it, give these Heathens and those others in whose lands we dwell the excuse to say, *Ne quæso dicant.* In this way Moses reasoned in favor of the People, and God was so convinced of the force of this argument that right there He revoked the sentence and, according to the Hebrew Text, not only repented of the execution, but also of the thought. *Et pœnituit Dominum mali, quod cogitaverat facere Populo suo:*[24] And the Lord repented of the thought and of the idea that He had had of punishing His People.

I therefore have much reason, my God, to hope that You shall leave this sermon repentant, for You are the same that You were, and no less a friend of Your name now than You were in times past: *Propter nomen tuum.* Moses told you: *Ne quæso dicant,* watch out, Lord, lest they say . . . And I say, and should say: Watch out, Lord, they already say . . . The insolent Heretics prosper, and they already say that You grant or allow them their

---

23. Exodus 32:12, "Let not the Egyptians say, I beseech thee: He craftily brought them out, that he might kill them in the mountains, and destroy them from the earth."

24. "And God repented of the evil that He had thought of doing to His people." Vieira paraphrases Exodus 32:14, *Placatusque est Dominus ne faceret malum quod locutus fuerat adversus populum suum,* "And the Lord was appeased from doing the evil which he had spoken against his people." In fact, he cites a version of the text that is more congenial to his sermon rather than the passage found in the Vulgate. Vieira draws instead on an edition of *Commentaria in Exodum* by the Dominican Jerónimo de Azambuja (also known as Hieronymus ab Oleastro, d. 1563) (Lisbon: João Blávio, 1557), pp. 79v–80v. See Frits Smulders, *António Vieira's Sermon against the Dutch Arms (1640)* (Frankfurt: Peter Lang, 1996), pp. 263–264.

successes. They already say that because their Religion, or what they call Religion, is the true one, that because of this God helps them and they are victorious. And because ours is wrong and false, that because of this He does not favor us and we are defeated. So they say, so they preach, and this is too bad because there will be no shortage of people who believe them. How is it possible, Lord, that what You permit can be an argument against Your Faith? How is it possible that our punishments give occasion for blasphemies against Your name? That the Heretic (it makes my tongue tremble just to pronounce it), that the Heretic says that God is Dutch? Oh do not permit such a thing, my God, do not permit such a thing, I beg You! I do not say it for us, for it would be of little importance if You were to punish us. I do not say it for Brazil, for it would be of little importance if You were to destroy it. I say it for You and for the honor of Your most holy name, the target of such impudent blasphemy: *Propter nomen tuum.* Since the perfidious Calvinist makes an argument of Religion out of the successes gained by him solely as the prize for our sins, and swaggers insolent and blasphemous as if his were the true one, let him see on what side the truth lies by the turn of that same wheel of Fortune that causes his vainglory. Let the winds and storms that scatter and defeat our Fleets defeat and destroy theirs. Let the diseases and plagues that diminish and weaken our armies scale their walls and depopulate their garrisons. Let the counsels that, when You want to punish, are corrupted be enlightened in us, and foolish and confused in them. Let victory change the Insignias, let us avenge the insults against the Catholic Crosses, let Your Wounds on our flags triumph, and let perfidy, humiliated and undeceived, know that only the Roman Faith that we profess is Faith, and only it is true and Yours.[25]

But there are still more who say *Ne quæso dicant Ægyptii*: Watch out, Lord, for we live among Heathens, some who are so today and others who were so yesterday; and what will these people say? What will the barbarian Tapuia without knowledge of God say?[26] What will the inconstant Indian who lacks the pious affection of our Faith say? What will the coarse Ethiopian say, he who was only sprinkled with Baptismal water without

---

25. The five wounds of Christ are symbolically represented on the Portuguese royal coat of arms, which would have been emblazoned on battle flags, much like the red cross of the Order of Christ.

26. Vieira uses the term Tapuia to refer to the peoples of the Brazilian interior, in contrast to the Tupi peoples of the coastal regions.

receiving any more doctrine? There is no doubt that all these, since they have no capacity to gauge the depths of Your judgments, will drink this error through their eyes. From the effects they see, they will say our Faith is false, and that of the Dutch the true one, and they will believe themselves to be more Christian by being like them. The Sect of the brutal and ignoble Heretic agrees more with the brutality of the barbarian; the laxity, the looseness of life, which was the origin and remains the instigation of the Heresy couples better with the depraved customs and the corruption of Heathenism. And what pagan will convert to the Faith that we preach, or what new Christian already converted will not be perverted, when either of them comes to understand and be persuaded that Heretics are rewarded for their Law and Catholics punished for theirs? Well, if these are the effects, unintended though they are, of Your rigor and punishment justly begun upon us, why is this punishment kindled and spread with so much damage unto those who are not complicit in our guilt, *Cur irascitur furor tuus*? Why does that which You Yourself have called fury continue unchecked? And why do You not immediately finish sheathing the sword of Your wrath?

If when so gravely offended by the Hebrew People You forgave them for a "What will the Egyptians say?", will it not be enough of a motive to consider what the Heretics say and what the Heathens will say for Your rigorous hand to suspend the punishment and forgive our sins, too, since, though great, they are lesser? The Hebrews adored the Idol, failed in their Faith, abandoned the cult of the true God, gave the name of God and Gods to a Calf. And thanks to Your infinite goodness we are and we have always been so far from the slightest fault or scruple in this matter that many have left their homeland, their home, their property, and even their wife and children, and they live as exiles in total misery, only so as not to live or communicate with men who have set themselves apart from Your Church.[27] Well, my Lord and my God, if for Your love and for Your Faith, without yet the danger of losing or risking it, the Portuguese make such gallantries—*Quare obivisceris inopiæ nostræ, & tribulationis nostræ*—why do You forget such religious miseries, such Catholic tribulations? How is it possible that Your Majesty will manifest itself in wrath against these most faithful servants and favor the unfaithful, the excommunicate, the impious?

---

27. Vieira again refers to the Portuguese exiles who fled Pernambuco in northeastern Brazil for the region of Bahia after the Dutch conquered that territory in 1630.

Oh, how we can complain at this point as the pitiful Job complained when, despoiled by the Sabeans and the Chaldeans, he saw himself, as we see ourselves, in the utmost oppression and misery! *Nunquid bonum tibi videtur, si calumnieris me, & opprimas me opus manuum tuarum, & consilium impiorum adjuves?*:[28] Does it seem right, Lord, does this seem right to You? That You should oppress and afflict me, Your servant? And favor and help Your enemies, the impious? Does it seem right to You that they should be the ones prospering, assisted by Your Providence, and we the ones You let slip from Your hand? We the ones forgotten by Your memory? We the example of Your rigors? We the spoils of Your wrath? Is it so small a thing to go into exile for You and leave everything? So small a thing to suffer toil and poverty, and the humiliations that accompany them, for Your love? Has Faith no longer merit? Has Piety no longer value? Does perseverance no longer please You? Well, if there is such a difference between us, though we are bad, and them, the perfidious ones, why do You help them and not favor us? *Nunquid bonum tibi videtur*: To You who are goodness itself, does this seem right?

III

Consider, my God, and forgive me if I speak inconsiderately. Consider from whom You take the lands of Brazil and to whom You give them. You take these lands from the Portuguese, to whom You gave them at the beginning; and it would be enough to say to whom You gave them to endanger the credit of Your name, because nothing can be called a liberal favor if it is tinged with repentance. Why did Saint Paul tell us, Lord, that, when You give, You do not repent, *Sine pœnitentia enim sunt dona Dei?*[29] But leaving this aside: You take these lands from the very same Portuguese that You chose, among all nations of the world, to be Conquerors for Your Faith, and to whom You gave Your own Wounds for their arms, as insignia and particular emblem. And is it right, Supreme Lord and Governor of the Universe, that the Sacred *Quinas* of Portugal and the Arms and Wounds of Christ will be followed by the Heretical Stripes of Holland, rebellious against their King and

---

28. Job 10:3, "Doth it seem good to thee that thou should calumniate me, and oppress me, the work of thy own hands, and help the counsel of the wicked?"

29. Romans 11:29, "For the gifts of God are without repentance."

God?[30] Is it right that these are to be seen waving victorious in the wind, while those are beaten down, dragged, and ignominiously surrendered? *Et quid facies magno nomini tuo?*[31] And what will You do (as Joshua said), or what will happen to Your glorious name, if such affronts come to pass?

Also, You take Brazil from the Portuguese, who conquered these immensely vast lands, as well as the most remote ones of the Orient, at the expense of so many lives and so much blood, more to dilate Your name and Your Faith (for that was the zeal of those Most Christian Kings) than to amplify and extend their Empire. You were served in this way to have us enter so honorably and so gloriously into these new worlds, and You permit in this way that we now leave (who would imagine such a thing of Your goodness!) with such affront and ignominy! Oh how I fear that there will be no lack of people who will say what the Egyptians said, *Callidè eduxit eos, ut interficeret, & deleret è terra*: That the generous hand with which You gave us so many dominions and Kingdoms did not signify favors of Your liberality, but cunning and dissimulation of Your wrath, so that out here, far from our homeland, You could kill us, destroy us, and utterly finish us. If this was to be the payment and the fruits of our toils, for what did we toil, for what did we serve, for what was so much and such illustrious blood shed in these Conquests? For what did we open those never-sailed seas?[32] For what did we discover unknown Regions and climes? For what did we battle winds and tempests with so much daring that there is hardly a shoal in the Ocean that is not infamous for the most wretched shipwrecks of the Portuguese? And after so many dangers, after so many misfortunes, after so many and such pitiful deaths, either unburied on deserted beaches or buried in the entrails of savages, of beasts, of fish, that the lands that we gained in this way should be lost like this? Oh how much better it would have been for us to never achieve or attempt such endeavors!

Holier than us was Joshua, less tested was his patience, and yet, on a similar occasion, he did not speak (when speaking to You) with a

---

30. *Quinas*, from the Latin for five, refers to the five shields found on the Portuguese royal arms and that are said to represent the five wounds of Christ. "Stripes of Holland" refers to the flag of the States General of the Dutch Republic. Recall that the Dutch War of Independence began in 1572 as a revolt against the ruler of the Netherlands, King Philip II of Spain.

31. Joshua 7:9, "And what wilt thou do to thy great name?"

32. Here Vieira uses the famous phrase *mares nunca dantes navegados* of Luís de Camões (c. 1524–1580) from *Lusíadas*, Canto 1:1.

different tone. After the children of Israel crossed to the oversea lands beyond the Jordan, just as we did to these,[33] part of the army went forth to mount an assault on the City of Hai, which in the echo of its name seemed already to predict the unfortunate outcome that the Israelites experienced there, because they were broken and scattered, although with fewer dead and wounded than we are used to here.[34] And what was Joshua to do in the face of this misfortune? He tears his imperial garments, he throws himself on the ground, he starts to cry out to Heaven, *Heu Domine Deus, quid voluisti traducere populum istum Jordanem fluvium, ut traderes nos in manus Amorrhæi?:*[35] My God and my Lord, what is this? For what did You tell us to cross the Jordan, for what did You have us take possession of these lands, if once here You were going to deliver us into the hands of the Amorrhites and condemn us? *Utinam mansissemus trans Jordanem!:*[36] Oh, would that we had never crossed this river!

So complained Joshua to God and so can we complain, and with much more reason than he. If this was to be the end of our navigations, if these fortunes awaited us in the conquered lands—*Utinam mansissemus trans Jordanem*—would that Your Divine Majesty had provided for us to never leave Portugal, or entrust our lives to the waves and winds, or know or set foot in foreign lands! To win them in order to not enjoy them was a curse, not a blessing; to take possession of them in order to lose them was the punishment of Your wrath, Lord, not the reward, or favor, of Your liberality. If You always meant to give these lands to the Dutch Pirates, why did You not give them away while they were still wild and uncultivated instead of now? Have these perverted and apostate people rendered so many services to You that You should send us here first to be their forerunners, to till the lands for them, to build the Cities for them, so that after these lands have been cultivated and enriched You can just hand them over? Should the Heretics and enemies of the Faith profit thus from Portuguese toil and

---

33. Vieira here uses the term *terras ultramarinas,* "the oversea lands," to force the comparison between the crossing of the Jordan River by the Israelites and the traversing of the Atlantic and the Indian Oceans by the Portuguese.

34. The name of the city Hai echoes the Portuguese interjection for pain, *ai!*

35. Joshua 7:7, "Alas, O Lord God, why wouldst thou bring this people over the river Jordan, to deliver us into the hand of the Amorrhite?"

36. Ibid., "Would we had stayed beyond the Jordan."

Catholic sweat? *En queis consevimus agros*: Behold for whom we have toiled for so many years![37]

But since, Lord, You so want and demand, do as it pleases You. Deliver Brazil to the Dutch, deliver the Indies to them, deliver the Spains to them (for the consequences of the loss of Brazil are no less dangerous), deliver as much as we have and possess to them (since You have already delivered such a great part), put the World in their hands; and as for us, the Portuguese and the Spaniards, leave us, repudiate us, ruin us, finish us. But I only say, and remind Your Majesty, Lord, that the very ones that You now disfavor and cast away, You may one day want and not have.

I would not have dared to speak thus, had I not taken the words out of the mouth of Job, who, being so pitiful, not surprisingly appears many times in this tragedy. This example of patience complained to God (since God wants us patient but not insensitive to pain), he complained of the harshness of his pains, quarrelling and questioning why their rigor should not slacken and be softened a little. And as the Lord showed Himself inexorable to all arguments and appeals, when he had nothing else to say he concluded thus: *Ecce nunc in pulvere dormiam, & si manè me quæsieris, non subsistam.*[38] Since You do not want, Lord, to give up or moderate the torment, since You want nothing but to continue with Your rigor and to carry it to its end, great though it is, kill me, consume me, bury me: *Ecce nunc in pulvere dormiam.* But I tell You and remind You of one thing only: If You look for me tomorrow, You will not find me, *Et si manè me quæsieris, non subsistam.* You will have the Sabeans, You will have the Chaldeans, let them be the theft and the lash of Your home; but You will not find a Job who will serve it, You will not find a Job who will venerate it, You will not find a Job who, for all his wounds, will not disrespect its authority. The same I say, Lord, for it is not surprising that he who sees himself in the same state will burst with the same emotions. Burn, destroy, consume us all; but the day may come when You want Spaniards and Portuguese, and do not find them. Holland will give You the Apostolic Conquerors who will carry the Standards of the Cross around the world. Holland will give You the Evangelical Preachers who will sow the Catholic doctrine in the lands

---

37. "See for whom we have sown our fields!" In Virgil's *Eclogue* 1, lines 71–73. Vieira's early modern edition of this text differs slightly from the modern standard version, *His nos consevimus agros*. Cf. Virgil, *Eclogues, Georgics, Aeneid: Books 1–6*, trans. H. Rushton Fairclough, ed. G. P. Goold (Cambridge, Mass.: Harvard University Press, 1916), p. 30.

38. Job 7:21, "Behold now I shall sleep in the dust: and if thou seek me in the morning, I shall not be."

of the barbarians, and water it with their own blood. Holland will defend the truth of Your Sacraments and the authority of the Roman Church. Holland will build Temples; Holland will raise Altars; Holland will consecrate Priests and offer the Sacrifice of Your Most Holy Body. In short, Holland will serve You and venerate You as religiously as it does every day in Amsterdam, Middelburg, Vlissingen, and in all of the other Colonies of that cold and swampy Hell.[39]

IV

I understand, Lord, that You can tell me that the propagation of Your Faith and the works of Your glory do not depend on us or on anyone, and that You are powerful enough, when men are wanting, to turn stones into sons of Abraham. But Your wisdom and the experience of all the centuries have also taught us that after Adam You have not created new men, that You make use of the ones You have in this world, and that You never admit any who are not good enough unless the best are lacking. This is what You did in the Parable of the Banquet. You called for the guests whom You had chosen and, because they excused themselves and would not come, You then admitted the blind and the lame and introduced them in the place of the others: *Cæcos, & claudos introduc huc.*[40] And if this is, my God, the regular disposition of Your divine Providence, how come we see it now so altered in us and so different with us? Who were these guests and who are these blind and lame ones? We were the guests whom You first called to these lands where You set the Table for us, a Table as generous and abundant as could be expected from Your greatness. The blind and the lame are the Lutherans and the Calvinists, blind without Faith, and lame without works in whose reproach lies the main error of their heresy.[41] If we who were the invited guests neither excused ourselves nor hesitated to come, but on the contrary broke through many obstacles that could have made us hesitate; if we came and sat at the Table, how can You exclude us now and cast us

---

39. When this sermon was given in 1640, the United Provinces of the Netherlands were still in the midst of their Eighty Years War of independence from Spain. Thus Vieira's *frio & alagado Inferno* was a work in progress, formed by the *colonias* of the various Dutch cities such as the ones he mentions. His invective in Bahia notwithstanding, Vieira would travel to the Netherlands as a diplomat for the newly independent Portugal.

40. Luke 14:21, "Bring in hither . . . the blind and the lame."

41. Here Vieira invokes the notion of *sola fide*, "by faith alone," defended by the Protestant reformers, against the combination of faith and works defended by the Catholics.

away from it? And how can You violently introduce the blind and the lame and give our places to the Heretics? If they were in everything else as good as we are, or we as bad as they are, why should at least the privilege and the prerogative of Faith not be of any help to us? In everything it seems, Lord, that with us You alter the styles of Your Providence and change the Laws of Your justice.

The ten Virgins from Your Gospel all surrendered to sleep, all fell asleep, all were equal in the same carelessness: *Dormitaverunt omnes, & dormierunt.*[42] And yet in five of them the Bridegroom overlooked this fault, and only because they kept the lamps lit did they deserve to participate in the wedding feast from which the others were excluded. If it is so, my Lord, if You have so judged it then (for You are that Divine Bridegroom), why is it of no help to us that we keep lit the lamps of Faith, which among the Heretics are so extinguished and so dead? Is it possible that You open the doors to those who bring the extinguished lamps and shut them to those who have theirs lit? Take note, Lord, that it is not fitting for Your divine Tribunal to hand down in the same case two sentences that are so contra-dictory. If those who let their lamps be extinguished were told, *Nescio vos;*[43] if the doors were closed to them, *Clausa est janua;*[44] who deserves to hear from Your mouth a tremendous *Nescio vos* but the Heretic who does not know You? And on whom should You slam the door in the eyes but on the Heretic who has eyes so blind?[45] But I see that not even this blindness or this ignorance, so deserving of Your rigor, delays the progress of their fortunes. Instead, their victorious weapons are coming swiftly upon us, and soon they will knock on the doors of this City of Yours. Of this City of Yours, I said, but I do not know if the name *Salvador* with which You honored it will save it and defend it, since it did not at another time.[46] Nor do I know if these pleas of ours, repeated and continued though they are, will find the way to Your divine gaze, since our righteous pain has been crying out to Heaven for so many years without Your clemency lending an ear to our clamors.

---

42. Matthew 25:5, "They all slumbered and slept."

43. Matthew 25:12, "I know you not."

44. Matthew 25:10, "The door was shut."

45. Vieira uses the term *olhos*, eyes, even though the idiomatic expression is *bater com a porta na cara*, slam the door in the face.

46. Bahia was besieged and captured by the Dutch in 1624, but was reconquered by the Portuguese the following year.

If that be the case (may You not permit it), and it has been determined in Your secret judgment that the Heretics should enter Bahia, the only thing I humbly and very truly bring before You is that before the execution of the sentence You take good note, Lord, of what may happen to You afterward, and that You examine that with Your heart while there is time, because it is better to repent now than when the evil has come to pass and cannot be remedied. You are present in the intention and in the allusion in my speech, and in the reason, grounded on You Yourself, that I have for speaking. Before the Flood, too, You were very choleric and irate against men, and as much as Noah prayed through all those hundred years, there was never a remedy that could placate Your wrath. Finally the floodgates of Heaven broke open, the sea rose to the mountaintops, the whole world inundated: Already Your justice should be satisfied. But all of a sudden, on the third day, the dead bodies started to float and those pale figures to emerge and appear in infinite multitudes.[47] And then the saddest and most disastrous tragedy was played out upon the waves, one that the Angels had never seen, one that there were no men left to see. You, too, saw that most pitiful show (as if this were a new sight for You), and even though You did not cry because You did not yet have eyes capable of tears, the entrails of Your Divinity were touched by such an intrinsic pain: *Tactus dolore cordis intrinsecùs.*[48] And, in the way of repenting that befits You, You repented of what You had done to the world. So complete was Your contrition that not only did You regret the past but You showed a firm determination never to do it again: *Nequaquam ultrà maledicam terræ propter homines.*[49]

This is who You are, Lord, this is who You are. And since You are thus, do not wrestle with Your heart. Why make a brave show against it now, when its sentiment and Yours will pay for it later? Since the executions of Your justice come at a price for Your goodness in repentance, watch what

---

47. Although the story of the flood in Genesis 7–8 does not mention the gruesome scene described by Vieira, several patristic sources mention human remains being eaten by the crow that Noah sent out before releasing the dove. See, for example, Jerome's Homily LVI (on Psalm 146); Augustine's *Contra Faustum*, Book 12; and Ambrose's treatise *de Noe et Arca*, chapters 15–18. The Ordinary Gloss also mentions these bodies, citing brief passages from Augustine, Ambrose, and Isidore of Seville. Medieval artists frequently included the image of a raven eating a corpse in representations of Noah's ark. See Anna Birgitta Rooth, *The Raven and the Carcass: An Investigation of a Motif in the Deluge Myth in Europe, Asia, and North America* (Helsinki: Academia Scientiarum Fennica, 1962), esp. pp. 92–154.

48. Genesis 6:6, "Being touched inwardly with sorrow of heart." This episode occurred before the Incarnation, so God did not have a human form.

49. Genesis 8:21, "I will no more curse the earth for the sake of man."

You do before You do it, lest something like this happen to You again. And so that You see this with human colors, which are no longer foreign to You, allow me first to act out live before You the sorrows and miseries of this future flood;[50] and if this play does not touch You and You have the stomach to see it without great pain, then unleash it all the same.

Let us then pretend (something which even when pretended and imagined causes horror), let us pretend that Bahia and the rest of Brazil fall into the hands of the Dutch. What will happen in that case? They will come into this City with the fury of victors and Heretics; they will not spare status, sex, or age; with the blades of the same scimitar they will measure all. The women will cry, seeing how their modesty inspires no decorum. The elderly will cry, seeing how their gray hair inspires no respect. The nobles will cry, seeing how their quality inspires no courtesy. The Religious and venerable Priests will cry, seeing how not even their sacred tonsures can defend them. Finally, everyone will cry, and the innocent most pitifully among all, because the heretical inhumanity will not forgive even these (as it did not on other occasions). I know, Lord, that only out of love of the innocent, at some point You said that it was not right to punish Nineveh.[51] But I do not know what times these are or what misfortune of ours this is, that even the same innocence does not soften You. Well, You, too, Lord, will be affected by part of the punishment (that which Christian piety feels most); it will reach You, too.

The Heretics will enter this Church and the others. They will snatch that Monstrance in which You are now being adored by the Angels. They will take the sacred Chalices and Vessels, and will use them for their abominable inebriations. They will knock over the figures and statues of the Saints from the Altars, deface them with slashes, and throw them into the fire. And the furious and sacrilegious hands will not show mercy either to the awe-inspiring images of Christ crucified or to those of the Virgin Mary. I am not surprised, Lord, that You should allow such offenses and affronts to Your Images, since You have already permitted them in Your most sacred Body. But to those of the Virgin Mary, to those of Your Most Holy Mother! I do not see how this befits a Son's piety and love. On Mount Calvary this Lady was always at the foot of the Cross, and although those tormentors were so discourteous and cruel, none of them dared touch

---

50. Vieira here refers to God as Christ, both man and God. The flood in the previous paragraph occurred before the Incarnation.

51. Jonah 3–4 relates the story of Nineveh.

or disrespect her. So it was, and so it was to be, for You had promised it through the Prophet: *Flagellum non appropinquabit tabernaculo tuo.*[52] Well, Son of the Virgin Mary, if you were so careful then about the respect and decorum due to Your Mother, how can You now permit so much insolence against her? Do not tell me, Lord, that it was the Person there, the Image here. The Ark of the Covenant was just an Image of the same Virgin, and only because Oza tried to touch it, You took his life.[53] So if there was such rigor then for whoever offended the Image of Mary, why is there none now? Back then any one of the other acts of insolence against sacred items was enough to warrant a most severe, albeit miraculous, demonstration from You. If Jeroboam's arm miraculously dried up right after he raised his hand against a Prophet, how can the Heretics keep their arms for yet other transgressions, after they dare affront Your Saints?[54] If Belshazzar, for drinking from the Vessels in the Temple in which Your blood was not consecrated, was deprived by You of his life and his Kingdom, why do those Heretics stay alive, they who convert your Chalices to profane uses? Are there no three fingers left to write the death sentence against the sacrilegious?[55]

In the end, Lord, with the Temples thus despoiled and the Altars knocked over, Catholic Christendom will be finished in Brazil. The divine cult will be finished. Grass will sprout in Churches as in the fields; there will be no one who enters. A Christmas day will come and there will be no memory of Your Birth. Lent will come, and Holy Week, and the Mysteries of Your Passion will not be celebrated. The paving stones will cry, as Jeremiah says those of the destroyed Jerusalem cried, *Viæ Sion lugent, eò quòd non sint, qui veniant ad solemnitatem:*[56] They will be seen desolate and solitary, and the devotion of the Faithful will not tread upon them as it used to on such days. There will be no Altars, or Masses, or Priests to say them; the Catholics will die without Confession or Sacraments. Heresies will be preached from these same pulpits and, instead of Saint Jerome and Saint Augustine, the infamous names of Calvin and Luther will be heard

---

52. Psalm 90:10, "Nor shall the scourge come near thy dwelling."

53. 2 Kings 6:6–7 recounts how Oza was struck dead for touching the Ark of the Covenant.

54. 3 Kings 13:1 and 4 recounts how Jeroboam's hand withered.

55. Daniel 5:1–5 recounts the feast of Belshazzar and the writing on the wall which served as his "death sentence."

56. Lamentations 1:4, "The ways of Sion mourn, because there are none that come to the solemn feast."

and cited. The innocents who stay, relics of the Portuguese, will imbibe the false doctrine. And we will reach the point where, if the children and grandchildren of those who are here are asked, "Child, to what Sect do you belong?", one will answer, "I am a Calvinist," another, "I am a Lutheran." Are we really to suffer this, my God? When You wanted to hand over Your sheep to Saint Peter, You examined him three times to see if he loved You: *Diligis me, diligis me, diligis me?*[57] And now You hand them over like this, not to shepherds but to wolves? Are You the same or are You another? Your flock to the Heretics? The Souls to the Heretics? Since I have spoken and mentioned the Souls, I do not want to tell You more. I know, Lord, that You shall be touched and repent, and that You shall not have the heart to see such sorrows and such damage. And if it is so (and so Your most pious entrails promise), if there is to be pain at all, if there is to be repentance afterward at all, let the wrath cease, let the executions cease now, for it is not right that You should be content at first by something which will weigh upon You later.

You honored man greatly, Lord, at the creation of the world, when You formed him with Your own hands, informing him and animating him with Your own spirit and imprinting in him the character of Your image and likeness. But it seems as if right from that very day You were not happy with him, because about all other things created by You the Scripture says that they seemed good to You: *Vidit Deus quód esset bonum.*[58] Only about man does it not say this. Human reason has ever since been perplexed and in suspense with admiration at this mysterious reticence, not able to grasp the cause why You, who were pleased with all Your works and made such a public show of it, with man alone, the most perfect of all, would not show pleasure. Finally, over one thousand seven hundred years later, the same Scripture which was mute about this mystery declared to us that You repented of having created man: *Pœnituit eum quòd hominem fecisset in terra.*[59] And that You Yourself said that he weighed on You—*Pœnitet me*

---

57. John 21:15–16, "Lovest thou me?" The third question, found in verse 17 of the Vulgate, is different: *Amas me?*

58. Genesis 1:10, "God saw that it was good."

59. Genesis 6:6, "It repented him that he had made man on the earth." Here Vieira refers to the moment of the great flood in the story of Noah, which he supposes was 1,700 years after the creation of the world. Debate over the dating of the flood was particularly intense in the early modern period in light of contemporary advances in biblical scholarship as well as astronomical science. A succinct overview is found in C. P. E. Nothaft, "Noah's Calendar: The Chronology of the Flood Narrative and the History of Astronomy

fecisse eos[60]—and then the secret that You had hidden for so long was patent and manifest to all. And You, Lord, say that it weighs on You and that You repent of having created man. This is why from the moment of his creation You were not pleased with him, nor did You want it said that You had been pleased with him, thinking, as was right, that for reasons unrelated to Your Wisdom and Providence, at no time would he please You or appear satisfying to You, the one whom You were later to regret, and repent of, having made: *Pœnitet me fecisse*. This is accordingly the truly divine condition and the highest governing principle of Your Providence: Never to take pleasure in what will cause repentance. It is also certain, according to the most pious entrails of Your mercifulness, that if You now permit the sorrows, the miseries, the damages that I have presented, they will certainly weigh upon You later and You shall repent. Repent, merciful God, while there is time! Set the eyes of Your mercy upon us! Hold back the hand of Your exasperated justice! Let Your love break the arrows of Your wrath! Do not permit so much irreparable harm! This is what they ask of You, those who prostrate themselves so many times before Your divine regard, these Souls, so faithfully Catholic, on their own behalf and on behalf of all Souls of this State.[61] And they do not make these humble pleas to You for the temporal losses that they concede and that You can impose upon them by other means, but rather for the eternal spiritual loss of so many Souls, for the injuries against Your Temples and Altars, for the extermination of the sacrosanct Sacrifice of Your Body and Blood, and for the insufferable absence, the absence of and longing for that Most Holy Sacrament which we do not know for how much longer we will have present.

V

Having reached the point beyond which I do not know how to go nor is it possible to go, it seems to me that Your divine and human goodness, Lord, is telling us that You would do what we ask easily and You would let Yourself be persuaded and convinced by these reasons of ours, were

---

in Sixteenth- and Seventeenth-Century Scholarship," *Journal of the Warburg and Courtauld Institutes* 74 (2011): pp. 191–211.

60. Genesis 6:7, "For it repenteth me that I have made them."

61. The official title of Portuguese Brazil was the Estado do Brasil, the State of Brazil, like the Portuguese Estado da Índia, the State of India, for which reason Vieira calls Brazil "this State."

Your divine Justice not crying out for the other side. And that, since You are equally just and merciful, You cannot but punish, for Brazil's sins are so many and so great. I confess, my God, that it is so and we all confess that we are very great sinners. But I am so far from being quieted by this response, that I view these many and great sins as being instead a new and powerful motive given by Yourself to better convince Your goodness.

The greatest force of my arguments has not rested until now on any foundation other than the credit, the honor, and the glory of Your most holy name: *Propter nomen tuum.* And what motive more glorious to that same name can I propose other than to say that our sins are many and great? *Propter nomen tuum, Domine, propitiaberis peccato meo: multum est enim:*[62] For the love of Your name, Lord, I am certain (said David) that You shall forgive my sins, for they are not just any sins, but they are many and great—*Multum est enim.* Oh motive worthy of God's breast alone! Oh consequence inevitable only in the highest goodness! So, to have his sins forgiven, a sinner argued with God that they were many and great. Yes, and not for love of the sinner or for love of the sins, but for love of the honor and glory of God Himself: the more and the greater the forgiven sins are, the greater His most holy name is, and the more it is augmented and exalted: *Propter nomen tuum, Domine, propitiaberis peccato meo: multum est enim.* David distinguishes greatness and multitude in God's mercifulness. Greatness—*Secundum magnam misericordiam tuam.*[63] Multitude—*Et secundum multitudinem miserationum tuarum.*[64] And since the greatness of the divine mercifulness is immense and the multitude of His mercies infinite, and immensity cannot be measured nor infinity counted, in order for the one and the other to have in some way proportionate matter for glory, it is important for the very greatness of mercifulness that sins be great, and for the very multitude of mercies that they be many: *Multum est enim.* Therefore I am right, Lord, in not surrendering to the argument that our sins are many and great. And I am also right in insisting on asking You why You do not give up punishing them: *Quare obdormis? Quare faciem tuam avertis? Quare oblivisceris inopiæ nostræ, & tribulationis nostræ?*

Job asked You the same when he said: *Cur non tollis peccatum meum, & quare non aufers iniquitatem meam?*[65] And although a great Interpreter

---

62. Psalm 24:11, "For thy name's sake, O Lord, thou wilt pardon my sin: For it is great."

63. Psalm 50:3, "According to thy great mercy."

64. Ibid., "According to the multitude of thy tender mercies."

65. Job 7:21, "Why dost thou not remove my sin, and why dost thou not take away my iniquity?"

of Your Scriptures argued on Your behalf, in the end he admitted defeat and confessed that Job was right in asking You. *Criminis in loco Deo impingis, quod ejus, qui deliquit, non miseretur?*[66], says Cyril of Alexandria: Enough, Job; do you incriminate and accuse God of punishing your sins? In those words, you confess that you committed sins and evil deeds; and with the same words you ask God why He punishes them? This is to give the reason while asking for the reason. The sins and evil deeds that you do not hide are the reason for the punishment. Well, if you give the reason, why do you ask for it? Because even though God, to punish sins, has the reason of His justice, He has a greater reason to forgive them and to give up the punishment, that of His glory: *Qui enim misereri consuevit, & non vulgarem in eo gloriam habet; obquam causam mei non miseretur?*[67] Job asks God for a reason, and he has good reason to ask for it (the same Saint who argued his case answers for him), because, if it is in God's nature to use mercifulness and if the glory that He acquires in forgiving sins is great and uncommon, what reason does He have or can He give that is enough for not forgiving them? Job himself had already declared the strength of this argument of his in the preceding words that he very forcefully spoke to God: *Peccavi, quid faciam tibi?*[68] As if he said: If I acted, Lord, as a man, sinning, what reason do You have for not acting as God, forgiving me? He still said, and meant to say, further: *Peccavi, quid faciam tibi?* I sinned, what else can I do for You? And what did you, Job, do for God by sinning? I did not do little for Him; because I gave Him an occasion to forgive me and, by forgiving me, to gain much glory. I shall owe Him, as the cause, for the grace that He shall grant me; and He shall owe me, as the occasion, for the glory He will attain.

And if it is so, Lord, without license or flattery, if it is so, merciful God, that when You forgive sins Your glory is augmented, which is the purpose of all Your actions, do not say that You cannot forgive us because our sins are many and great. Rather, because they are many and great, You should attribute that great glory to the greatness and bounty of Your mercifulness.

---

66. "You opportunely reproach God for a crime, since he shows no mercy to the one who committed it." In Cyril of Alexandria, in "Apologia Cyrilli Alexandrini Episcopi ad imperatorem Theodosium," *Opera Omnia* (Paris: Michel Sonnius, 1572), p. 83.

67. "Why does He who used to show mercy and from thence receive uncommon glory not have pity on me?" Vieira here modifies slightly Cyril of Alexandria's text. Ibid.

68. Job 7:20, "I have sinned: what shall I do to thee?"

It is by forgiving us and having pity on us that You shall display the sovereignty of Your Majesty, and not by punishing us, which diminishes more than accredits Your power. See it in this last punishment in which, against all the hopes of the world and of the day, You caused the defeat of our Armada, the greatest that ever crossed the Equator.[69] You were, Lord, able to defeat it; and what great glory of Your omnipotence was it, to be able to do what the wind can? *Contra folium, quod vento rapitur, ostendis potentiam.*[70] To displant a Nation, as You are doing to us, and to plant another is also a power that You ceded to a young man from Anathoth: *Ecce constitui te super Gentes, & super Regna, ut evellas, & destruas, & disperdas, & dissipes, & ædifices, & plantes.*[71] The power in which the majesty, the greatness, and the glory of Your infinite Omnipotence manifest themselves is that of forgiving and of being merciful: *Qui Omnipotentiam tuam, parcendo maximè, & miserando, manifestas.*[72] In punishing, You defeat us, who are weak creatures; but in forgiving, You defeat Yourself, who are all powerful and infinite. This victory alone is worthy of You, because only Your Justice can do battle against Your Mercifulness with equal weapons. And since the vanquished one is infinite, the victor's glory becomes infinite. So forgive, most benign Lord, for this great glory of Yours: *Propter magnam gloriam tuam.* Forgive for this immense glory of Your most holy name: *Propter nomen tuum.*

And if by any chance Your divine Justice still complains, most just rather than merciful God, surely that same justice could also be content with the rigors and punishments of so many years. Are You not, as the just one, that

---

69. Vieira refers to the ill-fated Portuguese-Spanish fleet that intended to dislodge the Dutch from Pernambuco in 1638. Despite being weakened by an outbreak of plague in the Cape Verde Islands, the fleet surprised the Dutch at Recife but did not engage them. Opting to wait for an even larger number of ships at Salvador, the Iberian captains squandered their chance for success. Their attack the following year was disastrous; the fleet was blown off course on its way to Pernambuco, delaying it long enough for the Dutch to prepare their defense. Despite being dramatically outnumbered, the Dutch ships managed to scatter the Iberian fleet in January 1640, a few months before Vieira preached this sermon. See Smulders, *António Vieira's Sermon*, pp. 320–324.

70. Job 13:25, "Against a leaf, that is carried away with the wind, thou shewest power."

71. Jeremiah 1:10, "Lo, I have set thee over the nations, and over the kingdoms, to root up, and pull down, and to waste, and to destroy, and to build, and to plant." Jeremiah 1 tells how he began to receive his prophecies as a young man.

72. "Who chiefly manifestest thine omnipotence by pardoning and having mercy." This phrase is from the prayer of the collect said on the tenth Sunday after Pentecost. See Prosper Guéranger, *The Liturgical Year*, trans. Laurence Shepherd, 15 vols. (Dublin: James Duffy, 1867-1890), vol. 11, p. 261.

just Judge about whom Your Prophet sings: *Deus Iudex justus, fortis, & patiens, numquid irascitur per singulos dies?*[73] Well, if Your wrath, again that of a just Judge, is not for every day, or for many days, why should it not be content with years, and so many years, of rigors? I know, Supreme Legislator, that in the cases of wrath, even when justified, Your most holy Law commands us to not let a day go by without forgiving before the Sun sets: *Sol non occidat super iracundiam vestram.*[74] Well, if Your very law expects from human weakness, which is so sensitive, such moderation for offenses, and commands it to forgive and to be placated in such a brief and precise span, and if You, who are infinite God and have a heart as large as Your very immensity, in the matter of forgiving show Yourself as an example to men, then how is it possible that the rigors of Your wrath will not soften after so many years, and that the Sun will set and rise again so, so many times, seeing the sword of Your vengeance always unsheathed and dripping blood? Sun of Justice is what I thought the Scriptures called You, because, even when at its most fiery and blazing, the rigor of Your rays would pass within the short span of twelve hours.[75] But the material Sun that illuminates us and surrounds us will disagree, because for so many days and so many years it has always seen You irate while passing over us twice from one Tropic to another.

I no longer argue with You, Lord, about what earth and men will say, rather about what Heaven and that same Sun will say. When Joshua ordered the Sun to stop, the words of the Hebrew language in which he spoke to it asked it not to stop, but to be quiet: *Sol tace contra Gabaon.*[76] The valiant Captain ordered the Sun to be quiet, because those fading beams with which it was burying itself in the West were muted tongues with which the same Sun muttered that Joshua was too vengeful. They were very loud voices with which the Law of God from Heaven reminded him and preached to him that he could not continue his vengeance, because it was going to set in the West: *Sol non occidat super iracundiam vestram.* And if God, as the Author of that same Law, ordered the Sun to stop and that

---

73. Psalm 7:12, "God is a just judge, strong and patient: Is he angry every day?"

74. Ephesians 4:26, "Let not the sun go down upon your anger."

75. Malachi 4:2, "The Sun of Justice shall arise."

76. In the Vulgate Joshua 10:12 reads *Sol, contra Gabaon ne movearis,* "Move not, o sun, towards Gabaon." Vieira possibly cites Alfonso de Madrigal, "el Tostado" (or Tostati, 1410–1455), whose commentary on this passage includes the rendering the preacher gives. See, for example, his *Commentaria in Primam Partem Iosue* (Venice: Ambrosium Dei, 1615), p. 307. See Smulders, *António Vieira's Sermon,* pp. 326–327.

day (the longest that the world ever saw) to exceed nature's limits by many hours and to be longer, it was so that, the just law agreeing with the just vengeance, on the one hand the rigor of the punishment would be applied, and on the other hand the rigor of the precept would be observed. Let the Gibeonite be punished, for it is fair to punish him; but let the Sun be still until the punishment is over, so that the victor's wrath, though just, will not exceed the limits of one day. Well, if this is, Lord, the span prescribed by Your Law, if You perform miracles, and such miracles, so that Your Law is preserved whole, and if Joshua orders the Sun to be quiet and mute so it will not complain and give voice against the continuation of his wrath, what do You want the same Sun to say when it is neither still nor mute? What do You want the Moon and the Stars to say when they are already tired of seeing our miseries? What do You want all of those Heavens to say, when they were created not to proclaim Your justice, but to sing Your glory: *Cæli enarrant gloriam Dei?*[77]

Finally, most benign Jesus, true Joshua and true Sun, let Your very name be the epilogue and conclusion to all our reasons: *Propter nomen tuum.* If the Sun finds Joshua's rigors strange because they exceed one day and Joshua orders the Sun to be quiet so it will not find them so, how can Your divine Justice find it strange that You employ mercifulness toward us, after You have applied so many and such rigorous punishments, which have continued not for a day or throughout many twelve-hour days, but for so many—soon to be twelve—and such long years?[78] If You are Jesus, which means Savior, be Jesus and be our Savior. If You are Sun, and Sun of Justice, before the Sun of this day sets, relax the rigors of Your Justice. Leave at once the rigorous Sign of Leo, and take a step toward the Sign of Virgo, a propitious and beneficial Sign.[79] Receive human influence from whom You received humanity. Forgive us, Lord, by the merits of the Most Holy Virgin. Forgive us by her prayers, or forgive us by her orders; because

---

77. Psalm 18:2, "The heavens shew forth the glory of God."

78. Vieira's chronology serves his rhetorical goals but is puzzling. The Dutch capture of Pernambuco occurred in 1630, ten years before this sermon was preached, but the first Dutch attack on Brazil—to which the preacher was an eyewitness—was the occupation of Bahia from 1624 until 1625. Vieira's description of that period in Bahia surely qualifies as a "rigorous punishment" by God. See his "Carta Anua da Província do Brasil," Bahia, September 30, 1626, in António Vieira, *Cartas*, ed. J. Lúcio de Azevedo, 3 vols. (Lisbon: Imprensa Nacional, 1970), vol. 1, pp. 3–70.

79. The signs of Leo and Virgo are sequential houses of the Zodiac which mark the later summer months, from late July until late September.

if, as Your creation, she asks Your pardon for us, as Your Mother she can order You, and does order You, to forgive us. Forgive us, in short, so that by Your example we shall forgive. And forgive us, too, by our example, because from this moment on we all shall forgive all through Your love: *Dimitte nobis debita nostra, sicut & nos dimittimus debitoribus nostris.*[80] *Amen.*

---

[80]. Matthew 6:12, the closing phrase of the Lord's Prayer, "Forgive us our debts, as we also forgive our debtors."

SERMAM
DE S. ANTONIO.
PREGADO

Na Cidade de S. Luis do Maranhaõ, anno de 1654.

Efte Sermaõ (que todo he allegorico) prègou o Autor tres dias antes de fe embarcar occultamente para o Reyno, a procurar o remedio da falvaçaõ dos Indios, pelas caufas que fe appontaõ no 1. Sermaõ do 1. Temo. E nelle tocou todos os pontos de doutrina (pofto que perfeguida) que mais neceffarios eraõ ao bem efpiritual, & temporal daquella terra, como facilmente fe pode entender das mefmas allegorias.

Vos eftis fal terra. Metth. 5.

§. I.

Os , diz Chrifto Senhor noffo , fallando com os Prègadores, fois o fal da terra : & chama-lhe fal da terra, porque quer (que façaõ na terra, o que faz o fal. O effeito do fal he impedir a corrupção, mas quando a terra fe vê taõ corrupta como eftá a noffa , havendo tantos nella, que tem officio de fal, qual ferá, ou qual pòde fer a caufa defta corrupção ? Ou he porque o fal naõ falga, ou porque a terra fe não deyxa falgar. Ou he porque o fal não falga , & os Prègadores naõ

Qq iiij prè-

Frontispiece of the Sermon of Saint Antony in António Vieira's *Sermoens... Segunda Parte* (Lisbon: Miguel Deslandes, 1682). Biblioteca Nacional de Portugal, shelfmark L-5256-A.

2

Sermon of Saint Anthony

Preached in the City of São Luís de Maranhão, the year of 1654

This Sermon (which is wholly allegorical) was preached by the Author three days before he embarked secretly for the Kingdom seeking to obtain a remedy for the salvation of the Indians, for the reasons stated in the first Sermon of the first Tome.[1] And in it the Author touched upon all the points of doctrine (its persecution notwithstanding) most necessary to that land's spiritual and temporal welfare, as can be easily understood by the said allegories.

Vos estis sal terra. MATTHEW 5[2]

I

You, says Christ our Lord, speaking with the Preachers, are the salt of the earth. And He calls them salt of the earth because He wants them to do on earth what salt does. The effect of salt is to prevent corruption, but when earth finds itself so corrupt as ours is, even with so many on it doing the job of salt, what is or what can be the cause of this corruption? Either it is because the salt does not salt, or because the earth does not let itself be salted. Either it is because the salt does not salt, and the Preachers do not preach the true doctrine; or because the earth does not let itself be salted, and the listeners, though the doctrine they are given is true, do not want to receive it. Either because the salt does not salt, and the Preachers say one

---

1. Vieira here refers to the Sexagesima Sermon, the first text in the 1679 editio princeps of his collected sermons. The context for both sermons was Vieira's return to Lisbon from Maranhão due to the anger of the settlers whom he denounced from the pulpit.

2. Matthew 5:13; "You are the salt of the earth." *Terra* here is a printing mistake in the editio princeps; it should be *Terræ*, as it appears later in the sermon.

thing and do another; or because the earth does not let itself be salted, and the listeners would rather imitate what the Preachers do than do what they say. Either because the salt does not salt, and the Preachers preach themselves, and not Christ; or because the earth does not let itself be salted and the listeners, instead of serving Christ, serve their own appetites. Is this not all true? Alas.

Having then posited that either the salt does not salt, or the earth does not let itself be salted, what is to be done about this salt and what is to be done about this earth? About the salt that does not salt, Christ said it right away: *Quod si sal evanuerit, in quo salietur? Ad nihilum valet ultra, nisi ut mittatur foras, & conculcetur ab hominibus.*[3] If the salt loses its substance and virtue, and the Preacher fails in his doctrine and example, the thing to do is toss it out as useless, to be tread upon by all. Who would have dared say such a thing if Christ Himself had not pronounced it? Just as there is no one more worthy of reverence or of being put on a pedestal than the Preacher who teaches and does what he should, so he who, with his word or his life, preaches the opposite is worthy of all contempt and of being stepped upon.

This is what should be done to the salt that does not salt. And to the earth that does not let itself be salted, what is to be done? Christ our Lord did not resolve this point in the Gospel; but we have the resolution for it from our great Portuguese Saint Anthony, whom we celebrate today, and it is the most gallant and glorious resolution ever found by a Saint. Saint Anthony was preaching in Italy, in the City of Rimini, against the many Heretics there, and, since errors of understanding are difficult to uproot, not only was the Saint not fruitful but the People were on the point of rising up against him, and were just short of taking his life. In this case, what was the generous spirit of the great Anthony to do? Shake the dust off his shoes, as Christ advises elsewhere? But with his bare feet Anthony could not make this protest, and feet to which nothing from the earth had stuck had nothing to shake off. What was he to do then? Retreat? Be quiet? Dissimulate? Stall for time? Prudence or human cowardice would perchance teach that, but the zeal of divine glory that burned in his chest did not surrender to such parties. So what did he do? He changed only the pulpit and the audience, but did not give up the doctrine. He leaves the squares, he goes to the beaches; he leaves the land, he goes to the sea. And there he starts to say in a loud voice: "Since men do not want to listen to

---

3. Matthew 5:13; "But what if the salt lose its savour, wherewith shall it be salted? It is good for nothing any more but to be cast out, and to be trodden on by men."

me, let the fish listen!" Oh wonders of the Most High! Oh powers of the One who created the sea and the land! The waves start to boil, the fish start to gather, the big ones, the biggest ones, the little ones; all lined up in order with their heads out of the water. Anthony preached and they listened.[4]

If the Church wants us to preach about Saint Anthony with the Gospel, then give us another passage. *Vos estis sal terræ*: It is a very good Text for the other Holy Doctors, but for Saint Anthony it falls rather short. The other Holy Doctors of the Church were salt of the earth, Saint Anthony was salt of the earth and salt of the sea. This is the subject that I was to take up today. But for many days now it has been in my thoughts that, on the feast days of the Saints, it is better to preach like them than to preach about them. All the more so since the salt of my doctrine, whatever it is, has had in this city a fortune so similar to that of Saint Anthony in Rimini that it is necessary to follow him in everything.[5] Many times I have preached to you in this Church and in others, in the morning and in the afternoon, during the day and at night, always with very clear, very solid, very true doctrine, that doctrine which is the most necessary and important for correcting and reforming the vices that corrupt this city.[6] What fruit I have gathered from this doctrine, and whether the earth has taken the salt or has taken at least some of it, you know the answer well and I feel sorry for you.

This understood, today I want to turn from the land to the sea in imitation of Saint Anthony and, since men do not benefit, preach to the fish. The sea is so close that they will hear me well. Others can leave the Sermon because it is not for them. Maria means *Domina maris*: Lady of the sea.[7]

---

4. The story of Anthony preaching to the fish is a commonplace in his hagiography. One version, which includes the quote from the saint reproduced by Vieira, is found in the life written by his fellow Jesuit Pedro de Ribadeneyra (1526–1611). See his *Flos Sanctorum, o Libro de las Vidas de los Santos* (Madrid: Luis Sánchez, 1616), p. 389.

5. Instead of *sal*, the original text reads *são*. According to Rodrigues Lapa, this can either be a printing error (and the author intended *sal*) or it can mean sane (*são*). See António Vieira, *Sermão de Santo António aos Peixes e Carta a D. Afonso VI*, ed. Rodrigues Lapa, 5th ed. (Lisbon: Textos Literários, 1961), p. 5.

6. This sermon was given in the Franciscan church of Santo António. It was common for religious communities to invite preachers from other orders to give sermons on the feast days of major saints who were from the community's own order. Accordingly, the Jesuit Vieira was invited to preach to the Franciscans on the feast of the Franciscan Saint Anthony.

7. This derivation is found in the work of influential Jesuit commentators such as Peter Canisius (1521–1597) and Cornelius Cornelii à Lapide (1567–1637) on the texts, traditions, and devotions related to the Virgin Mary. See, for example, Canisius, *De Maria Virgine incomparabili et Dei Genetrice sacrosancta, libri quinque* (Ingolstadt: David Sartorius, 1577), p. 3; and Lapide, *Commentaria in Pentateuchum Mosis* (Antwerp: Heirs of Martin Nuyts, 1616), p. 449.

And even though the topic is so out of use, I hope she will not fail to grant me the usual grace. *Ave Maria.*

II

Then what shall we preach to the fish today? They are no worse an audience. At least fish have two good qualities as listeners: They listen and do not speak. One thing only might disappoint the Preacher, the fact that fish are people who will not convert. But this is such an ordinary pain that custom makes it almost imperceptible. For this reason I will not speak today of Heaven or of Hell, and so this Sermon will be less sad than my other ones seem to men, since they always direct men to the remembrance of these two ends.

Vos estis sal terræ. You all will know, brother fish, that salt, son of the sea like you, has two properties that can be experienced in yourselves: to conserve what is healthy and to preserve it from corruption. The preaching of your Preacher Saint Anthony had these same properties, as should that of all Preachers. One is to praise the good, the other to reproach the evil: To praise the good in order to conserve it, and to reproach the evil in order to preserve against it. Do not think that this pertains only to men, because it also has its place among fish. So says the great Doctor of the Church Saint Basil: *Non carpere solum, reprehendereque possumus pisces, sed sunt in illis, & quæ prosequenda sunt imitatione.*[8] Not only is there something to remark and reproach in fish, says the Saint, but also something to imitate and praise. When Christ compared His Church to the fishing net, *Sagenæ missæ in mare,* He said that the fishermen gathered the good fish and threw out the bad, *Collegerunt bonos in vasa, malos autem foras miserunt.*[9] And where there is good and bad, there is something to praise and something to reproach. Bearing this in mind so that we proceed with

8. "Not only are we able to bring charges against the fish, but there is also something worthy of imitation in them." In Homily 7 in Basil's Nine Homilies on the Hexameron. Two patristic texts are the closest predecessors in spirit to Vieira's sermon, since they both identify human characteristics among different species of fish. In addition to this text by Basil, the Seventh Sermon (Fifth Book) of Ambrose's Homilies on the Hexameron contains long passages about fish and addresses fish as an audience. See Basil, *Exegetic Homilies,* trans. Agnes Clare Way (Washington, D.C.: Catholic University of America Press, 1963), p. 111, and Ambrose, *Hexameron, Paradise, Cain and Abel,* trans. John J. Savage (Washington, D.C.: Catholic University of America Press, 1961), pp. 159–226.

9. Matthew 13:47–48; "a net cast into the sea," and "they chose out the good into vessels, but the bad they cast forth." Vieira substitutes *elegerunt,* "chose," for *collegerunt,* "gathered."

clarity, I will divide your Sermon into two points, fish: In the first I will praise your virtues, in the second I will reproach your vices. And this way we will fulfill the salt's duties, for it is better for you to hear them while you are alive than to experience them after you are dead.

Starting thus by your praises, brother fish, it is right for me to tell you that, among all living and sentient creatures, you were the first that God created. He created you first, before the birds of the air; first, before the animals of the land; and first even before man. To man, God gave monarchy and dominion over all the animals of the three elements and, in the provisions by which He honored man with these powers, fish were the first ones named: *Ut præsit piscibus maris, & volatibus cœli, & bestijs, universæque terræ.*[10] Among all the animals of the world, fish are the most numerous and fish are the largest. What comparison is there in number between the species of birds and land animals and those of fish? What comparison is there in greatness between the Elephant and the Whale? Therefore Moses, Chronicler of creation, omitting the names of all animals, called only this one by its name: *Creavit Deus cete grandia.*[11] And the three musicians in the furnace of Babylon also sang of it as singular among all others: *Benedicite cete, & omnia quæ moventur in aquis Domino.*[12] Of these and other praises, of these and other excellences of your creation and greatness I could tell you, O fish, but this I leave for men who let themselves be carried away by such vanities, and also for those places where adulation is fitting, not the pulpit.

Arriving at your virtues, brothers, the ones that merit only true praise, the first that appears before my eyes today is that obedience with which, once called, you all came for the honor of your Creator and Lord; and that order, quietude, and attention with which you listened to the word of God from the mouth of His servant Anthony. Oh great praise indeed for fish, and great affront and confusion for men! Men persecuting Anthony, wanting to throw him out of town and, if they could, out of the world, because he reproved their vices, because he would not go easy on them and be indulgent with their faults. And at the same time innumerable fish gathering, responding to his voice, attentive and hanging on his words, listening in silence and with signs of admiration and assent (as if they had understanding) to what they did not understand. Whoever at this point

---

10. Genesis 1:26, "And let him have dominion over the fishes of the sea, and the fowls of the air, and the beasts, and the whole earth." Vieira changes the initial *et* to *ut*.

11. Genesis 1:21, "God created the great whales."

12. Daniel 3:79, "O ye whales, and all that move in the waters, bless the Lord."

were to look at the sea and at the land, and were to see on land men so furious and obstinate, and in the sea fish so quiet and so devout, what would he say? He might think that the irrational fish had converted into men, and men not into fish but into beasts. God gave the use of reason to men and not to fish. But in this case men had reason without its use, and fish had the use without the reason. You deserve great praise, fish, for this respect and devotion that you paid to the Preachers of the word of God, and all the more so since this was not the only time you behaved this way. Jonah, the Preacher of the same God, was aboard a ship when that great tempest arose. And how did men treat him, how did fish treat him? Men cast him into the sea to be eaten by fish, and the fish that ate him took him to the beaches of Nineveh, so that he would preach there and save those men.[13] Is it possible that fish assist in the salvation of men, and that men cast into the sea the ministers of salvation? See, fish, and do not fall into vainglory at how much better you are than men. Men had the stomach to throw Jonah into the sea, and the fish gathered Jonah in its stomach to take him to land alive.

But because in these two actions Omnipotence had a greater part than nature (as in all of men's miraculous actions), I proceed to the virtues that are naturally and properly yours. When Aristotle speaks of fish, he says that they are the only ones among animals that cannot be tamed or domesticated.[14] Among land animals, the dog is so domesticated, the horse so submissive, the bull so servile, the howler monkey so friendly or so flattering, and even lions and tigers can be tamed with art and treats. Among the animals of the air, leaving aside the birds that are raised and live with us, the parrot speaks to us, the nightingale sings to us, the goshawk helps us and entertains us; and even the great birds of prey, by clenching their claws, recognize the hand from which they receive their sustenance. By contrast, fish live in their seas and rivers, dive in their pools, hide in their caves, and none is so big that it will trust man, or so small that it will not flee from him. Authors commonly condemn this condition of the fish and ascribe it to lack of docility or to excessive roughness.[15] But I am of

---

13. The story of Jonah being thrown into the sea is in Jonah 1–3.

14. In Book 9 of the *Historia Animalium* Aristotle mentions how other animals, including dolphins, can be tamed, but he does not seem to discuss fish in this regard. See Jonathan Barnes, ed., *The Complete Works of Aristotle: The Revised Oxford Translation*, 2 vols. (Princeton, N.J.: Princeton University Press, 1984), pp. 980–981.

15. Basil's Homily 8 on the Hexameron makes this point about fish. See his *Exegetic Homilies*, p. 118.

a very different opinion. I do not condemn, rather I greatly praise, this reserve in fish; and it seems to me that, were this not their nature, it would be a sign of great prudence. Fish, the farther you are from men, the better: Interactions and familiarity with them, God forbid. However, if the animals of the land and of the air want to be familiar with them, let them, for they do so because of their lodgings. Let the nightingale sing to men, but in its cage; let the parrot tell them things, but on its chain; let the goshawk go hunting with them, but with its jesses; let the howler monkey make buffooneries for them, but on its block; let the dog be content with gnawing a bone for them, but taken by its leash to wherever it does not want to go; let the bull enjoy being called handsome or noble, but with the yoke on its neck, pulling the plow and the cart; let the horse glory in chomping on gilded bits, but under the crop and the spur; and if the tigers and lions eat their portion of meat that they did not hunt in the woods, let them be caged and enclosed with iron bars. And meanwhile you, fish, far from men and away from those courtesies, will live by yourselves alone, yes, but like fish in water. There are examples of all this truth from homes and indoors that I want to remind you of because there are Philosophers who say that you have no memory.[16]

In the time of Noah there was the Flood that covered and inundated the world; and of all animals, which ones made out best? Of the lions, two escaped, lion and lioness, and so it was with the other animals of the land. Of the eagles, two escaped, female and male, and so it was with the other birds. And of the fish? All escaped. Rather, not only did they all escape, they were much more numerous than before, because land and sea became all sea. For if all the animals of the land and all the birds died in that universal punishment, why did the fish not die as well? Do you know why? Saint Ambrose says: Because the other animals, being more domesticated or living closer to men, had more communication with them. Fish lived far away and withdrawn from men.[17] God could easily have made the waters poisonous so that they would kill all fish, just like they drowned all the other animals. You experience this in the strength of those weeds with which that same water kills you, once wells and lakes are infected. But since the Flood was a universal punishment that God gave men for their sins and the world for the sins of men, it was the most high

---

16. Basil makes this claim in Homily 8 on the Hexameron, ibid.

17. Ambrose makes this claim in Book Five of his sermons on the Hexameron. See his *Hexameron*, p. 167.

providence of divine Justice that there should be this diversity or distinction. In this way the world would see that from the company of men had come all evil, and that on account of it the animals that lived closer to them were also punished, and those that dwelt far away stayed free. See, fish, what a great good it is to be far from men. When asked what the best land in the world was, a great Philosopher answered the most deserted, because it would have men further away.[18] If Saint Anthony also preached this to you, and this was one of the benefits for which he exhorted you to give thanks to the Creator, he could well have argued to you on the basis of his own example, since the more he sought God, the more he fled from men. In order to flee men, he left his parents' house and retired to, or embraced, a Religion where he could profess perpetual enclosure. And because not even there would those he had left leave him, he first left Lisbon, then Coimbra, and finally Portugal. In order to flee, and hide from men, he changed his Habit, he changed his name, and he even changed himself, concealing his great wisdom under the appearance of an idiot, so he would not be recognized or searched for, but rather left alone by all, as happened to him with his own brethren at the General Chapter of Assisi.[19] From there he retired to the solitary life in a hermitage, which he would never have left, had God not manifested His will as if by force. And finally he ended his life in another desert; the more distant from men, the more united with God.

III

This is, fish, the common nature that I praise in all of you and the happiness for which I congratulate you, not without envy. Coming down to particulars, it would be an unending matter if I were to expand upon the virtues with which the Author of Nature endowed it and made it admirable in every one of you. I will mention only a few of you. The one that holds

---

18. It is unclear precisely to which philosopher Vieira refers. In his sermons he often mentions Seneca, who extolled the virtues of retirement, but not in the manner found here. Elsewhere Vieira reveals his familiarity with the biographies of the Greek sages found in Diogenes Laertius's *Lives of Eminent Philosophers*, whose account of Bias of Priene may also have given inspiration for this anecdote.

19. Saint Anthony, born in Lisbon in 1195 and baptized as Fernando, first joined the Canons Regular of Saint Augustine at São Vicente de Fora in his native city. He abandoned that community for another religious community in Coimbra, where he later encountered the Franciscans, whom he joined. As a Franciscan, he traveled first to Morocco and later to Italy. According to tradition, his presence at the General Chapter at Assisi in 1221 drew little notice; only afterward would he become renowned as a preacher.

first place among all for being so celebrated in Scripture is that Holy Fish of Tobias to whom the Sacred Text gives no other name but that of great, as it truly was in the interior virtues which alone constitute true greatness. Tobias was walking with the Angel Saint Raphael as his company and, as he went down to the riverbank to wash the dust of the road off his feet, lo and behold a great Fish came upon him with its mouth open, as if it meant to swallow him. Tobias screamed in awe, but the Angel told him to pick up the Fish by its fin and drag it to land, cut it open, take out its entrails, and keep them, because they would be of much use to him. Tobias did so. When he asked what virtue there was in the Fish's entrails that he had been ordered to keep, the Angel answered that the gall was good for healing blindness and the heart for casting out Demons: *Cordis ejus particulam, si super carbones ponas, fumus ejus extricat omne genus Dæmoniorum: & fel valet ad ungendos oculos, in quibus fuerit albugo, & sanabuntur.*[20] So said the Angel and so experience immediately demonstrated, because, since Tobias's Father was blind, his son applied a bit of gall to his eyes and he recovered his sight entirely. And after a Demon called Asmodeus killed Sarah's seven husbands, that same Tobias married her; and when he burnt part of the heart in the house, the Demon fled thence and never came back. And so that Fish's gall removed the blindness from the elder Tobit, and cast out the Demons from the house of the younger Tobias. Such a kind-hearted Fish, with such a useful gall! Who will not praise it highly? If this Fish were dressed up in a cowl and tied with a cord, it would certainly resemble a maritime portrait of Saint Anthony. Saint Anthony opened his mouth against the Heretics and inveighed against them, carried away by fervor and zeal for the Faith and divine glory. And what did they do? They screamed like Tobias and were shocked at that man, and were afraid that he wanted to eat them. O men, if only there were an Angel who would reveal to you that man's heart; and that gall which so embitters you, how useful and necessary for you it is! If you opened his breast and saw his entrails, you would certainly find and clearly know that he wants but two things from you, and with you: One is to illuminate, and heal your blindnesses; and the other to cast out the Demons from your house. And yet you persecute the one who wants to remove your blindnesses, the one who wants to free you from Demons? There was only one difference between

---

20. Tobias 6:8–9, "If thou put a little piece of its heart upon coals, the smoke thereof driveth away all kind of devils . . . And the gall is good for anointing the eyes, in which there is a white speck, and they shall be cured."

Saint Anthony and that Fish: The Fish opened its mouth against someone who was washing himself, and Saint Anthony opened his mouth against those who did not want to wash themselves. Ah residents of Maranhão, there is so much I could tell you now about this case! Open, open these entrails; see, see this heart. But oh yes, I almost forgot! I do not preach to you, I preach to the fish.

Moving on from the fish in Scripture to those in Natural History, who will not praise and greatly admire the oft-celebrated virtue of the Remora? On the feast of a Minorite Saint, the minor fish should come before the others.[21] Who would not admire, I say, the virtue of that little fish, so small in body and so great in strength and power? Though no larger than a palm, if it sticks to the rudder of an Indiaman, despite the sails and winds and the ship's weight and size, it will halt and stay it more than anchors, so that the carrack will not move or go forward.[22] Oh, if there were a Remora on land that had as much strength as that of the sea, how fewer dangers there would be in life and how fewer shipwrecks in the world! If there ever was a Remora on land, it was Saint Anthony's tongue, in which, as in the Remora, the words of Saint Gregory Nazianzen are attested: *Lingua quidem parva est, sed viribus omnia vincit.*[23] In his most eloquent Epistle, the Apostle Saint James compares the tongue to the Carrack's rudder and to the horse's curb.[24] Both comparisons wonderfully declare the virtue of the Remora, which, when stuck to the Carrack's rudder, is a curb for the Carrack and a rudder for the rudder. And such was the virtue and strength of Saint Anthony's tongue. The rudder of human nature is the will, the

---

21. The official name of the first order of Franciscans, Ordo Fratrum Minorum, is rendered in English as the Order of Friars Minor. Its members are called friars or minorites.

22. Basil mentions this quality of the remora, as does Pliny the Elder in Books 9 and 32 of his *Natural History*. See Basil, *Exegetic Homilies*, pp. 115–116, and Pliny, *Natural History*, trans. H. Rackham et al., 10 vols. (Cambridge, Mass.: Harvard University Press, 1940), vol. 3, p. 215, and vol. 8, pp. 467, 469.

23. "The tongue is a little thing, but its strength conquers all." This citation is based on Gregory Nazianzen's Poem 2.1.34, "On Silence at the Time of Fasting," in particular line 65, "The tongue is a little thing but has more power than anything else." Vieira's preferred biblical commentator Cornelius Cornelii à Lapide employs it in a discussion of James 3, noting that it comes from that poem, inter alia. Since much of Poem 2.1.34 discusses tongues and speaking, Lapide likely tried to capture the essence of Gregory's references in a succinct phrase. See Lapide, *Commentarii in Epistolas Canonicas* (Lyon: Jacques and Mathieu Prost, 1627), p. III, and Gregory of Nazianzus, *Autobiographical Poems*, trans. and ed. Carolinne White (Cambridge: Cambridge University Press, 1996), pp. 165–181, esp. 169. The editors are grateful to S. Abrams Rebillard for this reference.

24. These comparisons are found in James 3:2–5.

Pilot is reason: But how seldom do the precipitate impulses of the will obey reason? Nevertheless, upon such a disobedient and rebellious rudder, Saint Anthony's tongue has shown how much strength it had, like the Remora, to tame and stop the fury of human passions. How many, running after Fortune on the Carrack Pride with the sails swollen by the wind and by their very pride (which is wind, too), were going to break up in the shallows, the bow already touching ground, had Saint Anthony's tongue, like a Remora, not grasped the rudder until the sails eased, as reason commanded, and the exterior and interior storm ceased? How many aboard the Carrack Vengeance, with the artillery readied and the fuses lit, were racing at full sail into battle where they would burn or sink, had the Remora of Saint Anthony's tongue not halted their fury until the wrath and hatred were calmed and they were amicably saved with flags of peace? How many sailing on the Carrack Greed, overloaded to the topsail and straining at all seams because of its weight, incapable of fleeing or of defending itself, would fall into the hands of Corsairs with the loss of all they carried and of all they were after, had Anthony's tongue not halted them like the Remora until, relieved of an unjust cargo, they escaped danger and made port? How many on the Carrack Sensuality, which always sails in a fog without the Sun of day or the Star of night, fooled by the Sirens' song and letting themselves be carried by the current, would get blindly lost either in Scylla or Charybdis where no Ship or sailor would appear, had the Remora of Anthony's tongue not contained them, until the weather cleared and they could get on course? This is the tongue, fish, of your great Preacher, which was also your Remora while you listened to it; and because it is now mute (even though it is preserved whole) so many shipwrecks are seen and wept over on land.[25]

But from admiring such a great virtue of yours, let us proceed to praising, or envying, another but not lesser one. Equally admirable is the quality of that other little fish which the Latins called Torpedo.[26] Both these fish we know here more by renown than by sight. But this is how great virtues are: The greater they are, the more they hide. The fisherman stands with his rod in hand, the hook at the bottom and the float on the water, and

---

25. The relic of Anthony's tongue is preserved in its own reliquary, separate from his other remains, at the saint's shrine in Padua.

26. An electric ray of the Torpedinidae family. Vieira appears to have derived his description of this fish from Aristotle. See his *Historia Animalium*, Book 9 (620b: lines 13–23); in Barnes, *Complete Works of Aristotle*, p. 966.

when he feels the Torpedo nip the bait, his arm starts to tremble. Can there be a greater, quicker, and more admirable effect? So that in a moment the virtue of the little fish passes from the mouth to the hook, from the hook to the line, from the line to the rod, and from the rod to the fisherman's arm. Very rightly I said that this praise would be mentioned with envy. Would that the fishermen in our element had or were given this trembling quality in all that they fish on land! They fish a lot, but the grand scale does not surprise me. What surprises me is that they fish so much and tremble so little. So much fishing and so little trembling? One might wonder where there are more fishermen and more ways and forms of fishing, whether at sea or on land. Surely, on land. I do not want to expand on them, even if it were great consolation for the fish. It is enough to make the comparison with the rod, for this is the instrument in our case. In the sea, rods fish; on land, poles (and all sorts of poles) fish, staffs fish, canes fish, batons fish, and even scepters fish, and fish more than all because they fish Cities and entire Kingdoms.[27] Is it then possible that, fishing things of such weight, men do not feel hand and arm tremble? If I had preached to men and had Anthony's tongue, I would have made them tremble. Twenty-two such fishermen found themselves listening by chance to a Sermon by Saint Anthony, and the Saint's words made them all tremble in such a way that they all threw themselves trembling at his feet, all confessed to their thefts trembling, all returned what they could trembling (this is what causes more trembling in this sin than in others), all, in short, changed their lives and their jobs, and mended their ways.[28]

I want to finish this discourse on the praises and virtues of fish with one who may or may not have listened to Saint Anthony or learned to preach from him. The truth is that it preached to me and, if I had been another, it would have converted me, too. Sailing from here to Pará (it is right that fish from our shores not be excluded), I saw a school of little fish that I did not recognize run across the surface of the water, leaping every now and then; and since I was told that the Portuguese called them "Four Eyes," I tried to investigate with my eyes the reason for this name.[29] I found that they truly

---

27. Vieira's terms for different poles have other meanings beyond their literal senses, indicating the various forms of judicial and military authority.

28. Vieira likely refers to the conversion of "twenty-two famous thieves" on the occasion of one of Saint Anthony's sermons. The hagiographic text refers not to fishermen, *pescadores*, but to sinners, *pecadores*. See Ribadeneyra, *Flos Sanctorum*, p. 389.

29. A four-eyed fish of the *Anableps* genus.

have four eyes, wholly complete and perfect. Give thanks to God, I said to it, and praise the liberality of His divine Providence toward you. To Eagles, who are the lynxes of the air, He gave only two eyes; and to Lynxes, who are the eagles of the land, also two; but to you, little fish, four. I was even more surprised when I pondered the circumstance of place in this wonder. So many instruments of sight for a little sea animal on the shores of those most vast lands where God allows so many thousands of people to live in blindness for so many centuries? Oh how high and incomprehensible God's reasons are and how deep the abyss of His judgments!

Philosophizing thus on the natural cause of this Providence, I noticed that those four eyes are a little out of the usual place and that the eyes in each pair are united like the two bulbs of a sandglass, in such a way that the ones on top look directly up and the ones on the bottom directly down. And the reason for this new architecture is that these little fish, swimming always at the surface of the water, are not only persecuted by other, larger fish in the sea, but also by a great quantity of seabirds that live on those shores. And since they have enemies in the sea and enemies in the air, Nature doubled their sentinels and gave them two eyes to look straight up, for watching out for the birds, and two others to look straight down, for watching out for the fish. Oh how well a rational Soul would have informed these four eyes, and how it would have been put to good use in them, better than in many men! This is what that little fish preached to me, teaching me that if I have Faith and the use of reason, I must only look straight up and only straight down: Upward, to consider that there is a Heaven, and downward, to remember that there is a Hell. He did not refer me to a passage from Scripture, but taught me then what David meant in a passage that I had not understood: *Averte oculos meos, ne videant vanitatem.*[30] Turn away my eyes, Lord, so they will not see vanity. But could David not turn his eyes wherever he wanted? Not the way he wanted, no. He wanted his eyes turned in such a way that they would not see vanity, and this he could not do in this world no matter where he turned his eyes, because in this world all is vanity: *Vanitas vanitatem, & omnia vanitas.*[31] Thus, for David's eyes not to see vanity, God would have to turn them in a way that they would only see, and look at, the other world in both its hemispheres: Either the top one, looking straight up to Heaven only, or the bottom one, looking straight down to Hell only. And this is the favor

---

30. Psalm 118:37, "Turn away my eyes that they may not behold vanity."

31. Ecclesiastes, 1:2, "Vanity of vanities, and all is vanity."

that the great Prophet asked of God, and this the doctrine that such a little fish preached to me.

But even though Heaven and Hell were not made for you, brother fish, I conclude and end your praises by giving you thanks for the way you help those who draw sustenance from you go to Heaven and not to Hell. You are the ones who sustain the Carthusians and the friars at Buçaco, and all the holy Families who profess the most rigorous austerity.[32] You are the ones who help all true Christians endure penance during Lent. You are the ones with whom Christ celebrated His Easter, the two times He ate with His Disciples after being resurrected.[33] Let the birds and the animals of the land be praised for making the banquets of the rich splendid and costly, and let you be glorified for being the companions of the fasting and abstinence of the just. You all have such kinship and sympathy with virtue that, while God forbids even the worst and cheapest meat during fasting, He permits the best and most delicate fish. And though only two days of the week are called yours, no day is barred to you.[34] One place only did the Astrologers give you among the celestial Signs, but those on earth who sustain themselves by you alone are the ones who have their places in heaven most assured. Finally, you are the creatures of that element among all elements whose fecundity is proper to the Holy Spirit: *Spiritus Domini fœcundabat aquas.*[35] God bestowed the blessing upon you that you might grow and multiply; and in order for the Lord to confirm that blessing on you, remember not to fail the poor with their remedy. Understand that in the sustenance of the poor you have your growth assured. Take the

---

32. These two groups of religious were known for their extreme asceticism. The friars at Buçaco mentioned here were Discalced Carmelites who lived in the heart of a forest atop a mountain in central Portugal.

33. Luke 24:42 and John 21:13 both mention Jesus eating fish after the Resurrection.

34. The Catholic faithful were instructed to fast on Wednesdays and Fridays.

35. "The Spirit of the Lord fertilized the waters." The marginal notes from the editio princeps indicate that this passage comes from the Septuagint version of Genesis 1:5, but this is not the case. The most recent critical edition of this sermon notes that Vieira's version does not appear in any version of the Bible. This passage, however, seems to be a corruption of another, *Spiritus Dei fecundabat aquas* or *Spiritus Dei fovebat aquas*, which appears in early seventeenth-century texts as representing some ancient versions of the same passage. François de Sales (1567–1622) includes this citation in a sermon on Saint Peter, and the Jesuit exegete Antonio de Escobar y Mendoza (1589–1669) uses it in his comments on the Paraclete. See François de Sales, *Sermons* (Paris: 1643), p. 401, and Antonio de Escobar y Mendoza, *Ad Evangelia Sanctorum Commentarii Panegyricus Moralibus Illustrati*, 12 vols. (Lyon: Pierre Prost, 1642–1648), vol. 2, p. 187. Cf. António Vieira, *Sermões*, ed. Arnaldo do Espírito Santo, 2 vols. (Lisbon: INCM, 2008–2010), vol. 2, p. 438.

example of the sisters sardines. Why do you think the Creator multiplies them in such innumerable numbers? Because they are the sustenance of the poor. The Sturgeon and the Salmon are very few because they are served at the tables of Kings and the Powerful; but the fish that satisfies the hunger of Christ's poor, the same Christ multiplies and increases. Those two fish, companions to the five loaves in the Desert, multiplied to such an extent that they fed five thousand men.[36] So if dead fish that sustain the poor multiply so much, how much more and better the living ones shall. Grow fish, grow and multiply, and let God confirm His blessing upon you.

IV

But before you go, just as you heard your praises, hear now also your reproaches. They will help to confound you, since they cannot make you mend your ways. The first unedifying thing about you, fish, is that you eat one another. A great scandal this is, but the circumstance makes it even greater. Not only do you eat one another, but the big ones eat the little ones. If it were the other way around, it would be less evil. If the little ones were to eat the big ones, a big one would be enough for many little ones. But, since the big ones eat the little ones, a hundred or a thousand little fish are not enough for just one big fish. See how Saint Augustine finds this strange: *Homines pravis, perversisque cupiditatibus facti sunt veluti pisces invicem se devorantes.*[37] Men with their evil and perverse greed become like the fish that eat one another. So foreign a thing it is, not only to reason but to nature itself, that you live by eating one another, all of you being created in the same element, all of you citizens of the same homeland, and all of you, finally, brothers. Saint Augustine, who preached to men, in order to depict the ugliness of this scandal more forcefully pointed to it among fish; and I, who preach to fish, want you to see it among men to have you realize how ugly and abominable it is. Look, fish, from there in the sea, to the land. No, no; that is not what I mean. Are you turning your eyes to the woods and to the Wilderness? Over here, over here; to the City

---

36. The feeding of the five thousand is recounted in all of the gospels. See Matthew 14:13–21; Mark 6:31–44; Luke 9:10–17; and John 6:5–15.

37. "The perverse and depraved lusts of human beings have made them like fishes devouring each other." In Augustine, Exposition on Psalm 64, point 9. This short section of the commentary comes under the heading "the present world is a turbulent sea, full of varied fish," and echoes several of Vieira's themes. In Augustine, *Expositions on the Psalms*, ed. John Rotelle, trans. Maria Boulding, 6 vols. (Hyde Park, NY: New City, 2000–2004), vol. 3, p. 276.

is where you should look. You think that only the Tapuias eat one another; the butchery here is far greater, the whites eat one another much more often.[38] Do you see all that commotion, do you see all that running about, do you see all that racing to the squares and crossing of the streets, do you see all that going up and down the pavement, do you see that coming and going without rest or quiet? Well, all of that is men seeking ways to eat, and ways to eat one another.

One of them dies. Immediately, you see many others falling upon the wretch to tear him into pieces and eat him. The heirs eat him; the beneficiaries eat him; the legatees eat him; the creditors eat him; the officers in charge of orphans eat him, as do those in charge of the deceased and of the absent; the Doctor who treated him or helped him die eats him; the bleeder who drew blood from him eats him; the wife who begrudgingly gives him the oldest bed sheets in the house for a shroud eats him; the one who digs his grave eats him, as does the one who rings the bells, and so do the ones who chant as they bear him to his burial. In short, the earth has not yet eaten the poor dead man, and the whole world has already eaten him. If at least men were only eaten after death, it might be less horrible and less lamentable. But so that you know the extent of your cruelty, consider, fish, how men, too, eat one another alive, just like you do. Job was alive when he said: *Quare persequimini me, & carnibus meis saturamini?*[39] Why do you persecute me so inhumanely, you who fill yourself with my flesh? Do you want to see a Job like this? Look at one of these men who are persecuted by lawsuits or accused of crimes, and look at how many are eating him. The Bailiff eats him, the Jailor eats him, the Scribe eats him, the Solicitor eats him, the Attorney eats him, the Investigator eats him, the Witness eats him, the Judge eats him; he has not yet been sentenced and he has already been eaten. Men are worse than crows. The unfortunate who goes to the gallows is not eaten by the crows until after he has been executed and killed; and the one who is being judged has not yet been executed or sentenced, and has already been eaten.

And so that you see how these who are eaten on land are the little ones, eaten in the same way that you in the sea eat one another, listen to God lamenting this sin: *Nonne cognoscent omnes, qui operantur iniquitatem, qui*

---

38. Vieira's Tapuias were indigenous peoples of the Brazilian interior, considered in contrast to the Tupi peoples of coastal areas. He invokes the commonplace of the perceived savagery of the more distant peoples.

39. Job 19:22, "Why do you persecute me as God, and glut yourselves on my flesh?"

devorant plebem meam, ut cibum panis?[40] Do you think, says God, that the time will not come when those who commit the wickedness will know and pay their due? And what wickedness is this that God singularly calls "the wickedness" as if there were none other in the world? And who are those who commit it? The wickedness is men eating one another, and those who commit it are the biggest ones who eat the little ones: *Qui devorant plebem meam, ut cibum panis.* In these words, as far as you are concerned, fish, it is important to pay close attention to the many other warnings, as many as the words themselves. God says that men eat not simply His people, but decidedly His plebs, *Plebem meam*, because the plebs and the plebeians, the littlest, the least powerful ones, and the ones who are least noticed in the Republic, are the ones who are eaten. And He does not just say that they are eaten in any manner, but that they are swallowed and devoured: *Qui devorant.* Because the big ones who rule the Cities and the Provinces do not satisfy their hunger by eating the little ones one by one, or little by little; rather, they devour and swallow entire peoples: *Qui devorant plebem meam.* And in what manner do they devour and eat them? *Ut cibum panis*: Not like other foods, but like bread. The difference between bread and other foods is that there are meat days for meat and fish days for fish and different months of the year for fruits; however, bread is a food for every day, eaten always and continually. This is what the little ones suffer. They are the daily bread of the big ones. And just as bread is eaten with everything, so too are the miserable little ones eaten with everything and in everything, not having or doing any job where they are not weighed down, where they are not fined, where they are not defrauded, where they are not eaten, swallowed, and devoured: *Qui devorant plebem meam, ut cibum panis.* Does this seem right to you, fish? I can see by the movement of your heads that you are all saying no, and by the way you look at one another that you are surprised and shocked that there is such injustice and wickedness among men! Well, you do this same thing yourselves. The biggest ones among you eat the little ones and the very big ones do not just eat one by one, but eat entire schools; and you do it continually, without respect for the hour, not just during the day but also at night, in the light and in the dark, just as men do.

If perchance you think these injustices among yourselves are tolerated and go without punishment, you are mistaken. Just as God punishes them

---

40. Psalm 13:4, "Shall not all they know that work iniquity, who devour my people as they eat bread?"

in men, so He in His way punishes them in you. The oldest among you
who listen to me and who are present saw, or at least you would have heard
it murmured by the passengers in the canoes and even more lamented
by their miserable oarsmen, how in this State the biggest who were sent
here, instead of governing and increasing that State, have destroyed it,
because they satisfied all the hunger they brought with them by eating and
devouring the little ones. So it was. But if by chance there are among you
some of those who, following in the ships' wake, go with them to Portugal
and return to your home waters, you would have heard over there in the
Tagus how these same biggest ones, who here ate the little ones, when
they arrive there find other bigger ones who in turn eat them. This is the
style of divine Justice, so ancient and manifest that even the Pagans knew
and celebrated it:

> Vos quibus rector maris, atque terræ
> Jus dedit magnum necis, atque vitæ;
> Ponite inflatos, tumidosque vultus;
> Quidquid à vobis minor extimescit,
> Maior hoc vobis Dominus minatur.[41]

Take notice, fish, of that definition of God, *Rector maris, atque terræ*,
Governor of sea and land, so that you do not doubt that the same custom
that God maintains for men on land He observes also for you in the sea. It
is therefore necessary that you watch yourselves and that you do not belit-
tle the doctrine that the great Doctor of the Church Saint Ambrose gave
you when, speaking to you, he said: *Cave nedum alium insequeris, incidas
in validiorem.*[42] Let the fish that persecutes the weakest one in order to eat
it beware lest it find itself in the mouth of the strongest and be swallowed.
We see it here every day. The Jackfish goes chasing after the Catfish, like

---

41. "You, whom the ruler of the earth and sea / has granted dread power over life and death: /
drop your puffed-up, arrogant airs. / Whatever a lesser man fears from you / threatens you
from a greater master." Seneca, *Thyestes*, Act 3, lines 607–611. There were several early modern editions of Seneca's plays; this passage, for example, can be found in an edition of his
Tragœdiæ (Lyon: Jean Pillhotte, 1596), p. 77. Translated in Seneca the Younger, *Tragedies*, 2
vols., trans. John G. Fitch (Cambridge, Mass.: Harvard University Press, 2002–2004), vol.
2, p. 283.

42. "Be on your guard, while you are in pursuit of him, against an attack of a still stronger
foe." The Latin for this quote found in the editio princeps is slightly different from the same
passage in Ambrose's fifth sermon on the six days of Creation: *Cave ne dum illum persequeris,
incidas ipse in validiorem.* See Ambrose, *Hexameron*, p. 169.

the dog after the hare, and, blind, does not see right behind him the Shark with four rows of teeth that will swallow him in one bite. It is what Saint Augustine also told you with greater elegance: *Prædo minoris fit præda maioris.*[43] But these examples, fish, are not enough to persuade your gluttony that the same cruelty that you use with the little ones has already found its matching punishment in the voracity of the big ones.

Since you experience it thus with so much injury to yourselves, it is important that from now on you be more civic-minded and zealous of the common good. This must prevail against each one's particular appetite, so that it does not happen that, just as today we see many of you so reduced, you come to be completely consumed. Are so many outside enemies not enough for you, and so many persecutors as shrewd and tenacious as are the fishermen who night and day never cease to besiege you and make war against you in so many ways? Do you not see the nets knitted and set up against you, traps woven against you, lines twisted against you, hooks bent and barbed against you, slings and harpoons against you? Do you not see that even rods are lances against you, and floats weapons of aggression? Is it then not enough for you to have so many, and so well-armed outside enemies, that even at home you should be the cruelest enemies to yourselves, persecuting one another in a conflict worse than civil war, eating one another? Stop, stop right away, brother fish, and may such a pernicious discord someday come to an end. And since I have called you brothers, and you are brothers, remember the obligations of that name. Were you not so quiet, and so peaceful, and so friendly to all, big and little, when Saint Anthony preached to you? Well, remain so, and you will be happy.

You will tell me (the same way men tell me) that you have no other means of sustaining yourselves. And how do they sustain themselves, the many among you who do not eat others? The sea is very large, very fertile, very abundant; and with what it tosses onto the beaches alone, it can sustain a large part of those who live in it. Animals eating one another is voracity and abuse, and not a law of Nature. Animals of the land and of the air that today eat one another did not eat one another at the beginning of the world, something that was convenient and necessary for the multiplication of all species. So it was (even more clearly) after the Flood; only two of each species having escaped, they could scarcely be preserved if they ate one another. And finally, at the time of the same Flood, when all

---

43. "As the lesser creature was a prey to you, you will be the stronger raptor's prey." In Augustine, Exposition on Psalm 123, point 10, in his *Expositions*, vol. 3, p. 52.

lived together inside the Ark, the wolf was looking at the lamb, the hawk at the partridge, the lion at the deer, and each one at those they used to feed upon. And if by chance they had that temptation there, all resisted it and resigned themselves to the rations from the common store that Noah doled out to them. Now if the animals from the other, warmer elements were capable of this temperance, why should the animals of the water not be? After all, if on so many occasions, out of a natural desire for self-preservation and increase, those animals made a virtue of necessity, do so, too; or make a virtue without necessity, and it will be a greater virtue.

Another very general thing that not so much disappoints me as makes me sorry for many of you is that remarkable ignorance and blindness experienced in all voyages by those who sail to these parts. A seaman takes a hook, ties a piece of cloth to it after cutting it in two or three places, and casts it on a thin pole until it touches the water. On seeing it, the fish heads for it blindly and gets stuck, gasping until, hanging like that in the air or tossed up onto the deck, it finally dies. Can there be greater ignorance and more complete blindness than this? To lose one's life, fooled by a piece of cloth? You will tell me that men do the same. I will not deny it. An army goes to battle against another army, men throw themselves upon the points of the pikes, spears, and swords, and why? Because someone fooled them and made a bait for them with two pieces of cloth. Among vices, vanity is the shrewdest fisherman, the one that most easily fools men. And what does vanity do? It places as bait, on the tips of those pikes, spears, and swords, two pieces of cloth, either white, called the Habit of Malta, or green, called that of Avis, or red, called that of Christ and of Santiago; and men, wanting to wear this piece of cloth on their breast, do not notice that they gulp and swallow the iron.[44] And then what happens? The same as happens to you. The one that swallowed the iron was killed right there, or on another occasion; and the same pieces of cloth return once again to the hook to fish others. By this example I concede to you, fish, that men do the same as you, though I do not think that this was the basis for your answer or excuse, since here in Maranhão, even though so much blood is spilled, there are no armies, nor such an ambition for Habits.

But I will not for that matter deny that here, too, men let themselves be fished by the same deceit, less honorably and more ignorantly. Who

---

44. The military orders of Malta, Avis, Christ, and Santiago were knightly orders from the Middle Ages. Membership in them during the early modern period was largely a sign of status for noblemen.

fishes the lives of all men in Maranhão, and with what? A seaman with some pieces of cloth. A Shipmaster comes from Portugal with four scraps from shops, with four cloths and four silks, already out of date and out of use. And what does he do? He baits with those cloths the residents of our town, waves them once and waves them twice, each time raising the price; and the Bonitos, or the ones who want to look pretty, all starving for glad rags, are held there gagging and stuck with debts from one year to the next, and from one harvest to the next, and there goes life.[45] This is no exaggeration. Everyone working his whole life, either on the farm, in the cane field, at the sugar mill, or in the tobacco field; and this work of a lifetime, who takes it away? Not the coaches, or the litters, or the horses, or the squires, or the pages, or the lackeys, or the tapestries, or the paintings, or the tableware, or the jewels. So, where does the whole life go and what is it spent on? On the sad rags in which they go out on the street, and for that they kill themselves all year long.

Is this not, my fish, great madness on the part of men with which you excuse yourselves? Of course it is, you cannot deny it. Well, if it is great madness for those who have the obligation of dressing to waste their lives for two pieces of cloth, then what about you, whom God dressed from head to foot either with such showy and appropriately colored skins or with silver and golden scales, outfits that never tear or wear out with time, nor vary or ever change with fashion? Is it not greater ignorance and greater blindness on your part to let yourselves be fooled by two little strips of cloth and caught by the jaws? Look at your Saint Anthony, whom the world could hardly fool with such vanities. When he was a boy, and a noble, he left the finery that is so prized at that age and traded it for a serge cassock and a sash of a Canon Regular. And, once he saw himself dressed like that, finding that shroud still very costly, he traded the serge for coarse wool and the sash for the rope.[46] With that rope and with that cloth he fished many, and these were the only ones who were not fooled and were sober.

---

45. "Bonitos" refers to the fish of that name, as well as to people characterized as "pretty ones."

46. Saint Anthony first joined the Canons Regular of Saint Augustine, then left that order for the Franciscans. He thus traded his clothing for habits of increasingly coarser, and thus more ascetic, fabrics.

V

Coming down to particulars, I will now say, fish, what I have against some of you. Starting here with our shore: On the very day I arrived here, hearing the Grunts and seeing their size, I was moved as much to laughter as to anger.[47] Is it possible that being such little fish, you will be the grunters of the sea? If with a sewing line and a twisted needle a crippled person can fish you, why should you grunt so much? But that is exactly why. Tell me, why does the Swordfish not grunt? Because usually one who has lots of sword has little tongue. This is no general rule; but it is a general rule that God does not want Grunts, and that He is particularly careful to knock down and humiliate those who grunt a lot. Saint Peter, whom your ancestors knew very well, had such a good sword that he alone advanced against a whole army of Roman Soldiers. And had Christ not ordered him to sheath his sword, I promise you that he would have cut off more ears than just Malchus's.[48] However, what happened to him that same night? Peter had grunted and blustered how, if all were to falter, he alone would be constant, if necessary until death. And so much the opposite happened. He alone faltered, more than anyone, and the voice of a little woman was enough to make him tremble and deny.[49] Before that he had already faltered in the same hour when he promised so much of himself. Christ told him in the Garden to keep watch and, coming back after a little while to check whether he was doing that, He found him sleeping so carelessly that not only did He wake him from his sleep, but also from his bravado: *Sic non potuisti una hora vigilare mecum?*[50] You, Peter, are the valiant one who shall die for me, and you could not keep watch with me for one hour? A little while ago so much grunting, and now so much sleeping? But so it was. Grunting a lot before an occasion is a sign of sleeping through it. So what do you think, brother Grunts? If this happened to the greatest fisherman, what can happen to the littlest fish? Measure yourselves and you will see how little basis you have for bravado or grunting.

---

47. The fish to which Vieira refers is the *Haemulon plumierii*, the common grunt, called *roncador* in Portuguese, which also means one who boasts.

48. Vieira refers to the seizing of Christ in the Garden of Gethsemane, when Peter cut off the ear of Malchus, a servant of the high priest Caiaphas.

49. Here the reference is to the woman at the Temple who identified Peter as one of Jesus's followers, an accusation that he denied.

50. Matthew 26:40, "What? Could you not watch one hour with me?"

If Whales grunted, their arrogance would have an excuse in their greatness. But even in those same Whales that arrogance would not be justified. What the Whale is among fish, the Giant Goliath was among men. If both the River Jordan and the Sea of Tiberias communicate with the Ocean, as they must, since everything flows from it, you should know well that this Giant was the grunt of the Philistines. For forty continuous days he was on the field in arms, defying all of the camps of Israel, without anyone daring to fight him. And in the end what came of all that arrogance? A little shepherd with a crook and a slingshot was enough to bring him down to earth. The arrogant and the proud take on God; and those who take on God come out always on the bottom. So, my Grunt friends, the true counsel is to be quiet and to imitate Saint Anthony. There are two things in men that generally make them grunts, because both swell them: knowledge and power. Caiphas grunted with knowledge: *Vos nescitis quidquam.*[51] Pilate grunted with power: *Nescis quia potestatem habeo?*[52] And both against Christ. But Christ's faithful servant Anthony, having so much knowledge as I told you already, and so much power as you yourselves experienced, was never heard speaking of knowledge or power, let alone bragging about them. And because he was so quiet, he made such an uproar.

In the voyage that I mentioned and in all those I made across the Equinoctial Line, I saw south of it what I had many times seen and remarked in men, and I was surprised that such cunning would have extended to fish and caught on among them. These I now speak of are called with great propriety Shark suckers, because little though they are, they do not simply cling to other, bigger fish, but they stick in such a way to their backs that they never let them go.[53] Of some animals of lesser strength and industry, it is said that they follow hunting Lions at a distance in order to sustain themselves with their leftovers. These Suckers do the same, as safe close by as those others are afar, because the big fish cannot bend its head or turn its mouth to those it carries on its back, and so it sustains their weight and their hunger besides. If this way of life, more shrewd than generous, by chance spread and caught on from one element to another, it was doubtless learned by the fish from above, after

---

51. John 11:49, "You know nothing."

52. John 19:10, "Knowest thou not that I have power."

53. Fish from the genus *Echeneis,* now commonly called remoras.

our Portuguese sailed there.[54] The Viceroy or Governor cannot depart for the Conquests without being surrounded by Suckers that cling to him in order to satisfy their hunger here, something they could not do there. The least ignorant, undeceived by experience, let go and seek their livelihood by other means; but those who continue to cling to the mercy and fortune of the big ones end up like the Suckers in the sea.

The Shark circles the Carrack at the calms of the Line, carrying its Suckers on its back, sewn so closely to its skin that they look more like patches or natural spots than like guests or companions. A hook on a chain is cast its way with the rations of four Soldiers, and the Shark throws itself furiously at the prey, swallows everything in a bite, and gets caught. Half the crew races to haul it up, it smacks the deck strongly with its last jerks, and at last the Shark dies and with it the Suckers. It seems as if I am hearing Saint Matthew who, while not a fisherman Apostle, describes this very scene on land. Once Herod was dead, says the Evangelist, the Angel appeared to Joseph in Egypt and told him that he could now return to his homeland, because all those who wanted to take the Child's life were dead: *Defuncti sunt enim qui quærebant animam Pueri*.[55] The ones who wanted to take the Christ Child's life were Herod and all his people, all his family, all his adherents, all who followed and hung on his fortune. For is it possible that all of these would have died together with Herod? Yes, because, as the Shark dies, the Suckers die with him, too: *Defuncto Herode, defuncti sunt qui quærebant animam Pueri*.[56] Lo and behold, you tiny ignorant and miserable fish, how wrong and deceitful this way of life that you have chosen is. Take the example of men, since they do not take yours, or follow, as they should, that of Saint Anthony.

God has His Suckers, too. One of them was David, who said: *Mihi autem adhærere Deo bonum est*.[57] Let others cling to the great of the earth, I only want to cling to God. So, too, did Saint Anthony; just look at this Saint and see how he clings to Christ and Christ to him. Truly, one can wonder which of the two is the sucker. It seems it is Christ, because the little one is always the one who clings to the bigger one, and the Lord made

---

54. Vieira says that this was learned by *os peixes do alto*. There are two interpretations for *do alto*, one meaning "on the high (seas)" and the one chosen here referring to people of importance and their retainers sailing upon the water, giving their example "from above."

55. Matthew 2:20, "For they are dead that sought the life of the child."

56. Matthew 2:19–20, "Herod was dead . . . they are dead that sought the life of the child."

57. Psalm 72:28, "But it is good for me to adhere to my God."

Himself so tiny in order to cling to Anthony.[58] But Anthony also made himself a Minor, to further cling to God.[59] Hence it follows that all who cling to God, who is immortal, are safe from dying like the other Suckers do. So sure that, even in the case in which God made Himself Man and died, He only died so that those who would cling to Him would not die. This was clearly seen in those who were already attached to Him, when He said: *Si ergo me quæritis, sinite hos abire*, If it is me that you want, let these go their way.[60] And even though only men can cling in this manner and not you, my little fish, you should at least imitate those other animals of the air and of the land which, when they come close to the big ones and look for protection in their power, do not cling in such a way that they will die together with them. Scripture tells of that famous tree that represented the great Nebuchadnezzar and on whose branches all the birds of the Sky rested, in whose shade all the animals of the land gathered, the ones and the others sustaining themselves by its fruits. But it also tells that the moment this tree was cut down, the birds flew away and the other animals fled.[61] Although you may come near the big ones, do not get so attached, however, that you kill yourselves for them or die with them.

Consider, living Suckers, how and why the others that clung to that big fish died. The Shark died because he ate, and they died for what they did not eat. Can there be greater ignorance than to die for someone else's hunger and by someone else's mouth? Let the Shark die since it ate and its gluttony killed it; but that the Sucker should die for what it did not eat is the greatest disgrace that one can imagine! I did not think that in fish, too, there was original sin. We men were so unfortunate that someone else ate and we pay for it. All our death began with Adam and Eve's sweet tooth; and what a great disgrace that we should die for what someone else ate! But we cleanse ourselves of this disgrace with a little water, while you cannot cleanse yourselves of your ignorance with all the water in the sea.

I also need to have a word with the Flying Fish, and my complaint is not small. Tell me, Flyers, did God not make you fish? So why do you play at birds? God made the sea for you and the air for them. Be content

---

58. Vieira refers to the hagiographic tradition which depicts Saint Anthony with the infant Jesus.

59. Vieira plays on the similarity between *menor*, lesser/minor, and (*frade*) *Menor*, Friar Minor, that is, Franciscan.

60. John 18:8, "If therefore you seek me, let these go their way."

61. The tree in Nebuchadnezzar's dream is described in Daniel 4:1–10.

with the sea and with swimming, and do not seek to fly, because you are fish. If by chance you do not know yourselves, look at your bones and your scales and you will know that you are not birds, but fish, and not even among the best fish. You will tell me, Flyer, that God gave you larger fins than He gave others of your size. So just because you got larger fins, should you make them into wings? But alas you do, even though your punishment so often undeceives you. You wanted to be better than the other fish, and because of that you are the most unfortunate. The hook or the slingshot kills other fish from above, but neither slingshot nor hook kills you; your presumption and your whim do. The ship sails on with the Mariner asleep and the Flyer hits the sail or the rope and falls, palpitating. Hunger kills the other fish and the bait fools them; the vanity of flying kills the Flyer and its bait is the wind. How much better it would have been for him to dive under the keel and live than to fly over the rigging and fall dead. Great ambition it is that, the sea being so immense, the whole sea should not suffice for so little a fish, who craves another, larger element. But see, fish, the punishment for ambition. God made the Flyer a fish and it wanted to be a bird, and the same God allows it to suffer the dangers of a bird as well as those of fish. All the sails are nets for it as a fish, and all the ropes are snares for it as a bird. See, Flyer, how swiftly your punishment arrived. A little while ago you were swimming alive in the sea with your fins, and now you lie on a deck shrouded in your wings. Not content with being a fish, you wanted to be a bird, and now you are no longer fish or fowl; you can neither fly nor swim. Nature gave you water, you wanted nothing but air, and I already see you put on the fire. Fish, let each one be content with its element. If the Flyer had not wanted to go from the second to the third, it would not have ended up in the fourth.[62] It was perfectly safe from the fire while it was swimming in the water; but because it wanted to be a butterfly of the waves, its wings came to be burned.

In view of these examples, Fish, keep in mind this maxim, all of you: He who wants more than his lot loses what he wants and what he has got. He who can swim and wants to fly will in time neither fly nor swim. Listen to the case of a Flyer on earth. Simon Magus, who got his surname from the Magical Art in which he was most famous, pretending to be the true Son of God announced the day when, before the eyes of all Rome, he

---

62. According to the ancients, the order of the four elements was earth, water, air, fire.

would rise to Heaven.[63] And, indeed, he began to fly very high. However, the prayer of Saint Peter, who was present, flew more swiftly than he did. When the Magus fell from on high, God did not want him to die straight away but to break his feet before everyone's eyes, as indeed happened. I want you to pay attention not to the punishment as such but to its form. That Simon should fall is a very good thing; that he should die would also have been a very good thing, considering his boldness and his diabolical art. But that from a fall so high he should not burst or break his head or his arms but just his feet? Yes, says Saint Maximus, because it is just that one who has feet for walking and wants wings for flying should lose the wings as well as the feet. As the Holy Father elegantly puts it: *Ut qui paulo ante volare tentaverat, subito ambulare non posset: & qui pennas assumpserat, plantas amitteret.*[64] And Simon has feet and wants wings, can walk and wants to fly; so break his wings that he will not fly and also his feet that he will not walk. Lo and behold, Flyers of the sea, what happens to those on earth, so that each one will be content with his element. If the sea were to take example from the rivers, after Icarus drowned in the Danube there would not be so many Icaruses in the Ocean.

O Soul of Anthony, only you had wings and flew without danger, because you knew how to fly downward and not upward! Already in the Apocalypse Saint John saw that woman whose adornment used up all the lights in the Firmament, and he says that two great Eagle wings were given to her: *Datæ sunt mulieri alæ duæ Aquilæ magnæ.*[65] And for what? *Ut volaret in desertum.*[66] To fly to the desert. A remarkable thing; it was not in vain that the same Prophet called it a great wonder. This woman was in Heaven: *Signum magnum apparvit in Cælo, mulier amicta Sole.*[67] Well, if the woman was in Heaven and the desert on earth, how is she given wings to

---

63. Simon Magus is mentioned in Acts 8:9–24, but the story of his attempts to levitate belong to apocryphal traditions that were widely disseminated in the Middle Ages and the early modern period.

64. "The one who a little before had tried to fly was suddenly unable to walk, and he who had assumed wings was deprived of his feet." Maximus of Turin, "On the Anniversary of Saints Peter and Paul." Early modern editions of Maximus labeled this particular text his fifth sermon on the subject of Peter and Paul's feast. See, for example, Leo I, Maximus, Peter Chrysologus, Fulgentius, and Valerian, *Opera Omnia* (Paris: Morelli, 1623), p. 664–665, and *The Sermons of St. Maximus of Turin*, ed. and trans. Boniface Ramsey (New York: Newman, 1989), p. 16.

65. Revelation 12:14, "There were given to the woman two wings of a great eagle."

66. Ibid., "That she might fly into the desert."

67. Revelation 12:1, "A great sign appeared in heaven: A woman clothed with the sun."

fly to the desert? Because there are wings for going up and wings for going down. The wings for going up are very dangerous; the wings for going down very safe, and such were Saint Anthony's. Saint Anthony's Soul was given two Eagle wings, which were that sublime double wisdom, natural and supernatural, as we know. And what did he do? He did not spread his wings to go up, he folded them to go down. And so folded were they that, even though he was the Ark of the Testament, he was, as I already told you, reputed to be a Layman and without science.[68] Flyers of the sea (I do not speak to those on land), imitate your Holy Preacher. If it seems to you that you can use your fins as wings, do not spread them to go up lest you hit a sail or the side of a ship; fold them to go down, go stick yourselves in some cave at the bottom and, the better hidden you are there, the safer you will be.

But since we are in the sea caves, before we leave them, let us deal with our brother Octopus, against which none less than Saint Basil and Saint Ambrose have great complaints.[69] The Octopus, with that hood on its head, looks like a Monk; with those rays spread, looks like a Star; with that lack of bones, looks like softness itself, like gentleness itself. And under such a modest appearance or such a holy hypocrisy, according to the uniform testimony of the two great Doctors of the Latin and Greek Churches, the said Octopus is the greatest traitor of the sea. The Octopus's treachery resides first in dressing or painting itself with the same colors as anything to which it clings. The colors that are finery in the Chameleon are malice in the Octopus; the shapes that are a fable in Proteus are truth and artifice in the Octopus. If it is in the seaweed, it turns green; if it is on the sand, it turns white; if it is in the mud, it turns dun; and if it is on some rock, as it most ordinarily is, it turns the color of that rock. And what follows from here? It follows that another fish, oblivious to the treachery, passes by incautious; and the bandit, waiting in ambush in its own disguise, suddenly shoots its arms at it and makes it a prisoner. Would Judas have done more? He would not have done more, because he did not even do as much. Judas embraced Christ, but others arrested Him; the Octopus is the one who embraces and moreover arrests. Judas made the sign with his arms, and the Octopus made ropes of his own arms. Judas, it is true,

68. The bull of canonization by Pope Gregory IX for Saint Anthony referred to him as "Ark of the Testament" in recognition of his knowledge of sacred scripture. Vieira's *sciencia* is rendered here as science, meaning knowledge.

69. Basil, *Exegetic Homilies*, p. 110; and Ambrose, *Hexameron*, pp. 176–177.

was a traitor, but with lanterns in hand. He planned his treachery in the dark, but carried it out in good light. The Octopus, darkening itself, makes others blind to it; and the first treachery and theft that he makes is of the light, so that it will not reveal the colors. See, perfidious and vile Fish, what your wickedness is; for, in comparison to you, Judas seems less of a traitor.

Oh what an insulting excess and so unworthy of so pure, so clear, and so crystalline an element as Water, natural mirror not only of earth but also of Heaven. The Prophet says in celebration that, in the clouds of the air, even the water is dark: *Tenebrosa aqua in nubibus aeris*.[70] And he said specifically in the clouds of the air to attribute the darkness to the other element and not to water, which in its own element is always clear, diaphanous, and transparent, in which nothing can be hidden, concealed, or dissimulated. And that in this same element a monster so deceitful, so false, so shrewd, so cunning, and so recognizably treacherous should be created, conserved, and allowed to act with so much harm to the public good? I see, Fish, that, thanks to the knowledge that you have of the lands where your seas break, you respond to me agreeing that on them, too, there are falsehoods, deceits, pretenses, swindles, traps, and much greater and more pernicious treacheries. And on this same point that you argue, you could also apply to those similar to you yet another characteristic that is very much their own; but since you would rather be quiet about it, I will be quiet, too.[71] With great confusion, however, I confess everything to you, and much more than what you say, since I cannot deny it. But cast your eyes upon Anthony, your Preacher, and you will see in him the purest exemplar of candor, sincerity, and truth, where there never was malice, pretense, or deceit. And

---

70. Psalm 17:12, "Dark waters in the clouds of the air."

71. This passage is obscure. Clearly Vieira means more than simply hypocrisy. It is possible that he refers to the illegal enslavement of the native peoples by the Portuguese settlers. This issue was the source of repeated friction between the Jesuits and the colonists, discord that led to the Jesuits' retreat from Maranhão in 1637. When Vieira led a new Jesuit contingent to re-establish the Amazon mission in 1653, his group agreed that, for the survival of the mission, they would not speak of this issue unless they were asked by the colonists to do so. Vieira was nevertheless invited to preach on the topic in his first sermon in São Luís, and so he preached his "Sermão das Tentações" on the first Sunday of Lent 1653. But it does not appear that he publicly addressed indigenous slavery again and maintained that silence until the following year, when he pronounced these words. On the Jesuits' agreement, see J. Lúcio de Azevedo, *História de António Vieira*, 2. vols. (Lisbon: Livraria Classica, 1918–1921), vol. 1, pp. 215–216; on Vieira's "Sermão das Tentações," see Thomas Cohen, *The Fire of Tongues: António Vieira and the Missionary Church in Brazil and Portugal* (Stanford, Calif.: Stanford University Press, 1998), pp. 59–66.

know, too, that for all of this to exist in each one of us, it used to be enough to be Portuguese, one did not have to be a Saint.

I have finished, Brother Fish, your praises and reproaches, and I have fulfilled, as I promised, both obligations of salt, though of the sea and not of the earth: *Vos estis sal terræ*. There is only one very necessary warning that I should give to you who live in these seas. Since they are so full of reefs and shoals, you know well how many ships are lost and wash up onshore, enriching the sea and impoverishing the land. It is thus important to be wary of this wealth, for in it lies great danger, because all those who profit from the goods of the shipwrecked are excommunicated and doomed. This penalty of excommunication, one that is most serious, was not applied to you, but to men. But God has many times shown that when animals commit materially that which is forbidden by this Law, they, too, incur its penalties in their own way; and at that moment they begin to languish until they end miserably. Christ ordered Saint Peter to go fishing, and in the mouth of the first fish that he caught he would find a coin with which to pay a certain tribute.[72] If Peter was to catch more fish than this, supposing this was the first, from its price and that of the others he could make the money with which to pay that tribute of only one silver coin of little weight. What a mystery it is that the Lord orders that it should be taken from the mouth of this fish and that this one should die before the others. Pay attention now. Fish do not mint coins at the bottom of the sea, or have contracts with men from which they can earn money. Therefore, the coin that this fish had swallowed belonged to some ship that had been wrecked in those seas. And the Lord wanted to show that those penalties which Saint Peter or his successors fulminate against men who take the goods of the shipwrecked, the fish, too, incur them in their own way, dying before the others, and with the same money that they swallowed stuck in their throats. Oh how good a doctrine this would be for the land, were I not preaching to the sea. To men, there is no more miserable death than to die with a foreign object stuck in the throat, because it is a sin which not even Saint Peter or the Supreme Pontiff himself can absolve. To be sure, men incur eternal death, of which fish are incapable; fish, however, rush to their temporal death, as in this case, if, as I have said, they do not materially abstain from the goods of the shipwrecked.

---

72. The story of the tribute money is in Matthew 17:23–28.

VI

With this last warning I give you leave, or I take leave of you, my Fish. And so that you can go comforted by the Sermon, since I do not know when you will hear another, I want to give you some relief for a very old discomfort which you all have borne since Leviticus was published. In the Ecclesiastical Law, or the Ritual of Leviticus, God chose certain animals that were to be sacrificed to Him; but all of them were either land animals or birds, with fish totally excluded from sacrifices. And who doubts that such a universal exclusion justified great discomfort and regret on the part of all the inhabitants of an element so noble that it was worthy of providing the matter for the first Sacrament?[73] The principal reason why fish were excluded was that other animals could go to the sacrifice alive, and fish generally not, only dead; and God does not want a dead thing to be offered to Him or to arrive at His Altars. This point, too, would be very important and necessary for men, were I to preach to them. Oh how many souls arrive at that Altar dead, because they arrive, and are not horrified to arrive, in a state of mortal sin! Fish, give great thanks to God for delivering you from this danger, because it is better to not arrive at the Sacrifice than to arrive dead. Let other animals offer God their sacrifice; as for you, offer Him your not arriving at the sacrifice. Let others offer blood and life as sacrifice to God; as for you, offer respect and reverence as sacrifice to Him.

Ah Fish, how much I envy you that natural irregularity! How much better it would be for me to not take God in my hands than to take Him so unworthily! In all wherein I surpass you, fish, I recognize many advantages in you. Your brutishness is better than my reason and your instinct better than my will. I speak, but you do not offend God with words. I remember, but you do not offend God with memory. I reason, but you do not offend God with understanding. I yearn, but you do not offend God with desire. You were created by God to serve man and you achieve the end for which you were created. I was created to serve Him, and I cannot achieve the end for which I was created. You shall not see God, and you will be able to come before Him very confidently because you have not offended Him. I hope to see Him, but with what face shall I come before His divine regard, if I do not cease to offend Him? Ah, I almost want to say that it would have been better for me to be like you; for the Supreme Truth said of a man who had the same obligations as I have that it would have been better for him to not

---

73. Vieira here refers to the water of baptism.

be born, or to not be born a man: *Si natus non fuisset homo ille.*[74] And since we who are born men respond so poorly to the obligations of our birth, be content, Fish, and give great thanks to God for yours.

Benedicite cete, & omnia, quæ moventur in aquis Domino:[75] Praise God, Fish, the big and the small; and, divided into two immense choirs, praise Him all in unison. Praise God, because He created you in such numbers. Praise God, who has distinguished you with so many species. Praise God, who has dressed you in such variety and beauty. Praise God, who provided you with all the instruments necessary for life. Praise God, who gave you such a large and pure element. Praise God, who, coming into this world, lived among you and called to Himself those who lived with you and on you. Praise God, who sustains you. Praise God, who preserves you. Praise God, who multiplies you. Praise God, finally, by serving and sustaining man, the end for which He created you. And just as at the beginning He gave you His blessing, may He give it to you now as well. Amen. Since you are not capable of Glory or Grace, your Sermon does not end in Grace and Glory.

---

74. Matthew 26:24, "If that man had not been born."

75. Daniel 3:79, "O ye whales, and all that move in the waters, bless the Lord."

SERMAM
DA
SEXAGESIMA
Prégado na Capella Real.

*Este Sermaõ prégou o Author no anno de 1655. vindo
dà Miſſaõ do Maranhaõ, onde achou as difficulda-
des, que nelle ſe apontaõ: as quaes vencidas, com no-
vas ordens Reaes voltou logo para a meſma Miſſaõ.*

Semen eſt Verbum Dei. Luc. 8.

§. I.

 SE quizeſſe
Deos, que eſte
taõ illuſtre, &
taõ numeroſo
auditorio ſahiſſe hoje taõ
deſenganado da préga-
çaõ, como vem enganado
com o Prégador! Ouça-
mos o Euangelho, & ou-
çamolo todo : que todo
he do caſo, que me leuou,
& trouxe de tam longe.
*Ecce exijt, qui ſeminat,
ſeminare.* Diz Chriſto,
que ſahio o Prégador E-
uangelico a ſemear a pa-
A laura

Frontispiece of the Sexagesima Sermon in António Vieira's *Sermoens . . . Primeyra Parte* (Lisbon: João da Costa, 1679). Biblioteca Nacional de Portugal, shelfmark L-5255-A.

3

The Sexagesima Sermon

Preached in the Royal Chapel
The Author preached this sermon in the year of 1655,
coming from the Maranhão Mission, where he encountered
the difficulties that are indicated here.
Once these were conquered,
the author returned immediately to the same Mission
with new Royal orders.

Semen est Verbum Dei.
LUKE 8[1]

I

And what if God wanted such an illustrious and numerous audience to leave today as undeceived by the preaching as it comes deceived by the Preacher? Let us listen to the Gospel and let us listen to it all, since it is all about the affair that took me so far and brought me back.

Ecce exijt, qui seminat, seminare:[2] Christ says that the Evangelical Preacher went out to sow the divine word. This text sure seems like it comes from the books of God. Not only does it mention sowing, but it also deals with going out. *Exijt*, because on the day of the harvest our sowing will be measured and our paces counted. The world, to you who till in its way, neither satisfies what you expend nor compensates for how much you walk. God is not like that. For those who till in God's way, the very going out is sowing, because from paces, too, they gather fruit. Among the sowers of the Gospel, there are some who go out to sow and others who sow without going out. Those who go out to sow are the ones who

---

1. Luke 8:11, "The seed is the word of God." Vieira changed *Domini* to *Dei.*

2. Matthew 13:3, "Behold the sower went forth to sow." The Rheims-Challoner translation for *exijt* is "go forth," but Vieira uses *sair*, "to go out." Throughout the sermon Vieira moves between the three texts of the Parable of the Sower: Matthew 13:3–8, Mark 4:3–9, and Luke 8:5–8.

go preach in India, in China, in Japan; those who sow without going out are the ones who are content with preaching in the homeland. All may have their reasons, but for all there is a reckoning. Those who have their field at home will have their sowing paid. Those who go such a long way in search of their field shall have their sowing measured and their paces counted. Ah Day of Judgment! Ah Preachers! Those of you who work here will find yourselves with more Palace, those of you who work there with more paces: *Exijt seminare.*[3]

But from right here where I stand I see that you remark (and remark about me) that Christ says the sower of the Gospel went out, yet does not say he returned. Because for Evangelical Preachers, the men who profess to preach and to propagate the Faith, it is right to go out, but it is not right to return. What were the properties of those Animals in Ezechiel that pulled the triumphal car of God's glory and signified the Preachers of the Gospel? *Nec revertebantur, cùm ambularent*: Once gone, they did not return.[4] The pair of reins by which they governed themselves was the impetus of the spirit, as the text says. But that spirit had impulses to carry them forth, not to bring them back; because it is better not to go out if one goes out only to return. So you argue very rightly, and I say so as well. But I ask: And what if, when that Evangelical sower went out, he were to find the field taken? What if the thorns were to arm themselves against him, what if the stones were to rise against him and block his paths, what should he do then? The sower of our Gospel experienced all these obstacles that I mention and all these setbacks. He started to sow (says Christ) but with scant fortune. Part of the wheat fell among thorns, and the thorns choked it: *Aliud cecidit inter spinas, & simul exortæ spinæ suffocaverunt illud.*[5] Another part fell on stones, and dried up on the stones for lack of moisture: *Aliud cecidit super petram, & natum aruit, quia non habebat humorem.*[6] Another part fell on the path, and men trampled it and birds ate it: *Aliud cecidit secus viam, & conculcatum*

---

3. Vieira here contrasts *passos*, paces or strides, with *paço*, palace. The royal chapel where he delivered this sermon was located in Lisbon's Paço da Ribeira.

4. Ezechiel 1:12, "And they turned not when they went." The editio princeps includes a marginal note to Gregory the Great, likely to his Two Books of Homilies on Ezechiel, in particular Book 1, Homily 5, which deals with this passage. See, for example, his *Opera*, 4 vols. (Rome: Typographia Vaticana, 1608–1613), vol. 3, pp. 44–52.

5. Luke 8:7, "Some fell among thorns, and the thorns growing up with it, choked it."

6. Luke 8:6, "Some fell upon a rock: and as soon as it was sprung up, it withered away, because it had no moisture." Luke's *supra* becomes Mark's *super* in this passage.

est, & volucres cæli comederunt illud.[7] Now see how all the world's creatures armed themselves against this sowing. All the creatures in the world can be reduced to four kinds: rational creatures like men; sentient creatures like animals; vegetative creatures like plants; insentient creatures like stones; and that is all. Did any one of these fail to arm itself against the sower? None. Insentient nature persecuted him in the stones; vegetative nature in the thorns; sentient nature in the birds; rational nature in the men. And notice the wheat's misfortune: Where it could expect nothing but reason, it found greater offense. Stones dried it, thorns choked it, birds ate it. And men? They trampled it: *Conculcatum est. Ab hominibus* (says the Gloss).[8] When Christ sent the Apostles to preach throughout the world, this is how He spoke to them: *Euntes in mundum universum, prædicate omni creaturæ.*[9] Go and preach to every creature. How is that again, Lord? Are animals not creatures? Are trees not creatures? Are stones not creatures? Are the Apostles to preach to the stones? Are they to preach to the tree trunks? Are they to preach to the animals? Yes, says Saint Gregory following Saint Augustine.[10] Because, since the Apostles were going to preach to all the nations of the world, many of them barbarian and uneducated, they were bound to find men who had degenerated into all species of creatures. They were bound to find human men; they were bound to find brutish men; they were bound to find trunk men; they were bound to find stone men. And when Evangelical Preachers go preach to every creature, to have all creatures arm themselves against them? Great misfortune!

And yet that of the sower of our Gospel was not the greatest misfortune. The greatest is the one experienced in the field that I went to and to which I now come. Everything that wheat suffered here, the sowers suffered

---

7. Luke 8:5, "Some fell by the way side, and it was trodden down, and the fowls of the air devoured it."

8. "It was trampled. By men." Vieira indicates the Ordinary Gloss, the scriptural commentary that often accompanied the Bible texts in later medieval and early modern editions, but the passage is not found in that gloss for Luke 8:5. It is, however, associated with Luke's gospel in the gloss on Matthew 13:4. See *Biblia Sacra cum Glossa interlineari, ordinaria*, 6 vols. (Venice: 1588), vol. 5, p. 44.

9. Mark 16:15, "Go ye into the whole world, and preach the gospel to every creature."

10. Vieira's assertion is cryptic. Indeed, in the *Catena Aurea*, a collection of sayings from church fathers compiled by Thomas Aquinas (1225–1274), a quotation from Gregory follows after one from Augustine on precisely the conundrum created by Christ's command. But Gregory is the only one who expands on the need to preach to all creatures. See Thomas Aquinas, *Catena Aurea*, 4 vols. in 6 books (Oxford: J. Parker, 1841–1845), vol. 2, book 1, pp. 343–345.

there. If you pay close attention, here there was withered wheat, choked wheat, eaten wheat, and trampled wheat. Withered wheat: *Natum aruit, quia non habebat humorem*. Choked wheat: *Exortæ spinæ suffocaverunt illud*. Eaten wheat: *Volucres cæli comederunt illud*. Trampled wheat: *Conculcatum est*. All this the Evangelical sowers of the Maranhão mission have suffered for the past twelve years. There were Missionaries choked, because some drowned in the mouth of the great Amazon River. There were Missionaries eaten, because the barbarians on the Island of the Aruans ate others. There were Missionaries withered, because this is how the ones who went on a journey to the Tocantins returned, withered from hunger and disease; like the one who, wandering twenty-two days lost in the bush, slaked his thirst only with the dew that he licked off leaves.[11] See if *Natum aruit, quia non habebat humorem* does not fit his case. And that, on top of being withered, being choked, and being eaten, they should still be trampled and persecuted by men![12] *Conculcatum est?* I do not complain nor do I say it, Lord, for the sowers; I say it for the field only, for the field only do I feel it. For the sowers, these are glories. Withered, yes, but withered for the love of You. Choked, yes, but choked for the love of You. Eaten, yes, but eaten for the love of You. Trampled and persecuted, yes, but trampled and persecuted for the love of You.

Now my question returns. And what would the Evangelical sower do in this case, or what should he do, seeing his first works so unsuccessful? Would he leave the tilling behind? Would he give up his sowing? Would he stay in the field idle, just because he had gone there? Probably not. But if he were to return home very quickly to fetch some tools with which to clear the land of stones and thorns, would this be giving up? Would this be withdrawing? Certainly not. We have the evidence in that same text by Ezechiel with which you argued. We have seen before how the text said that those Animals of God's chariot, once gone, did not return: *Nec revertebantur, cùm ambularent*. Read now two lines below and you will see that the same text says that those Animals

11. Vieira refers to the various missions launched from São Luís into the Brazilian hinterlands, whether to the west toward the Island of Marajó and the Amazon river valley or to the south along the Araguaia and Tocantins rivers. His expression "twelve years" counts from the death of mission founder Luís Figueira in 1643. See Thomas Cohen, *The Fire of Tongues: António Vieira and the Missionary Church in Brazil and Portugal* (Stanford, Calif.: Stanford University Press, 1998), p. 69.

12. Vieira alludes to the mutinous resistance that the Jesuits faced from the colonists in Maranhão.

returned like a lightning bolt: *Ibant, & revertebantur in similitudinem fulguris coruscantis.*[13] Well, if the Animals went out and returned like a lightning bolt, how can the text say that, when they went out, they did not return? Because whoever goes out and then comes back like a lightning bolt does not return. To go out and come back like lightning is not to return, it is to move ahead. Thus did the sower of our Gospel. He was not discouraged by the first, or the second, or the third loss. He continued ahead with the sowing and was so fortunate that this fourth and last part of the wheat more than compensated the losses of the rest. The wheat sprouted, grew, shot up, ripened, was gathered, was measured, and it was found that one grain multiplied a hundredfold, *Et fecit fructum centuplum.*[14]

Oh what great hopes this sowing gives me! Oh what a great example this sower gives me! The sowing gives me great hopes because, even when the first labors are lost, the last ones will be successful. The sower gives me a great example because, after losing the first, the second, and the third parts of the wheat, he profited from the fourth and last part and from it gathered much fruit. Since the three parts of life were lost, since the thorns carried off one part of the years, since the stones carried off another part, since the paths, and so many paths, carried off another part, why should this fourth and last part, this final quarter of life, be lost as well? Why should it not bear fruit? Why should life's years not also have what every year has? The year has time for flowers and time for fruit. Why should life not have its autumn, too? Some flowers fall, others dry up, others wilt, others are carried away by the wind; the few that cling to the trunk and convert into fruit are the only fortunate ones, the only discreet ones, the only enduring ones, the only ones that benefit, the only ones that sustain the world. Is it right that the world should die of hunger? It is right that the last days should be spent in flower? It is not right, nor does God want it so, nor shall it be so. This is why I said at the beginning that you came here deceived by the Preacher. But so that you can go away undeceived by the Sermon, in it I will deal with a matter of great weight and importance. It will serve as a prologue to the Sermons that I shall preach to you as well as to the others that you shall hear this Lent.

---

13. Ezechiel 1:14, "Ran and returned like flashes of lightning."

14. Luke 8:8, "Yielded fruit a hundredfold."

II

Semen est Verbum Dei

The wheat sowed by the Evangelical Preacher, says Christ, is the word of God. The thorns, the stones, the path, and the good ground upon which the wheat fell are the diverse hearts of men. The thorns are the hearts disturbed by cares, by wealth, by delights; and in these the word of God is choked. The stones are hard and obstinate hearts; and in these the word of God dries up and, even if it sprouts, does not take root. The paths are hearts restless and upset by the impermanence and commotion of the things of the world, some that go, some that come, others that cut across, and all pass. And on these paths the word of God is trampled, because it is either ignored or despised. Finally, the good ground is the kind heart, or the men with kind hearts. And in these the divine word takes hold and bears fruit with such fecundity and abundance that for each one a hundred are gathered: *Et fructum fecit centuplum.*

This great fructifying of the word of God is what I consider today, and it causes a doubt or amazement that leaves me in suspense and confounded upon ascending the pulpit. If the word of God is so effective and powerful, how come we see such little fruit from the word of God? Christ says that the word of God bears fruit at the rate of a hundred to one; and I would be content if it were to bear fruit at the rate of one to a hundred. If with every hundred Sermons one man were to convert and mend his ways, the world would already be holy. This argument of Faith, founded on Christ's authority, is made stronger still by experience, when times past are compared to the present. Read the Ecclesiastical Histories and you will find them all filled with the admirable effects of the preaching of God's word: So many sinners converted, such change of life, such reformation of customs! The great despising the wealth and vanities of the world; Kings renouncing their scepters and crowns; the youth and the nobility going off to the deserts and to caves! And today? None of this. Never in the history of God's Church has there been so much preaching or have there been so many preachers as today. So if the word of God is sown to such an extent, how does it bear so little fruit? There is not one man who by a Sermon will look within himself and change; there is no young man who will repent; there is no old man who will be undeceived. What is this? Just as God is no less omnipotent today, so His word today is no less powerful than it was before. Well, if the word of God is so powerful, if the word of God has so many preachers today, why do we not see any fruit today from the word of God? Such a great and important question will be the matter of the Sermon. I want to start by preaching to myself. To myself it will be, and to you, too: To myself, so I learn to preach; to you, so you learn to listen.

III

The scarcity of fruit borne by the word of God in the world may stem from one of three causes: Either it is due to the preacher, or to the listener, or to God. For a soul to convert by means of a Sermon, there must be three concurrences: The preacher must concur with the doctrine, persuading; the listener must concur with comprehension, understanding; God must concur with grace, illuminating. For a man to see himself, three things are necessary: Eyes, a mirror, and light. If he has a mirror and is blind, he cannot see himself for lack of eyes; if he has a mirror and eyes, and it is night, he cannot see himself for lack of light. Thus the need for light, the need for a mirror, and the need for eyes. What is the conversion of a soul if not a man entering into himself and seeing himself? For this sight eyes are necessary, light is necessary, a mirror is necessary. The preacher concurs with the mirror, which is the doctrine; God concurs with the light, which is the grace; the man concurs with the eyes, which are the knowledge. Now if we posit that the conversion of souls through preaching depends on these three concurrences, of God, of the preacher, and of the listener, which one should we understand to be at fault? The listener, the preacher, or God?

Firstly, God is not at fault, nor can He be at fault. This is a proposition of Faith, defined at the Council of Trent, and we have it in our Gospel. Of the wheat that the sower scattered on the ground, one part thrived and three were lost. And why were these three lost? The first was lost because the thorns choked it; the second, because the stones dried it; the third, because men trampled it and birds ate it. This is what Christ says, but notice what He does not say. He does not say that any part of that wheat was lost because of the Sun or the rain. The reason why seeds are ordinarily lost is the instability and intemperance of the weather: Either there is too little or too much rain, too little or too much Sun. So why does Christ not introduce in the Gospel Parable some wheat that would be lost because of the Sun or the rain? Because the Sun and the rain are Heaven's influences, and when the word of God does not bear fruit, it is never Heaven's fault, it is always our fault. The seeds may fail to bear fruit because of the tangle of the thorns, or the hardness of the stones, or the straying of the paths, but for the lack of Heaven's influences it never is nor can be. For His part, God is always ready to warm with the Sun and to water with the rain; with the Sun to illuminate, and with the rain to soften, if our hearts so wish: *Qui solem suum oriri facit super bonos, & malos, & pluet super justos, & injustos.*[15] If God gives His Sun and His rain to the good and to the bad, how can He deny it to the bad who want to make themselves good? This point is so clear that we need not be detained with further proof. *Quid debui facere vineæ meæ, & non feci?* said God through Isaiah.[16]

So, since it is certain that it is not because of God that the divine word fails to bear fruit, it follows that it is either the fault of the preacher or the fault of the listeners. Which one can it be? Preachers blame the listeners, but that is not right. If it were the fault of the listeners, the word of God would not bear much fruit. But when it does not bear any fruit and has no effect, it is not because of the listeners. Let me prove it. Listeners are either bad or good: If they are good, the word of God bears great fruit in them; if they are bad, even though it does not bear fruit in them, it has an effect. We find this in the Gospel. The wheat that fell on the thorns sprouted but was choked: *Simul exortæ spinæ suffocaverunt illud.* The wheat that fell on the stones also sprouted but dried up: *Et natum aruit.* The wheat that fell on good ground sprouted and bore fruit, multiplying greatly: *Et natum fecit fructum centuplum.* So the wheat that fell on the good ground sprouted and bore fruit; the wheat that fell on the bad ground did not bear fruit, but it sprouted. Because the word of God is so fecund that among the good it bears much fruit, and it is so effective that among the bad, even if it does not bear fruit, it has an effect. Cast upon the thorns, it did not bear fruit; but it sprouted even among the thorns. Cast upon the stones, it did not bear fruit; but it sprouted even on the stones. The worst listeners in the Church of God are the stones and the thorns. And why? Because they are sharp as thorns and hard as stones. Listeners with sharp understanding and listeners with hardened wills are the worst there are. Listeners with sharp understanding are bad listeners, because they come only to listen to subtleties in the hope of gallantries, to evaluate thoughts, and sometimes also to sting those who do not sting them. *Aliud cecidit inter spinas*: The wheat did not sting the thorns, instead the thorns stung it; the

---

15. Matthew 5:45, "Who maketh his sun to rise upon the good, and bad, and raineth upon the just and the unjust."

16. Isaiah 5:4, "What is there that I ought to do more to my vineyard, that I have not done to it?"

same happens here. You think the Sermon stung you, and it is not so; it is you who sting the Sermon. This is why those with sharp understanding are bad listeners. But those with hardened wills are even worse. Because a sharp understanding can be wounded by its very edge, and a sharpness can be defeated by another, greater one. But against hardened wills sharpness is no good; it only causes more damage, because the sharper the arrows, the more easily they break against the stone. Oh deliver us God from hardened wills, even worse than stones. The staff of Moses softened the stones and yet could not soften a hardened will: *Percutiens virga bis silicem, & egressæ sunt aquæ largissimæ. Induratum est cor Pharaonis.*[17] And even though listeners with sharp understanding and listeners with hardened wills are the most rebellious, such is the strength of the divine word that, despite the sharpness, it sprouts among thorns, and, despite the hardness, it sprouts on stones. We could argue with the farmer of the Gospel about not cutting the thorns and not digging up the stones before sowing, but he left the stones and thorns in the field on purpose, so that the strength of what he sowed would be seen. The strength of the divine word is such that, even without cutting or clipping the thorns, it sprouts among thorns. The strength of the divine word is such that, even without digging up or softening the stones, it sprouts on stones. Hearts tangled like thorns, hearts dry and hard like stones, hear the word of God and have confidence; take the example of those same stones and thorns. Those thorns and those stones resist Heaven's sower now; but the time will come when those same stones will acclaim Him and those same thorns will crown Him.[18] When Heaven's sower left the field, departing this world, stones were rent to acclaim Him, and thorns were woven to make Him a crown. And if the word of God triumphs even over thorns and stones, if the word of God sprouts even on stones and among thorns, when today the word of God does not triumph over free wills or sprout among hearts, it is not the fault of the listeners or due to their indisposition.

If we accept these two demonstrations and posit that the lack of fruit and effect of the word of God is not due to either God or the listeners, it follows as clear consequence that it is due to the preacher. And so it is. Do

---

17. Numbers 20:11, "[Moses] struck the rock twice with the rod, there came forth water in great abundance," and Exodus 7:13, "Pharao's heart was hardened."

18. A marginal note in the editio princeps indicates two moments from the Passion: Matthew 27:51, *Petræ scissæ sunt*, "The rocks were rent," and Matthew 27:29, *Coronam de spinis, posuerunt super caput ejus*, "A crown of thorns, they put it upon his head."

you know, Christians, why the word of God does not bear fruit? Because of the preachers. Do you know, Preachers, why the word of God does not bear fruit? Because of us.

IV

But since there are so many qualities in a preacher and so many laws that govern preaching, and preachers can be at fault in them all, where does the fault lie? There are five circumstances to be considered in the preacher: the Person, the Science, the Matter, the Style, the Voice.[19] The person he is; the science he has; the matter he deals with; the style he follows; the voice he speaks with. We have all these circumstances in the Gospel. We shall examine them one by one and search for the cause.

Is today's lack of fruit from the word of God perchance due to the circumstance of the person? Is it because in the old days preachers were holy, exemplary and Apostolic Men, and today preachers are myself and others like me? This is a good reason. What defines the preacher is his life and example. Because of this, Christ in the Gospel did not compare him to the sower, but to one who sows. Take note. Christ does not say: The sower went out to sow. Rather, He says: The one who sows went out to sow, *Ecce exijt, qui seminat, seminare.*[20] Between the sower and one who sows there is a great difference: The soldier is one thing, and one who fights is another; the governor is one thing, and one who governs is another. In the same way, the sower is one thing, and one who sows is another; the preacher is one thing, and one who preaches is another. Sower and Preacher are names; one who sows and one who preaches denote actions. And actions give the preacher his being. To have the name of preacher, or to be a preacher by name, is of no importance; actions, life, example, works convert the

---

19. Vieira's *ciencia* has been rendered here as *science*. The word has the broad meaning of "knowledge," and not the modern meaning of "facts derived from scientific investigation." English authors in the seventeenth century, including Shakespeare and Milton, use the word with this original, expansive meaning, and therefore we have tried to reproduce Vieira's original word. The term *conhecimento*, knowledge, also existed in his day, and the choice to employ *ciencia* was his.

20. Matthew 13:3, "Behold the sower went forth to sow." This passage in the Rheims-Challoner translation of the Bible betrays Vieira's intention to distinguish between the sower and the one who sows, *qui seminat*. Had he worked from the Greek instead of the Vulgate Latin text, he would not have been able to make this distinction since *ho speirōn* can be read as both the sower and the one who sows. The translators would like to thank Ben Sadock for this observation.

world. What do you think is the best concept that the preacher brings to the pulpit? It is the concept the listeners have of his life.[21] In the old days, the world was converted; why is no one converted today? Because today words and thoughts are preached; in the old days, words and works were preached. Words without works are shots without bullets, they stun but they do not wound. David's sling brought down the Giant. It did not bring him down with the snap, but rather with the stone: *Infixus est lapis in fronte ejus.*[22] The voices of David's harp cast out the demons from Saul's body; but these were not voices pronounced with the mouth, they were voices formed with the hand: *David tollebat citharam, & percutiebat manu sua.*[23] This is why Christ compared the preacher to the sower. Preaching that is speaking is done with the mouth; preaching that is sowing is done with the hand. To speak to the wind, words suffice; to speak to the heart, works are necessary. The Gospel says that the word of God bore fruit a hundred to one. What does this mean? Does it mean that from one word, a hundred words sprouted? No. It means that from few words many works sprouted. Words that bear works, see if they can be mere words! God wanted to convert the world and what did He do? He sent His Son made man to the world. Take note. The Son of God qua God is word of God, not work of God: *Genitum, non factum.*[24] The Son of God qua God and Man is both word of God and work of God: *Verbum caro factum est.*[25] So God did not entrust the conversion of men even to His word unaccompanied by works. The effectiveness of the salvation of the world consisted in the union of the Word of God with the greatest work of God. Divine *Verbum* is Divine word; but it matters little that our words are divine, if they are unaccompanied by works. The reason for this is that words are heard, works are seen. Words enter through the ears, works enter through the eyes; and our soul surrenders much better through the eyes than through the ears. In Heaven there is no one who does not love God, or who can avoid loving Him. On earth there are so few who love Him; all offend Him. Is God not the same and as

---

21. Listeners would have recognized this reference to concepts as being in contrast to the more specific term *conceito*, identified with the contemporary style called *conceptismo*. In the Portuguese Baroque, this style consisted of elaborate word games and surprising paradoxes. Vieira will present a caricature and longer criticism of this style in Part V below.

22. 1 Kings 17:49, "The stone was fixed in his forehead."

23. 1 Kings 16:23, "David took his harp, and played with his hand."

24. "Begotten, not made" is a phrase in the Nicene Creed.

25. John 1:14, "The Word was made flesh."

worthy of being loved in Heaven as on earth? So how is it that in Heaven all are obliged and compelled to love Him, and not on earth? The reason is that God in Heaven is God seen and God on earth is God heard. In Heaven the knowledge of God enters the soul through the eyes: *Videbimus eum sicuti est.*[26] On earth the knowledge of God enters it through the ears: *Fides ex auditu.*[27] And what enters through ears is believed, what enters through eyes is compelled. Would that listeners saw in us that which they hear from us, the jolt and the effects of the Sermon would be very different.

A preacher goes preaching the Passion, arrives at the Praetorium of Pilate, tells of how Christ was mocked as King, says that they took a purple robe and placed it upon His shoulders; and the audience listens very attentively. He says that a crown of thorns was woven and forced onto His head; all listen with the same attention. He further says that they tied His hands and placed in them a reed as a scepter; our listeners continue in the same silence and suspense. At this point a curtain is drawn and the image of the *Ecce Homo* appears: Behold all prostrated on the ground, behold all beating their breasts, behold the tears, behold the shouts, behold the howls, behold the slaps. What is this? What new thing appeared in this Church? Everything that the curtain revealed, the preacher had already said. He had already spoken of that purple robe, he had already spoken of that crown and of those thorns, he had already spoken of that scepter and of that reed. Well, if this did not produce any jolt then, how does it produce such a great one now? Because first the *Ecce Homo* was heard, and now the *Ecce Homo* is seen. The preacher's account entered through the ears; the representation of that figure enters through the eyes. Do you know, Father Preachers, why our sermons produce few jolts? Because we do not preach to the eyes, we only preach to the ears. Why did the Baptist convert so many sinners? Because just as his words preached to the ears, his example preached to the eyes. The words of the Baptist preached penitence: *Agite pœnitentiam,*[28] Men, do penance; and the example exclaimed *Ecce homo,* behold the man who is the portrait of penance and asperity. The words of the Baptist preached fasting and reproached the delights and excesses of gluttony; and the example exclaimed *Ecce homo,* behold the man who sustains himself with grasshoppers and wild honey. The words of the Baptist

---

26. 1 John 3:2, "We shall see him as he is."

27. Romans 10:17, "Faith cometh by hearing."

28. Matthew 3:2, "Do penance." Vieira reverses the order of the words in this passage from the original: *Pœnitentiam agite.*

preached composure and modesty, and condemned pride and the vanity of finery; and the example exclaimed *Ecce homo*, behold the man dressed in camel skins with bristles and cilice close to his flesh. The words of the Baptist preached detachment and withdrawal from the world, and flight from temptations and men; and the example exclaimed *Ecce homo*, behold the man who left the courts and the cities, and lives in a desert and in a cave. If the listeners hear one thing and see another, how shall they convert? Jacob placed his spotted rods before the sheep when they conceived, and because of that the lambs were born with spots.[29] If, when the listeners receive our concepts, they have our stains before their eyes, how are they to conceive virtues? If my life is an apology against my doctrine, if my words are already refuted by my works, if one thing is the sower and the other he who sows, how can there be any fruit?

This could be a very good and very strong reason for the lack of fruit from the word of God, but the example and the experience of Jonah go against it. Jonah was a fugitive from God, disobedient, recalcitrant, and, even after he was swallowed and vomited up, irate, impatient, uncharitable, unmerciful. And he had more zeal and concern for his self-regard than for God's honor or for the salvation of souls, wishing to see Nineveh overthrown, and overthrown before his eyes, despite the many thousands of innocents there. However, with one sermon this same man converted the greatest King, the greatest Court, and the greatest Kingdom in the world, and not a Kingdom of men of faith but one of idolatrous heathens. The cause we seek is therefore another. What can it be?

V

Can it be perchance the style that is used today in the pulpits? Such a contorted style, such a difficult style, such an affected style, a style so contrary to all art and all nature? This, too, is a good reason. Style should be very easy and very natural. This is why Christ compared preaching to sowing: *Exijt, qui seminat, seminare.* Christ compares preaching to sowing because sowing is an art that has more nature than art. In the other arts, everything is art: In Music, everything is done by beat; in Architecture, everything is done by rule; in Arithmetic, everything is done by count; in

---

29. A marginal note in the editio princeps indicates the passage Genesis 30:39, *Factumque est ut in ipso calore coitus, oves intuerentur virgas, et parerent maculosa,* "And it came to pass that in the very heat of coition, the sheep beheld the rods, and brought forth spotted."

Geometry, everything is done by measure. Sowing is not like this. It is an art without art; fall where it may. See how our farmer of the Gospel sowed. The wheat fell on thorns and sprouted: *Aliud cecidit inter spinas, & simul exortæ spinæ.* The wheat fell on stones and sprouted: *Aliud cecidit super petram, & natum.* The wheat fell on good ground and sprouted: *Aliud cecidit in terram bonam, & natum.* As the wheat fell, it sprouted.

So shall it be with preaching. Things shall fall and things shall sprout, so natural that they go falling, so proper that they come sprouting. How different is today's violent and tyrannical style! To see the sad Passages of the Scripture arrive as though coming to be martyred! Some come carted, others come dragged, others come pulled, others come forced, others come disjointed; tied up is the only way they do not come. Is there greater tyranny? And then, in the midst of it all, one hears: How elevated that is! The point is not to elevate, it is to make fall: *Cecidit.* Take note of an allegory specific to our language. Even though the sower's wheat fell four times, it only sprouted three. For the Sermon to come sprouting, it shall have three ways of falling. It shall fall with inclination, it shall fall with cadence, it shall fall with ease. Inclination is for things, cadence for words, ease for disposition. Inclination is for things because they shall be well introduced and in their proper place; they shall have inclination. Cadence is for words because they shall not be harsh or dissonant; they shall have cadence. Ease is for disposition because it shall be so natural and unaffected that it appears easy and not studied, *Cecidit, cecidit, cecidit.*

Since I speak against modern styles, I want to invoke in my defense the style of the most ancient preacher that there has ever been in the world. And who was that? The most ancient preacher that there has ever been in the world was Heaven. *Cæli enarrant gloriam Dei, & opera manuum eius annuntiat firmamentum,* says David.[30] If we posit that Heaven is a preacher, he must have sermons and must have words. Yes, he does, says David; he has words and he has sermons, and what is more they are very well heard: *Non sunt loquellæ, neque sermones, quorum non audiantur voces eorum.*[31] And what sermons and what words of Heaven are these? The words are the stars; the sermons are their composition, order, harmony, and course. See how Heaven's style of preaching agrees with the style that Christ taught on earth. In one and the other there is sowing: Earth sown with wheat;

---

30. Psalm 18:2, "The heavens shew forth the glory of God, and the firmament declareth the work of his hands."

31. Psalm 18:4, "There are no speeches nor languages, where their voices are not heard."

Heaven sown with stars. Preaching shall be like sowing, and not like paving or tiling. In order, but like the stars: *Stellæ manentes in ordine suo.*[32] All
the stars are in their order, but it is an order that produces influence, not
an order that produces artifice. God did not make Heaven a chessboard
of stars the way preachers make their sermons chessboards of words. If
on one side there is White, on the other there will be Black; if on one side
there is Day, on the other there will be Night; if on one side they say Light,
on the other they will say Shade; if on one side they say Descended, on the
other they will say Ascended. Enough! Are we never to see two words at
peace in a sermon? Must all words always face off against their opposites?
Let us learn from Heaven the style of disposition and also that of words.
What shall the words look like? Like stars. Stars are very distinct and very
clear. So shall the style of preaching be, very distinct and very clear. And
do not fear that the style will seem low for all that: Stars are very distinct,
and very clear, and most high. The style can be very clear and very high: So
clear that those with little knowledge will understand it; and so high that
those with great knowledge will have much to understand in it. The rustic
finds instructions for his farming in the stars, and the sailor for his navigation, and the mathematician for his observations and his judgments.
This way the rustic and the sailor who cannot read or write understand the
stars, and the mathematician who has read all who have written does not
grasp and understand all that there is in them. So can the sermon be: Stars
that all see and very few measure.

Yes, Father, yet that style of preaching is not learned preaching. But
what if it were? This unfortunate style that is used today is called learned
by those who want to honor it; those who condemn it call it obscure, but
in so doing they still do it much honor. The learned style is not obscure;
it is dark, raw dark, and pitch black. Is it possible that, being Portuguese
and listening to a preacher in Portuguese, we shall not understand what
he says? Just as there is a Lexicon for Greek and a Calepino for Latin, so
it is necessary that there be a vocabulary for the pulpit.[33] At least I would
use it for proper nouns, since the learned have unbaptized the Saints, and
every Author whom they cite is an enigma. So said the Penitent Scepter;
so said the Evangelist Apelles; so said the Eagle of Africa, the Honeycomb
of Clairvaux, the Purple of Bethlehem, the Golden Mouth. What a way

---

32. Judges 5:20, "The stars remaining in their order."

33. Ambrogio Calepino (c. 1440–1510) wrote a widely consulted Latin dictionary in the early
sixteenth century.

of citing! They say that the Penitent Scepter is David, as if all Scepters were not penance. They say that the Evangelist Apelles is Saint Luke; the Honeycomb of Clairvaux, Saint Bernard; the Eagle of Africa, Saint Augustine; the Purple of Bethlehem, Saint Jerome; the Golden Mouth, Saint Chrysostom. And who would prevent someone else from thinking that the Purple of Bethlehem is Herod, that the Eagle of Africa is Scipio, and that the Golden Mouth is Midas? If there were a lawyer who would invoke Bartolus and Baldus this way, would you trust him with your plea?[34] If there were a man who would talk like this in conversation, would you not take him for a fool? Well, how can that which would be foolishness in conversation be discretion in the pulpit?

This reason, too, seemed good to me. But the learned defend themselves for what is polished and studied with the great Nazianzen, with Ambrose, with Chrysologus, with Leo; and for what is obscure and hard with Clement of Alexandria, with Tertullian, with Basil of Seleucia, with Zeno of Verona, and others. And we cannot deny the reverence to such Authors; although we wish that those who pride themselves for drinking from these streams had their profundity. What, then, can be the cause of our complaint?

VI

Can it be the matter, or matters, that the preachers take up? Today a method called postillating the Gospel is used, in which many matters are taken up, many subjects are raised; and those who rouse much game and do not follow any of it will, not surprisingly, go home with empty hands. This, too, is a good reason. The Sermon shall have one subject only, and one matter only. This is why Christ said that the farmer of the Gospel had not sown many kinds of seeds, but only one: *Exijt, qui seminat, seminare semen.* He sowed one seed only, and not many; because the Sermon shall have one matter only, and not many. If the farmer had sown wheat first, and over the wheat had sown rye, and over the rye had sown maize and millet, and over the corn had sown barley, what would have sprouted? A wild brush, a green confusion. Behold what happens to Sermons of this kind. Since they sow such variety, they cannot gather what is right. Whoever sows mixtures can hardly gather wheat. If a carrack were to take a course to the

---

34. Bartolus de Saxoferrato (1313–1357) and Baldus de Ubaldis (1327–1400) were two of the most important late medieval jurists.

North, another to the South, another to the East, another to the West, how could it make a voyage? This is why there is so much working and so little sailing in the pulpits. One subject goes with a wind, another subject goes with another wind; what will be gathered but wind? The Baptist converted many in Judea, but how many matters did he take up? Only one: *Parate viam Domini*, the Preparation for the Kingdom of Christ.[35] Jonah converted the Ninevites, but how many subjects did he take up? Only one: *Adhuc quadraginta dies, et Ninive subvertetur*, the Overthrow of the City.[36] So Jonah in forty days preached one subject only, and we want to preach forty subjects in one hour? Therefore we preach none. The sermon shall be of one color only, it shall have one object only, one subject only, one matter only.

The preacher shall take up one matter only. He shall define it, so it will be known. He shall divide it, so it will be discernible. He shall prove it by Scripture. He shall declare it with reason. He shall confirm it by example. He shall amplify it with the causes, the effects, the circumstances, the adequacies that shall be followed, the inadequacies that shall be avoided. He shall answer questions. He shall resolve the difficulties. He shall impugn and refute with all strength of eloquence arguments to the contrary. And, after this, he shall gather, he shall bind, he shall conclude, he shall persuade, he shall finish. This is a sermon, this is preaching. And speaking from on high is what this is not. I do not deny . . . I do not mean that the sermon shall not have a variety of discourses. But those shall all stem from the same matter, and continue and end in it. Do you want to see all of this with your eyes? So see here: A tree has roots, has a trunk, has branches, has leaves, has switches, has flowers, has fruits. So shall the sermon be. It shall have strong roots, solid ones, because it shall be grounded in the Gospel. It shall have a trunk, because it shall have one subject only and deal with one matter only; from this trunk several branches shall sprout, which are several discourses stemming from the same matter and continuing in it. These branches shall not be dry, but covered in leaves, because the discourses shall be dressed and adorned by words. This tree shall have switches that are for the reprehension of vices. It shall have flowers that are maxims. And as a finishing touch it shall have fruits, the fruit and end of the order in the sermon. So there shall be fruit, there shall be flowers, there shall be switches, there shall be leaves, there shall be branches, but everything stemming from and grounded in one trunk only that is

---

35. Matthew 3:3, "Prepare ye the way of the Lord."

36. Jonah 3:4, "Yet forty days, and Ninive shall be destroyed."

one matter only. If everything is trunks, it is not a sermon, it is wood. If everything is branches, it is not a sermon, it is shavings. If everything is leaves, it is not a sermon, it is fluff. If everything is switches, it is not a sermon, it is a bundle. If everything is flowers, it is not a sermon, it is a bouquet. If everything is fruit, it cannot be, because there is no fruit without a tree. So that in this tree, which we can call the Tree of Life, there shall be what is beneficial in fruit, what is beautiful in flowers, what is rigorous in switches, what is dressed by leaves, what is extended in branches; but all this stemming and formed from one trunk only, and one not suspended in the air, but grounded in the roots of the Gospel: *Seminare semen.* Behold how the sermons shall be; behold how they are not. And so it is no wonder that they do not bear much fruit.

All that I have said could have been extensively demonstrated, not only with the precepts of the likes of Aristotle, Cicero, Quintilian, but also with the observed practice of the prince of the Evangelic Orators Saint John Chrysostom, of Saint Basil the Great, Saint Bernard, Saint Cyprian, and with the most famous orations of Saint Gregory Nazianzen, master of both Churches. And even though in these same Fathers, as in Saint Augustine, Saint Gregory, and many others, one finds the Gospels postillated with names of sermons and homilies, it is one thing to expound and another to preach; it is one thing to teach and another to persuade. And it is of this last thing that I speak, one with which Saint Anthony of Padua and Saint Vincent Ferrer produced so much fruit in the world. But, for all that, I still do not think that this is the true cause I seek.

VII

Is it perchance the lack of science that is common among preachers? There are many preachers who live off that which they have not gathered, and who sow that which they have not tilled. After Adam's sentence, land does not usually bear fruit except to those who eat their bread by the sweat of their brow. This, too, seems like a good reason. The preacher shall preach what is his and not what belongs to others. For this reason Christ says that the farmer of the Gospel sowed his wheat: *Semen suum.* He sowed his own and not that of others, because that of others is not good to sow, nor is that which is stolen, even if what is stolen is science. Eve ate the apple of science and I used to complain of this Mother of ours: Since she ate the apple, why did she not keep the seeds? Would it not be good that the tree should come down to us, since its troubles did? So why did Eve not do so? Because the apple was stolen. And that which belongs to others is good for eating, but it is not good for sowing. It is good for eating because they say it is tasty. It is not good for sowing because it does not sprout. Someone may have seen something that belongs to another sprout at home. But certainly, if it sprouts, it shall not sink roots; and that which does not sink roots cannot bear fruit. Behold why many preachers do not produce fruit: because they preach that which belongs to others and not to them, *Semen suum.* To preach is to enter into battle against vices; and the weapons of another, even of Achilles, never gave victory to anyone.[37] When David entered the field against the Giant, Saul offered him his weapons, but he would not accept them.[38] With someone else's weapons no one can win, even if he is David. Saul's weapons serve only Saul, and David's David. One's own crook and sling are more useful than another's sword and lance. A preacher who fights with someone else's weapons is at no risk of bringing down a giant.

Christ turned the Apostles into fishers of men, which meant ordaining them as preachers.[39] And what did the Apostles do? The Text says that they were *Reficientes retia sua*, remaking their nets.[40] These were the Apostles' nets and no one else's. Take note: *Retia sua* does not say that they were theirs because they bought them, but that they were theirs because they made them. They were not theirs because they cost them their money, but because they cost them their work. In this way the nets were theirs. And because in this way they were theirs, for that reason they were fishermen's nets that were to fish men. With someone else's nets or nets made by someone else's hands, fish can be fished, men cannot be fished. The reason is that in fishing with understanding, only one who knows how to make the net knows how to cast it. How do you make a net? The weave is made of thread and knots; how is one who does not thread or tie to make a net? And how is one who cannot thread, who cannot tie, to fish men? The net has lead weights that sink to the bottom and has cork that stays afloat on the water. In preaching there are some things of greater weight

---

37. Book 16 of *The Iliad* recounts how Patroclus borrowed the armor and weapons of Achilles for his fateful confrontation with the Trojan army.

38. 1 Kings 17:38–39 recounts how David tried on Saul's armor before his battle with Goliath.

39. A marginal note in the editio princeps indicates the passage Matthew 4:19, *Faciam vos fieri piscatores hominum,* "I will make you to be fishers of men."

40. Matthew 4:21, "Mending their nets."

and more depth, and other things that are more superficial and lighter. And only those who make the net can manage what is light and what is heavy. In the mouth of those who do not make what they preach, even lead is cork. Reasons shall not be grafted, they shall sprout. To preach is not to recite. One's own reasons sprout from understanding; those of others come out clinging to memory. And men are not convinced by memory, but by understanding.

The Holy Spirit descended upon the Apostles. And when the tongues descended from Heaven, I thought they were to be put in their mouths, but they were put upon their heads. Well, why upon the head and not in the mouth, which is the tongue's place? Because that which the preacher shall say shall not come out of his mouth only, it shall come out of his mouth but from his head. That which comes only out of the mouth stops at the ears; that which sprouts from judgment penetrates and convinces the understanding. These tongues of the Holy Spirit have yet more mystery. The Text says that the tongues were not all put upon all the Apostles, but each tongue upon each Apostle: *Apparuerunt dispertitæ linguæ tanquam ignis; seditque supra singulos eorum.*[41] And why each one upon each one and not all upon all? Because not all tongues serve all, but each one serves one only. One tongue upon Peter only, because Peter's tongue does not serve Andrew. Another tongue upon Andrew only, because Andrew's tongue does not serve Philip. Another tongue upon Philip only, because Philip's tongue does not serve Bartholomew. And so with the rest. Or else see it in the style of each one of the Apostles upon whom the Holy Spirit descended. We have Scriptures by five only, but the difference with which they wrote, as the Learned know, is admirable. The quills were all taken from the wings of that Divine Dove, but the style, so diverse, so particular, so specific to each, shows well that it was each one's own: Matthew's easy; John's mysterious; Peter's serious; James's strong; Thaddeus's sublime. And all with such valor in their sayings that each word was a thunderbolt, each clause a flash of lightning, and each reason a triumph. To these five add Saint Luke and Saint Mark, who were also there, and you will find the number of those seven thunders that Saint John heard in the Apocalypse: *Loquuta sunt septem tonitrua voces suas.*[42] They were thunders that spoke and whence came voices, but those voices were theirs: *Voces*

---

41. Acts 2:3, "There appeared to them parted tongues as it were of fire, and it sat upon every one of them."

42. Revelation 10:3, "Seven thunders uttered their voices."

suas, theirs and not others', as Ansbert noted, *Non alienas, sed suas.*[43] In short, to preach something that belongs to others is to preach something alien and with something alien nothing good was ever made.

However, I do not rest wholly on this reason because, as Saint Luke noted, we know of the great Baptist that he preached what Isaiah had preached, and by no other name but that of sermons: *Prædicans baptismum pœnitentiæ in remissionem peccatorum, sicut scriptum est in libro sermonum Isaiæ Prophetæ.*[44] I leave aside what Saint Ambrose took from Saint Basil; Saint Prosperus and Bede from Saint Augustine; Theophylactus and Euthymius from Saint John Chrysostom.

VIII

Finally, is the voice with which preachers today speak the cause that we have sought for so long? In the old days they would preach crying out; today they preach conversing. In the old days, the first element of the preacher was a good voice and good lungs. And truly, since the world is governed so much by the senses, cries can sometimes do more than reason. This would also be a good reason, but we cannot confirm it with the sower, since we have already said that his was not a work of the mouth. Yet what the Gospel denied to us in the metaphoric sower, it gave to us in the true sower, Christ. As soon as Christ ended the Parable, the Gospel says that He started to cry out: *Hæc dicens clamabat.*[45] The Lord cried out and did not reason about the Parable, because the audience was such that He trusted cries more than reason.

The Baptist was asked who he was. He answered: *Ego vox clamantis in deserto*, I am a voice crying out in this desert.[46] The Baptist defined himself this way. The definition of the preacher, I thought, was a Voice that reasons, and not a Voice that cries out. So why did the Baptist define himself

---

43. "Their voices" and "Not those of others, but theirs." A marginal note in the editio princeps indicates that this phrase is from Ambrosius Ansbertus (or Autpertus), but it is likely that Vieira drew the citation from an early modern Portuguese Jesuit exegete, Brás Viegas (1553–1599), who refers to Ansbertus in a commentary on Revelation which draws on many Patristic and later sources. See Brás Viegas, *Commentarii exegetici in Apocalypsim Ioannis Apostoli* (Évora, Portugal: Manuel de Lira, 1601), p. 455.

44. Luke 3:3–4, "Preaching the baptism of penance for the remission of sins; As it is written in the book of the sayings of Isaias the prophet."

45. Luke 8:8, "Saying these things, he cried out."

46. John 1:23, "I am the voice of one crying out in the wilderness."

by his crying out and not by his reasoning? Not by reason but by cries? Because there are many people in this world with whom cries can do more than reason, and such were the ones to whom the Baptist preached. See it clearly in Christ. After Pilate examined the charges that were brought against Him, he washed his hands and said: *Ego nullam causam invenio in homine isto*, I find no cause in this man.[47] During all this time, the People and the Scribes outside were crying out that He should be crucified: *At illi magis clamabant, crucifigatur.*[48] So Christ had reason on His side and cries against Him. And which could do more? Cries were able to do more than reason. Reason could not free Him, cries were enough to put Him on the Cross. And since cries can do so much in the world, it is right that preachers sometimes cry out; it is right that they shout. This is why Isaiah called preachers clouds: *Qui sunt isti, qui ut nubes volant?*[49] A cloud has lightning, it has thunder, it has bolts. Lightning for the eyes, thunder for the ears, bolts for the heart: With lightning, it illuminates; with thunder, it overawes; with bolts, it kills. But the bolt wounds one, lightning many, thunder all. So shall the voice of the preacher be: A thunder from Heaven that will overawe and shake the world.

But what shall we say about the Prayer of Moses? *Concrescat ut pluvia doctrina mea: fluat ut ros eloquium meum*, Let my doctrine come down like rain from Heaven and my voice and my words like the dew that is softly and quietly distilled?[50] What shall we say about the ordinary example of Christ that Isaiah celebrated so much? *Non clamabit, neque audietur vox ejus foris*, He shall not exclaim, he shall not cry out, but He shall speak with a voice so soft that no one outside will be able to hear it.[51] And there is no doubt that familiar preaching, and preaching that is whispered, not only draws greater attention than that which is shouted, but naturally and without force insinuates itself, enters, penetrates, and settles in the soul.

In conclusion, the cause why preachers today produce no fruit with the word of God is neither the circumstance of the Person, *Qui seminat*, nor that of the Style, *Seminare*, nor that of the Matter, *Semen*, nor that of the Science, *Suum*, nor that of the Voice, *Clamabat*. Moses had a weak

---

47. Luke 23:14, "I find no cause in this man."

48. Matthew 27:23, "But they all cried out the more, Let him be crucified."

49. Isaiah 60:8, "Who are these, that fly as clouds?"

50. Deuteronomy 32:2, "Let my doctrine gather as the rain, let my speech distil as the dew."

51. Isaiah 42:2, "He shall not cry, nor . . . shall his voice be heard abroad."

voice; Amos had a rough style; Solomon multiplied and varied the subjects; Balaam did not have an exemplary life, his animal had no science; and nevertheless they all persuaded and convinced by speaking.[52] Well, if no one of these reasons that we discussed, nor all of them together are the main cause or sufficient cause for the scarce fruit that the word of God bears today, what shall we finally say is the true cause?

IX

The words that I took as a Theme say it: *Semen est Verbum Dei.* Do you (Christians) know the cause why today so little fruit is born of so much preaching? It is because the words of the preachers are words, but they are not words of God. I speak of that which is ordinarily heard. The word of God (as I said) is so powerful and so effective that not only does it bear fruit in good ground, but it even sprouts on stones and among thorns. But if the words of the preachers are not the word of God, is it any wonder that they do not have the efficacy and the effects of the word of God? *Ventum seminabunt, & turbinem colligent,* says the Holy Spirit: Whoever sows winds gathers whirlwinds.[53] If the preachers sow wind, if what is preached is vanity, if the word of God is not preached, how is the Church of God not to suffer storms instead of gathering fruit?

But you will say to me: Father, do today's preachers not preach from the Gospel, do they not preach from the sacred Scriptures? So how do they not preach the word of God? This is the problem. They preach words of God, but they do not preach the word of God. *Qui habet sermonem meum, loquatur sermonem meum vere,* says God through Jeremiah.[54] The words of God preached in the sense in which God said them are the word of God; but preached in the sense that we want, they are not the word of God but possibly the word of the Demon. The Demon tempted Christ to

---

52. Marginal notes in the editio princeps refer the reader to Exodus 4:10 in Latin translations of the Septuagint Bible, where Moses declares that he is of *voce gracila,* "weak in speech", instead of the same passage in the Vulgate where he declares *impedioris et tardioris linguæ sum,* "I have more impediment and slowness of tongue." The notes also indicate Amos 1:1, "The words of Amos, who was among the herdsmen of Thecua"; Ecclesiastes 1, in which "the son of David, king of Jerusalem"—that is, Solomon—proposes in verse 13 "to seek and search out wisely concerning all things that are done under the sun"; and Numbers 22 and 23, which recount the story of Balaam, his donkey, and the angel.

53. Hosea 8:7, "They shall sow wind, and gather a whirlwind." Vieira exchanges *metent* in the Vulgate for *colligent.*

54. Jeremiah 23:28, "He that hath my word, let him speak my word with truth."

make bread from stones. The Lord answered him: *Non in solo pane vivit homo, sed in omni verbo, quod procedit de ore Dei.*[55] This sentence was taken from the eighth chapter of Deuteronomy. The Demon, seeing that the Lord defended Himself from temptation with Scripture, carries Him to the Temple and, citing Psalm ninety, speaks to Him thus: *Mitte te deorsum; scriptum est enim, quia Angelis suis Deus mandavit de te, ut custodiant te in omnibus vijs tuis,* Cast yourself down from there, because it has been promised in the sacred Scriptures that Angels will take you in their arms so that You will not harm Yourself.[56] And so it was that Christ defended Himself from the Devil with Scripture, and the Devil tempted Christ with Scripture. All the Scriptures are the word of God. So, if Christ takes Scripture to defend Himself against the Devil, how can it be that the Devil takes Scripture to tempt Christ? The reason is that Christ took the words of Scripture in their true sense, and the Devil took the words of Scripture in a different, twisted sense. And the same words that, taken in the true sense, are words of God, taken in a different sense are weapons of the Devil. The same words that, taken in the sense in which God said them, are a defense, taken in the sense in which God did not say them are temptation. Behold the temptation with which the Devil wanted to knock Christ down then and with which he makes war against Him today from the pinnacle of the temple. The pinnacle of the temple is the pulpit, because it is its highest place. The Devil tempted Christ in the desert, tempted Him on the mountain, tempted Him at the temple. In the desert, he tempted Him with gluttony; on the mountain, he tempted Him with ambition; at the temple, he tempted Him with wrongly interpreted Scriptures. And that is the temptation the Church suffers most today, one that in many places has brought down the faith in Christ, if not Christ Himself.

Tell me, Preachers (those to whom I speak, truly unworthy of such a sacred name), tell me: Those useless subjects that you so often raise; those tasks, in your opinion so ingenious, that you undertake; did you ever find them in the Prophets of the Old Testament, or in the Apostles and Evangelists of the New Testament, or in the Author of both Testaments, Christ? Certainly not, because, from the first word of Genesis to the last

---

55. Matthew 4:4, "Not in bread alone doth man live, but in every word that proceedeth from the mouth of God."

56. Matthew 4:6, "Cast thyself down, for it is written: That he hath given his angels charge over thee," and Psalm 90:11, "To keep thee in all they ways."

word of Apocalypse, there is no such thing in all the Scriptures.[57] Well, if in the Scriptures there is not what you say and preach, how is it that you think you preach the word of God? More. In those places, in those Texts that you cite to prove what you say, is that the sense in which God said them? Is that the sense in which the Fathers of the Church understand them? Is that the sense of the very Grammar of the words? Surely not, because you often take them for what they sound like and not for what they mean, and perhaps not even for what they sound like. Well, if that is not the sense of the words of God, it follows that they are not words of God. And if they are not words of God, why should we complain that the preaching does not bear fruit? Enough with bringing the words of God to say what we want, and we shall not want to say what they say![58] And that we should see the audience nod at these things when we should be banging our heads against the walls for hearing them! I do not truly know what amazes me more, our concepts or your applause![59] Oh how lofty the preacher made it! And so it is: But what did he make lofty? A false witness to the Text, another false witness to the Saint, another to the understanding and the sense of both. Should the world then be converted by false witnesses to the word of God? If this seems too great a censure to any of you, hear me out.

Christ stood charged before Caiaphas, and the Evangelist Saint Matthew says that in the end two false witnesses came: *Novissime venerunt duo falsi testes.*[60] These witnesses mentioned they had heard Christ say that, if the

---

57. A marginal note in the editio princeps refers the reader to a passage from Jerome's *Commentary on Galatians: Sola scripturarum ars est quam sibi passim onmes vendicant, & cùm aures populi sermone composito mulserint hoc legem Dei putant: nec scire dignantur quid Prophetæ, quid Apostoli senserint; sed ad sensum suum incongrua aptant testimonia: quasi grande sit, & non vitiosissimum dicendi genus, depravare sententias, & ad voluntatem suam scripturam trahere repugnantem.* The passage, however, comes from his letter to Paulinus (Letter 53:7), "The art of interpreting the scriptures is the only one of which all men everywhere claim to be masters. . . . Such men when they charm the popular ear by the finish of their style suppose every word they say to be a law of God. They do not deign to notice what Prophets and apostles have intended but they adapt conflicting passages to suit their meaning, as if it were a grand way of teaching—to misrepresent a writer's views and to force the scriptures reluctantly to do their will." See Philip Schaff and Henry Wace, eds., *A Select Library of Nicene and Post-Nicene Fathers of the Christian Church,* 2nd ser., 14 vols. (New York: Christian Literature Company, 1890–1900), vol. 6, p. 99.

58. This phrase is obscure in the original Portuguese. The second *want* can also signify need: "We shall not need to say what they say." In other words, we shall not need to explain, or interpret, them.

59. Concepts here refer to *conceptismo,* the contemporary literary fashion which Vieira criticizes.

60. Matthew 26:60, "Last of all there came two false witnesses."

Jews were to destroy the temple, He would rebuild it again in three days. If we read the Evangelist Saint John, we will find that Christ had truly said these words. Well, if Christ had said that He would rebuild the temple within three days and this is exactly what the witnesses mentioned, how can the Evangelist call them false witnesses, *Duo falsi testes?* Saint John himself gave the reason: *Loquebatur de templo corporis sui.*[61] When Christ said that in three days He would rebuild the temple, the Lord was speaking of the mystical temple of His body, which the Jews destroyed by death and the Lord rebuilt by resurrection. And since Christ was speaking of the mystical temple and the witnesses mentioned the material temple of Jerusalem, even though the words were true, the witnesses were false. They were false, because Christ said the words in one sense and they mentioned them in another. And to mention the words of God in a different sense from that in which they were said is to bear false witness against God, is to bear false witness against the Scriptures. Ah Lord, how many false witnesses are borne against you! How many times I hear that You say that which You never said! How many times I hear that they are Yours, those words which are my fantasies—for I will not exclude myself from this number of people! Small wonder, then, that our fantasies, and our vanities, and our fables do not have the effectiveness of the word of God!

Wretched are we, and wretched our times! For in them the prophecy of Saint Paul came to be fulfilled: *Erit tempus, cùm sanam doctrinam non sustinebunt.*[62] The time will come, says Saint Paul, when men will not suffer the sane doctrine, *Sed ad sua desideria coacervabunt sibi magistros prurientes auribus,* but for their appetite they will have a great number of preachers in a heap and without difference, who will do nothing but flatter their ears, *A veritate quidem auditum avertent; ad fabulas autem convertentur,* men will close their ears to the truth and open them to fables.[63] Fable has two meanings: It means pretense and it means comedy; and much preaching in our time is both. It is pretense because it is subtleties and airy thoughts not grounded in truth. It is comedy because listeners come to the preaching as to a comedy. And there are preachers who come to the

---

61. John 2:21, "He spoke of the temple of his body." Vieira uses *loquebatur* instead of the Vulgate's *dicebat.*

62. 2 Timothy 4:3, "There shall be a time, when they will not endure sound doctrine."

63. 2 Timothy 4:3–4, "But according to their own desires, they will heap to themselves teachers, having itching ears. And will indeed turn away their hearing from the truth, but will be turned unto fables."

pulpit as comedians. The end of comedies in Portugal was counted among the blessings of the present time; but this did not happen.[64] They did not end, they changed; they moved from the theater to the pulpit. Do not think I exaggerate when I call much of today's preaching comedy. I wish I had the comedies of Plautus, Terence, and Seneca here and you would see if you would not find exposed in them many deceits of life and the vanity of the world; many points of moral doctrine that have much more truth and that are much more solid than those heard today from pulpits. A great misery it is, surely, that greater directions for life are found in the lines of a profane and heathen poet than in the preachings of a Christian orator, and one who, in addition to being Christian, is often a religious!

In calling sermons comedy Saint Paul showed restraint, because there are many sermons that are not comedy but farce. On such an occasion one of those preachers who profess to be dead to the world ascends the pulpit dressed, or shrouded, in a penitential habit (all, more or less rough, are penitential; and all, from the day we profess them, are shrouds). The sight is for horror, the name for reverence, the matter for compunction, the dignity for an oracle, the place and the expectation for silence; and when it is broken, what is heard? If there were a foreigner in the audience who did not know us and who saw this man enter and speak in public in those clothes and in such a place, he would think that he was to hear a trumpet from Heaven, that each word was to be a bolt for the hearts, that the preacher was to preach with the zeal and the fervor of an Elijah, that with the voice, with the gestures, and with the actions he was to render vices into dust and ash. This is what the foreigner would think. And we, what do we see? We see coming out of the mouth of that man, in those clothes, a very affected and very polished voice; and what do we see him start to do right away, with great bluster? To motivate vigils, to credit debts, to refine courtesies, to flatter precipices, to shine dawns, to melt crystals, to faint jasmines, to dress springs, and a thousand other indignities of this sort.[65] Is this not a farce most worthy of being laughed at, were it not so worthy

---

64. Vieira refers to the small number of comedies (as opposed to plays with tragic or religious themes) performed after Portuguese independence from Castile was proclaimed in 1640. That event, and the ensuing years of war, greatly reduced the quantity of formerly numerous Spanish troupes performing in Portugal. The banning of comedies in Castile and Aragon from 1646 until 1651 further reduced that number. See Margarida Vieira Mendes, *A Oratória Barroca de Vieira*, 2nd ed. (Lisbon: Caminho, 2003), p. 164, and J. E. Varey and N. D. Shergold, "Datos históricos sobre los primeros teatros de Madrid: Prohibiciones de Autos y Comedia y sus consequencias (1644–1651)," *Bulletin Hispaniqueii* 62.3 (1960): pp. 286–325.

65. Vieira here parodies the clichés of his contemporaries.

of being cried about? In comedy, the king dresses as a king and speaks as a king; the lackey dresses as a lackey and speaks as a lackey; the rustic dresses as a rustic and speaks as a rustic; but for a preacher to dress as a religious and to speak as a—I do not want to say it out of reverence for this place. Since the pulpit is a theater, and the sermon a comedy, can we not at least play the part well? Should the words not agree with the dress and the job? Did Saint Paul preach like this, did those Patriarchs who dressed in these habits and dressed us in them preach like this? Do we not praise and admire their preaching? Do we not pride ourselves with being their sons? So why do we not imitate them? Why do we not preach the way they preached? Saint Francis Xavier preached in this very pulpit; Saint Francis Borgia preached in this very pulpit; and I, who wear the same habit, why should I not preach their doctrine, even if I lack their spirit?

X

You will tell me what I am told, and what I have already experienced, that if we preach this way the listeners will mock us and dislike listening. Oh what a good reason for a servant of Jesus Christ! Mock and dislike though they will, let us do our job. The doctrine that they mock, the doctrine that they dislike, is the one we should preach to them, and for that very reason: Because it is the most beneficial and the one they need the most. The wheat that fell on the path was eaten by the birds. These birds, as Christ Himself explained, are the Demons who take the word of God from the hearts of men: *Venit Diabolus, & tollit verbum de corde eorum.*[66] So why did the Devil not eat the wheat that fell among thorns, or the wheat that fell on stones, but only the wheat that fell on the path? Because the wheat that fell on the path, *Conculcatum est ab hominibus,* was trampled by men; and the doctrine that men trample, the doctrine that men despise, that is the one that the Devil fears. Those other concepts, those other thoughts, those other subtleties that men like and cherish, those the Devil does not fear or take caution against, because he knows that such is not the preaching that will pull souls from his claws. But that doctrine that falls, *Secus viam*; that doctrine that seems common, *Secus viam*; that doctrine that seems trivial, *Secus viam*; that doctrine that seems trodden, *Secus viam*; that doctrine that puts us on the path and on the way to our salvation (which is the one men trample and the one men despise), that is the one the Demon fears

---

66. Luke 8:12, "The devil cometh, and taketh the word out of their heart."

and takes caution against. That is the one he tries to eat and take from the world. And, for exactly that reason, that is the one the preachers should preach and the one the listeners should seek. But if they do not do so and instead mock us, let us mock their mockery as much as their applause. *Per infamiam, & bonam famam,* says Saint Paul.[67] The preacher shall know how to preach with fame and without fame. The Apostle says more. He shall preach with fame, and with infamy. That the preacher should preach in order to be famous, that is the way of the world. But infamous, and preaching what is right, even with discredit to his fame? That is what it means to be a preacher of Jesus Christ.

So what if the listeners like it or dislike it! Oh what a worthy warning! What doctor is there who will take note of the sick person's taste when he is working on giving him health? Heal, and dislike; let them be saved and embittered; for that is why we are doctors of souls. What do you think are the stones upon which part of the Gospel's wheat fell? When Christ is explaining the Parable, He says that the stones are those who hear the preaching with joy: *Hi sunt, qui cum gaudio suscipiunt verbum.*[68] Well, is it good that listeners enjoy it and in the end remain stones? Let them not enjoy it and be softened. Let them not enjoy it and break. Let them not enjoy it and bear fruit. This is how the wheat that fell on good ground bore fruit, *Et fructum afferunt in patientia,* Christ concludes.[69] So bearing fruit does not pair with enjoyment but with suffering; let us bear fruit and let them be patient. The preaching that bears fruit, the preaching that is beneficial, is not that which pleases the listener, it is that which is upsetting to him. When the listener trembles at the preacher's every word; when the preacher's every word is a wrench for the listener's heart; when the listener leaves the sermon for home confused and astonished, having lost something of himself; then this is the preaching that is right, then it can be expected to bear fruit: *Et fructum afferunt in patientia.*

Finally, so that preachers know how they shall preach and listeners to whom to listen, I end with an example from our Kingdom, one almost from our times. Two famous preachers were preaching in Coimbra, both well known for their writings; I do not name them, because I shall

---

67. 2 Corinthians 6:8, "By evil report and good report."

68. Luke 8:12–13, "Those are they . . . who receive the word with joy."

69. Luke 8:15, "And bring forth fruit in patience."

differentiate one from the other.[70] It was disputed among some of the
Doctors of the University which of the two was the greater preacher.
And since there is no judgment without inclination, some said this one;
others, that one. But one professor who had great authority among the
rest reached the following conclusion: Between two such great men I do
not dare to interpose a judgment; I will only mention a difference that
I always experience. When I hear one, I leave the sermon very happy
with the preacher; when I hear the other, I leave very unhappy with
myself. With this I finish. One day you were so deceived by me that you
were leaving the sermon very happy with the preacher; now I wish I
could undeceive you so much that you would leave very unhappy with
yourselves. Sowers of the Gospel, behold what we should intend in our
sermons: Not that men leave happy with us, but that they leave very
unhappy with themselves; not that our concepts seem right to them,
but that their customs, their lives, their pastimes, their ambitions,
and, in short, all their sins seem wrong to them. Provided they become
unhappy with themselves, let them be unhappy with us. *Si hominibus
placerem, Christi servus non essem*, said the greatest of all preachers,
Saint Paul: if I pleased men, I would not be a servant of God.[71] Oh let us
please God and cease to care about men! Let us pay close attention to
the existence in this very Church of higher tribunes than those we see:
Spectaculum facti sumus Deo (as Saint Bernard reads it), *Angelis, & hominibus.*[72] Above the tribunes of Kings are the tribunes of Angels and the
tribune and the tribunal of God who hears us and shall judge us. What
reckoning will a preacher give to God on the Day of Judgment? The
listener will say, I was not told. But the preacher? *Væ mihi, quia tacui*,
woe is me, I did not say what was right![73] Do not be like this anymore,
for the love of God and of us. We are at the gates of Lent, the time when,

---

70. Early editions of this sermon indicated that the two preachers were the Dominican Frei
Francisco Foreiro (1522–1581) and the Jesuit Sebastião Barradas (1543–1615). Vieira's Jesuit
predecessor Barradas comes out the better in this anecdote. See Mendes, *Oratória Barroca*,
p. 383.

71. Galatians 1:10, "If I pleased men, I should not be the servant of Christ."

72. "We are made a spectacle to God, and to angels, and to men." This rendering of 1
Corinthians 4:9 changes *mundo*, the world, to *Deo*, God. Vieira appears to cite a passage
from the version of Letter 87 by Bernard of Clairvaux (1090-1153) that is included in chapter
16 of early modern editions of the *Vita Christi* of Ludolph of Saxony (d. 1378). Bernard's letter
to Oger describes the virtues of a good religious in terms similar to those Vieira employs
here.

73. Isaiah 6:5, "Woe is me, because I have held my peace."

above all, the word of God is sown in the Church and when she arms herself against vices. Let us preach and let us all arm ourselves against sins, against prides, against hatreds, against ambitions, against envies, against greeds, against lusts. Let Heaven see that it still has those on earth who stand on its side. Let Hell know that there are still those on earth who will make war against it with the word of God. And let that same earth know that it is still capable of flowering again and of bearing much fruit: *Et fecit fructum centuplum.*

SERMAM
DO
BOM LADRAM,
PRÉGADO
Na Igreja da Mifericordia de Lisboa,
Anno 1655.

Domine, memento mei, cùm veneris in Regnum tuum:
Hodie mecum eris in Paradifo. Luc. 23.

§. I.

Ste Sermaõ, que hoje fe préga na Mifericordia de Lisboa, & nam fe préga na Capella Real, pareciame a mim, que lá fe havia de prégar, & naõ aqui. Daquella pauta havia de fer, & nam defta. E porque ? Porque o Texto em que fe funda o mefmo Sermaõ, todo pertence à Mageftade da-

406

quelle lugar, & nada à piedade defte. Hũa das coufas que diz o Texto, he que foram fentenciados em Jerufalem dous ladroens, & ambos condenados, ambos executados, ambos crucificados, & mortos, fem lhe valer procurador, nem embargos. Permitte ifto a Mifericordia de Lisboa? Naõ. A primeira diligencia que faz, he eleger por Procurador das Cadeas hum Irmão de grande authoridade,

---

Frontispiece of the Sermon of the Good Thief in António Vieira's *Sermoens . . . Terceira Parte* (Lisbon: Miguel Deslandes, 1683). Biblioteca da Ajuda, Lisbon, shelfmark B-XX-17.

4

Sermon of the Good Thief

*Preached at the Church of the Misericórdia in Lisbon, the
year of 1655.*

*Domine, memento mei, cum veneris in Regnum tuum:
Hodie mecum eris in Paradiso.*

LUKE 23[1]

I

This sermon, which I am preaching today at the Misericórdia of Lisbon
and not at the Royal Chapel, in my mind ought to be preached there and
not here.[2] It should be on that schedule and not on this one. And why?
Because the Text upon which this Sermon is based belongs entirely to the
Majesty of that place, and not at all to the piety of this one. One of the things
the Text says is that two thieves were sentenced in Jerusalem and both condemned, both executed, both crucified and killed, without recourse to an
advocate or an injunction. Does the Misericórdia of Lisbon permit such a
thing? No. The first measure it takes is to elect a Brother of great authority,
power, and industriousness as an Advocate for Jails. And the first mark
of this Advocate is to make it a point of honor that no criminal should be
executed during his term of office. This part of the story does not therefore
pertain to the Misericórdia of Lisbon. The other part (which I took as my
Theme) pertains entirely to the Palace and to the Royal Chapel. In it, the
King is addressed, *Domine*; in it, his Kingdom is discussed, *cùm veneris in
Regnum tuum*; in it, memorials are presented to him, *memento mei*; and in
it the King himself dispatches them immediately and without remanding

---

1. Luke 23:42–43, "Lord, remember me when thou shalt come into thy kingdom . . . this day
thou shalt be with me in paradise."

2. The Santa Casa da Misericórdia, the Holy House of Mercy, was a charitable brotherhood
whose mother chapter was founded in Lisbon in 1499. Its church was located very close to
the Royal Palace, and its members in Lisbon were drawn from the nobility as well as the
administrative and mercantile elite at the capital.

them to other Tribunals, *hodie mecum eris in Paradiso*. The thing that might inhibit me from preaching on this matter would be the mismatch between the doctrine and the place. But from this scruple, of which many preachers take no notice, Jonah's Preaching freed me. Jonah did not preach in the Palace, but through the streets of Nineveh, a City of greater distances than this one of ours, and the Sacred Text says that his preaching immediately reached the King's ears, *Pervenit verbum ad Regem*.[3] How I wish that what I am determined to preach today would reach all Kings, and Foreign ones even more than ours! They all should imitate the King of Kings; and they all have a lot to learn from this last action of His life. The Good Thief asked Christ to remember him in His Kingdom, *Domine, memento mei, cùm veneris in Regnum tuum*. And the remembrance the Lord had of him was that they were both to see themselves together in Paradise, *Hodie mecum eris in Paradiso*. This is the remembrance that all Kings should have, and I wish those to whom they listen most closely would persuade them of that. Let them remember not only to take the thieves to Paradise but to take them along with them, *Mecum*. Neither can Kings go to Paradise without taking thieves along with them, nor can thieves go to Hell without taking Kings along with them. This is what I shall preach.

Ave Maria.

II

For Kings to take thieves along with them to Paradise not only is not for them to keep indecent company, but it is such a glorious and truly Royal action that by it Christ Himself crowned and proved the truth of his Reign, as soon as He admitted the title of King on the Cross. But what we see practiced in all the Kingdoms of the world is so much the opposite that, rather than the Kings taking the thieves along with them to Paradise, it is the thieves who take the Kings along with them to Hell. And if it is so, as I will now demonstrate with evidence, no one can find strange the clarity or openness with which I speak and will speak in a matter that involves such sovereign respect; rather, everyone will be surprised at the silence and condemn the neglect with which Preachers conceal such a necessary doctrine, because it is the one that should be most often heard and declaimed in Pulpits. Let this subject therefore today be new, though it should be very old and very frequent. I will pursue it all the more, and with

---

3. Jonah 3:6, "The word came to the King."

greater hope of producing fruit, seeing how ennobled the present audience is with the authority of so many Ministers from all of the superior Tribunals, upon whose counsel and conscience the consciences of Kings are customarily discharged.

III

And so that such an important and grave discourse may rest upon solid and irrefutable foundations, I posit first that without the restitution of what belongs to others there can be no salvation. So conclude all Theologians agreeing with Saint Thomas; and so it is defined in the Chapter *Si res aliena* with words taken from Saint Augustine, which are as follows: *Si res aliena propter quam peccatum est, reddi potest, & non redditur, pœnitentia non agitur, sed simulatur. Si autem veraciter agitur, non remittitur peccatum, nisi restituatur ablatum, si, ut dixi, restitui potest.*[4] This means: If what belongs to others, and has been taken or retained, can be returned and is not returned, the penance for this and other sins is not true penance; rather, it is simulated and faked, because the sin cannot be forgiven if what was stolen is not returned when the one who stole it has the possibility of returning it. The only exception to this rule became the happiness of the Good Thief and was the reason why he was saved, and why the bad one, too, could have been saved without returning anything. Since both left the shipwreck of this life stripped naked and strapped to a pole, only their extreme poverty could absolve them of the larcenies they had committed, because, being impeded from making restitution, they were excused from it. However, if the Good Thief had owned property with which he could return all or part of what he had stolen, all his Faith and all his penitence, so celebrated by the Saints, would not have been enough to save him had he not returned it. This fortunate man lacked two things to be saved, one as the thief that he had been, another as the Christian that he was becoming. As the thief that he had been, he lacked the means of restitution; as

---

4. "If the offense committed has involved theft, and restitution is not made, although it is possible to make it, there is no repentance but only pretense. If, however, there is true repentance, the sin will not be forgiven unless there is restitution of stolen goods, but, as I said, where restitution is possible." Augustine, Letter 153, 6:20; in his *Letters*, trans. Wilifred Parsons, 3 vols. (Washington, D.C.: Catholic University of America Press, 1953), vol. 3, pp. 296–297. Also cited with minor variations in Thomas Aquinas, *Summa Theologica* 2a2æ, 62: 2, "On Restitution"; translation in the edition of the Fathers of the English Dominican Province, 22 vols. (London: Burns, Oates & Washburn, 1913–1942), Part 2, vol. 2, no. 2 (vol. 10), p. 171.

the Christian that he was becoming, he lacked Baptism. But just as the blood that he spilled on the Cross made up for his lack of Baptism, so his nakedness and his impediment made up for the lack of restitution; and because of that he was saved. Now think, as you consider this, of all those who stole in life and made no restitution, neither in life nor in death, and who instead, as they died, left much property in their wills and massive inheritances to their heirs. Think of where they are going, or where their Souls may have gone, and whether they could have been saved.

So rigorous was this precept of restitution in the Old Law that, if one who stole had no means with which to make restitution, God commanded him to be sold and to make restitution with the price he fetched, *Si non habuerit quod pro furto reddat, ipse venundabitur.*[5] So while a man was his own master and the owner of his freedom, even if he had nothing else, the Law did not judge him to be impeded from making restitution or excuse him from it until he sold himself and made restitution with the price he fetched. There can be no doubt that such a Law was just, since it was God's Law. And even though in the Law of Grace God Himself diminished this circumstance of rigor that belonged to Positive Law, nevertheless in Natural Law, which is indispensable and enjoins restitution on those who are able and have the means to make it, He was so far from changing or moderating anything that not even Christ Himself on the Cross would promise Paradise to the Thief in that case, unless he first made restitution. Let us place another Thief alongside this one and see, in Christ's own admirable judgment, the difference between one case and the other.

Just as Christ Our Lord said to Dismas, *Hodie mecum eris in Paradiso,* today you will be with Me in Paradise, so he said to Zacchaeus, *Hodie salus domui huic facta est,* today salvation came into this house of yours.[6] But what should be noted carefully is that to Dismas the Lord promised salvation immediately, and to Zacchaeus not immediately but much later. And why, if both were thieves and both converted? Because Dismas was a poor thief, and he did not have the wherewithal to return what he had stolen; Zacchaeus was a rich thief and had plenty with which to make restitution, *Zacheus Princeps erat publicanorum, & ipse dives,* says the Evangelist.[7] And even if he had not said so, the state of the one and the other thief would

---

5. Exodus 22:3, "If he have not wherewith to make restitution for the theft, he shall be sold."

6. Luke 19:9, "This day is salvation come to this house."

7. Luke 19:2, "Zacheus, who was the chief of the publicans, and he was rich."

amply declare it. Why? Because Dismas was a condemned thief and, had he been rich, it is obvious he would not have wound up on the gallows; Zacchaeus, however, was a tolerated thief, and his very wealth gave him the immunity to steal without punishment, and even without blame. And since Dismas was a poor thief and did not have the wherewithal to make restitution, there was no impediment to his salvation, and Christ therefore granted it to him that very moment. On the contrary, Zacchaeus, being a rich thief and having plenty with which to make restitution, could not have his salvation assured by Christ before he made restitution; and for that reason Christ delayed the promise to him. The Evangelist's narration itself is the best proof of this difference.

Zacchaeus knew Christ by His fame alone, and greatly desired to see Him. The Lord passed through his town and, since he was small in stature and the crowd was large, disregarding the authority of his person or of his office, *Princeps publicanorum*, he climbed a tree to see Him; and not only did he see Him, but he was seen and clearly seen. The Lord set those divine eyes on him, called him by his name, and told him to come down from the tree immediately, because it was important to Him to be his guest that day, *Zachee festinans descende, quia hodie in domo tua oportet me manere.*[8] So the Savior came into the house of Zacchaeus, and here it would appear to be fitting for Christ to tell him that salvation had then come into his house; but the Lord did not say this, or anything else. Zacchaeus welcomed Him and celebrated His arrival with all the manifestations of joy, *Excepit illum gaudens*, and the Lord kept the same silence.[9] He sat at the table overflowing with delicacies and even more with good will, which is the best dish for Christ, and He continued in the same suspense. On top of this, Zacchaeus said that he would give half of his property to the poor, *Ecce dimidium bonorum meorum do pauperibus*, and since the Lord is the One who, on the Day of Judgment, will reward only the merits of the alms with the Kingdom of Heaven, who would not think that He would immediately respond to this great gesture of liberality toward the poor with the promise of salvation?[10] But not even at this point was Zacchaeus worthy of hearing what Christ later told him. Well, Lord, if Your piety and truth have so often said that whatever one does for the poor, one does for You, and this man is serving

---

8. Luke 19:5, "Zacheus, make haste and come down; for this day I must abide in thy house."

9. Luke 19:6, "Received him with joy."

10. Luke 19:8, "Behold, Lord, the half of the goods I give to the poor."

You in Your Person with so many courtesies and in the person of the poor with so many endeavors; if You have invited Yourself to be his guest in order to save him, and his salvation is the urgency that brought You to his house; if You called him and he answered with such diligence; if You told him to hurry, *Festinans descende*, and he did not delay a moment; then why do You defer the grace You wish to grant him for so long, why do You not finish absolving him, why do You not assure his salvation? Because this same Zacchaeus, as head of the publicans, *Princeps publicanorum*, had stolen from many and, rich man that he was, *Et ipse dives*, had the means to return what he had stolen, therefore as long as he remained a debtor and did not return what belonged to others, however many good works he did, not even Christ could absolve him, and however much wealth he piously dispensed, not even Christ could save him. All the other works that Zacchaeus did after that fortunate sight were very commendable, but, as long as he did not do that of restitution, he was not capable of salvation. Let him return what he stole and he will immediately be saved; and so it was. Zacchaeus added that all he had improperly acquired he would return fourfold, *Et si quid aliquem defraudavi, reddo quadruplum.*[11] And at that very moment the Lord, who until then had been quiet, unlocked the treasuries of His grace and announced his salvation, *Hodie salus domui huic facta est.* So, even as the Savior came into Zacchaeus's house, salvation stayed outside because, as long as restitution did not leave that house, salvation could not enter. Salvation cannot enter without sin being forgiven and sin cannot be forgiven without the restitution of what has been stolen, *Non dimittitur peccatum, nisi restituatur ablatum.*[12]

IV

This first truth being posited as certain and infallible, the second thing that I posit with the same certainty is that the restitution of what belongs to others on pain of losing salvation is not only obligatory for subjects and private individuals, but also for Scepters and Crowns. Some Princes think, or must think, that just as they are superior to everyone, so are they masters of everything, and that is a mistake. The law of restitution is a Natural Law and a Divine Law. As a Natural Law it is obligatory for Kings because

---

11. Luke 19:8, "And if I have wronged any man of any thing, I restore him fourfold."

12. "The sin will not be forgiven unless there is restitution of stolen goods." Cited in Augustine, Letter 153, 6:20; in his *Letters*, vol. 3, pp. 296–297.

nature made all men equal; and as a Divine Law it is also obligatory for them because God, who made them greater than others, is greater than them. This truth is only contradicted by practice and use. But in relation to this very use, Saint Thomas, the Doctor I invoke today, who on these matters is the greatest authority, argues thus: *Terrarum Principes multa à suis subditis violenter extorquent: quod videtur ad rationem rapinæ pertinere: grave autem videtur dicere, quòd in hoc peccent: quia sic ferè omnes Principes damnarentur. Ergo rapina in aliquo casu est licita.*[13] This means: Rapine or theft is to take what belongs to others violently and against their will; Princes take many things violently from their vassals and against their will; therefore it seems that theft is licit in some cases, because if we say that Princes sin in this matter, all of them, or almost all, would be condemned, *Ferè omnes Principes damnarentur.* Oh how terrible and fearsome a consequence; how worthy of being profoundly contemplated by Princes and those who have a part in their decisions and counsels! The Angelic Doctor himself answers his argument, and although I do not usually bother my listeners with extensive Latin, I shall cite his very words: *Dicendum, quod si Principes à subditis exigunt quod eis secundùm justitiam debetur propter bonum commune conservandum, etiamsi violentia adhibeatur, non est rapina. Si verò aliquid Principes indebitè extorqueant, rapina est, sicut & latrocinium. Unde ad restitutionem tenentur, sicut & latrones. Et tanto gravius peccant quàm latrones, quanto periculosiùs, & communiùs contra publicam justitiam agunt, cujus custodes sunt positi.*[14] I answer (says Saint Thomas) that if Princes take from subjects that which, according to justice, is their due for the preservation of the common good, even if they carry it out with violence, it is not rapine or theft. However, if Princes take by violence that which is not their due, it is rapine and larceny. Thence it follows that they are obliged to make restitution, as thieves are; and that their sin is more grave than that of those

---

13. "Earthly princes violently extort many things from their subjects: and this seems to savour of robbery. Now it would seem a grievous matter to say that they sin in acting thus, for in that case nearly every prince would be damned. Therefore in some cases robbery is lawful." In Thomas Aquinas, *Summa Theologica* 2a2æ, 66: 8, "On Injustice"; translation in the edition of the Fathers of the English Dominican Province, Part 2, vol. 2, no. 2 (vol. 10), p. 234.

14. "It is no robbery if princes exact from their subjects that which is due to them for the safe-guarding of the common good, even if they use violence in so doing: but if they extort something unduly by means of violence it is robbery even as burglary is. . . . Wherefore they are bound to restitution, just as robbers are, and by so much do they sin more grievously than robbers, as their actions are fraught with greater and more universal danger to public justice whose wardens they are." Ibid., p. 235.

thieves by as much as the damage with which they offend the public justice that they are placed to defend is more dangerous and more common.

Here ends what the Prince of Theologians says of Princes. And since the
word rapine, or larceny, applied to men from the highest sphere is so far from
the flattery they are used to hearing that it is seems to contain some disso-
nance, the Holy Doctor tacitly excuses his manner of speaking and proves his
doctrine with two Texts by others, a divine one by the Prophet Ezechiel, and
another, just short of divine, by Saint Augustine. Ezechiel's Text is part of the
relation of the faults for which God so severely punished the two Kingdoms
of Israel and Judah, the one with the Assyrian captivity and the other with
the Babylonian; and the reason he gives and ponders extensively is that their
Princes, instead of guarding their Peoples like shepherds, robbed them
like wolves, *Principes ejus in medio illius, quasi lupi rapientes prædam.*[15] God
Himself chose only two Kings, Saul and David; and He raised both up from
shepherds so that, from the experience of those flocks that they guarded, they
would know how they should handle their vassals. But their successors, out
of ambition and greed, degenerated so much from this love and care that,
instead of guarding their vassals and grazing them like sheep, they robbed
them and ate them like wolves, *Quasi lupi rapientes prædam.*

Saint Augustine's Text speaks generally of all Kingdoms in which
such oppressions and injustices are common, and he says that between
those Kingdoms and thieves' dens (called larcenies by the Saint) there is
only one difference. And what is it? That Kingdoms are great larcenies
or robberies, and larcenies or robberies are small Kingdoms: *Sublatâ
justitiâ quid sunt Regna, nisi magna latrocinia? Quia & latrocinia quid
sunt, nisi parva Regna?*[16] This is what that pirate said to Alexander the
Great. Alexander was sailing in a powerful fleet over the Erythraean
Sea to conquer India, and when a pirate who went about stealing from
fishermen was brought into his presence, Alexander reproached him
greatly for engaging in such an evil craft. However, he who was neither fearful nor dull answered thus: How is it, Master, that by stealing
in a boat I should be a thief, and by stealing in a fleet you should be an

---

15. Ezechiel 22:27, "Her princes in the midst of her, are like wolves ravening the prey."

16. "In the absence of justice, what is sovereignty but organized brigandage? For, what are
bands of brigands but petty kingdoms?" In Saint Augustine, *The City of God* 4: 4; translated
in the edition of Demetrius Zema and Gerald Walsh, 3 vols. (Washington, D.C.: Catholic
University of America Press, 1950), vol. 1, p. 195.

Emperor?[17] So it is. Stealing a little is a fault, stealing a lot is greatness; stealing with little power makes pirates, stealing with much makes Alexanders. But Seneca, who knew well how to distinguish qualities and interpret meanings, defined both with the same name, *Eodem loco pone latronem, & piratam, quo Regem animum latronis, & piratæ habentem.*[18] If the King of Macedonia or any other does what the thief and the pirate do, the thief, the pirate, and the King all have the same place and deserve the same name.

When I read this in Seneca, I was not so surprised that a Stoic Philosopher would dare write such a sentence in Rome while Nero reigned over it; what surprised me the most and nearly embarrassed me was that in a time of Catholic Princes our Evangelical Orators, fearful either to criticize or to caution, would not preach the same doctrine. These mute men of eloquence should know that they offend Kings more with what they keep silent than with what they say, because the confidence with which such things are said is a sign that they do not pertain to the Kings, who therefore cannot be offended; and the caution with which such things are kept silent argues that the Kings will be offended, because these things pertain to them. But let us move forward quickly to the third and final posit, since all three are necessary for us to get to the point.

V

Finally, I posit that the thieves of whom I speak are not those wretches condemned to this kind of life by poverty and their vile fortune, since their very wretchedness either excuses or mitigates their sin, as Solomon says: *Non grandis est culpa, cùm quis furatus fuerit: furatur enim ut esurientem impleat animam.*[19] The thief who steals in order to eat neither goes nor takes anyone to Hell; the ones who not only go but take others there, those I am

---

17. The well-known story of Alexander and the pirate in the form that Vieira tells it is recounted in Augustine's *City of God* 4: 4. It derives from a fragment in Cicero's *De Republica* (Book 3, 14, 24) and was repeated in the works of several medieval and early modern authors such as John of Salisbury (c. 1120–1180) and Tomasso Garzoni (1549–1589). See John of Salisbury, *Policraticus* 3: 14, and Tomasso Garzoni, *La Piazza Universale di tutte le Professione del Mondo* (Venice: Giovanni Battista Somasco, 1587), p. 867.

18. "Imagine in a like situation a brigand or a pirate or a king with the temper of a brigand or a pirate." In Seneca, *De Beneficiis* Book 2; in Lucius Annaeus Seneca, *Moral Essays*, trans. John W. Basore (Cambridge, Mass.: Harvard University Press, 2006), p. 89.

19. Proverbs 6:30, "The fault is not so great when a man hath stolen: for he stealeth to fill his hungry soul."

talking about, are different thieves of a greater caliber and from a higher sphere. They are the ones whom, under the same name and the same predicament, Saint Basil the Great distinguishes very well, *Non est intelligendum fures esse solùm bursarum incisores, vel latrocinantes in balneis; sed & qui duces legionum statuti, vel qui commiso sibi regimine civitatum, aut gentium, hoc quidem furtim tollunt, hoc vero vi, & publice exigunt:*[20] Thieves are not only, says the Saint, those who cut purses or peep at people going to bathe in order to swipe their clothes; the thieves who more properly and worthily deserve this title are those to whom Kings entrust their armies and legions, or the government of Provinces, or the administration of Cities, and who either by cunning or by force rob and plunder peoples. Other thieves rob a man, these rob Cities and Kingdoms; others steal at their own risk, these without fear or danger; others, if they steal, are hanged, these steal and hang. Diogenes, who saw everything with a keener sight than other men, saw that a great troop of officers and Ministers of justice were taking some thieves to be hanged, and he started to shout: There go the big thieves off to hang the little ones![21]

How fortunate Greece was to have such a Preacher! And more fortunate would other nations be if justice did not suffer such affronts in them! How often in Rome was a thief seen going to the gallows for stealing a sheep, and on the same day a Consul or a Dictator being carried in triumph for robbing a Province? And how many thieves might these same triumphant thieves have hanged? Of one called Seronatus, Sidonius Apollinarius said with a subtle counterposition, *Non cessat simul furta, vel punire, vel facere*: Seronatus is always busy with two things, punishing thefts and committing them.[22] This was no zeal for justice, but rather envy. He wanted to remove thieves from the world, in order to steal on his own.

---

20. "Now we must not understand by thieves, only such as cut strips off hides, or commit robberies in the baths. But all such also as, when appointed leaders of legions, or installed governors of states or nations, are guilty of secret embezzlement, or violent and open extractions." Saint Basil, cited by Saint Thomas Aquinas in the *Catena Aurea*, a collection of comments by church fathers on the gospels; translated in *Catena Aurea: Commentary on the Four Gospels, collected out of the Works of the Fathers by S. Thomas Aquinas*, 4 vols. in 6 books (Oxford: J. H. Parker, 1841–1845), vol. 3, book 2, p. 611.

21. This anecdote is found in the life of Diogenes the Cynic included in Diogenes Laertius's *Lives and Opinions of Eminent Philosophers* 6: 45. See Diogenes Laertius, *Lives of Eminent Philosophers*, trans. R. D. Hicks, 2 vols. (New York: Putnam, 1925), vol 2., p. 47.

22. "He is ceaselessly busy either in punishing thefts or in committing them." Sidonius Apollinaris, Book 2, Letter 1, in Sidonius, *Poems; Letters: Books 1–2*, Ttans. W. B. Anderson (Cambridge, Mass.: Harvard University Press, 1936), p. 415.

VI

Now that I have declared, not with my own words but with those of very good Authors, how honored and invested with authority the thieves of whom I speak are, these are the ones about whom I said and say that they take Kings along with them to Hell. Were they to go there alone and were the Devil to take them, unfortunate though it would be, it would be as they wanted. But that they should take Kings along with them is a pain that cannot be suffered; and therefore one cannot keep silent about it. But if Kings, far from taking what belongs to others, instead are the ones who are robbed and the most robbed of all, then how is it that these bad thieves take these good Kings along with them to Hell? Not by one but by many ways, ways that seem intangible and hidden and yet are very clear and manifest. First, because Kings give them the offices and powers with which they steal; second, because Kings maintain them there; third, because Kings advance and promote them to other, greater offices; and finally, because though Kings are obliged on pain of losing their salvation to make restitution for all these damages, neither in life nor in death do they do so. And who says this? You already know that it has to be Saint Thomas. Saint Thomas poses the question whether the person who has not stolen, or received, or come to possess any part of what has been stolen can be obliged to return it. And not only does he decide affirmatively but, expressing more strongly what I am saying, he takes Kings as his example. The Text goes, *Tenetur ille restituere, qui non obstat, cùm obstare teneatur. Sicut Principes, qui tenentur custodire justitiam in terra, si per eorum defectum latrones increscant, ad restitutionem tenentur: quia redditus, quos habent, sunt quasi stipendia ad hoc instituta, ut justitiam conservent in terra:*[23] He who has the obligation to prevent theft, if he has not prevented it, is obliged to return what has been stolen. And even Princes who through their own fault let thieves multiply are obliged to make restitution, in so much as the rents with which their peoples serve and assist them are like stipends, instituted and consigned by these peoples for Princes to guard them and keep them in a state of justice. This Theology is so natural and clear that

---

23. "He who does not prevent the theft, whereas he is bound to do so, is obliged to make restitution; for instance, persons in authority who are bound to safeguard justice on earth, are bound to restitution, if by their neglect thieves prosper, because their salary is given to them in payment of their preserving justice here below." Cited in Thomas Aquinas, *Summa Theologica* 2a2æ, 62: 7, "On Restitution"; translated in the edition of the Fathers of the English Dominican Province, Part 2, vol. 2, book 2 (vol. 10): p. 182.

even Agamemnon, a Heathen King, acknowledged it when he said: *Qui non vetat peccare, cùm possit, jubet.*[24]

And if Princes incur this obligation of making restitution for the thefts committed by occasional and involuntary thieves, how will they answer for those to whom they themselves and by their own choice accord the jurisdictions and powers with which to rob those peoples? That is not, nor can it be, the intent of Princes, but it suffices that those officials, either of War, or of the Treasury, or of Justice, who commit the thefts are their choices and creatures, for Princes to pay for whatever they do. Let us take the example of fault from where there can be none. God placed Adam in Paradise with jurisdiction and power over all living creatures, and with absolute lordship over all things created, except one tree alone. *Adão* lacked only a few letters to be *ladrão*, and *fruto* did not lack any to be *furto*.[25] Finally, he and his wife (women are often the go-betweens) stole that one thing in the world that was not theirs. So here we have Adam chosen, here we have him in office, here we have him a thief. And who was the one who paid for the theft? What a case, admirable above all others! The one who chose the thief and who gave him the office paid for the theft. The one who chose Adam and who gave him the office was God; and it was God who paid for the theft so greatly at His own cost, as we know. God Himself said so, mentioning how much the atonement for the theft and its damages had cost Him, *Quæ non rapui, tunc exolvebam.*[26] Did you see the human body that I, God as I am, dressed Myself in? Did you see how much I suffered? Did you see the blood I spilled? Did you see the death between thieves to which I was condemned? Well then, with all that I was paying for what I did not steal. Adam was the one who stole, and I the one who paid, *Quæ non rapui, tunc exolvebam.* So, my Lord, how was your Divine Majesty at fault in Adam's theft? It was not My fault at all, nor would it have been My fault, even if I were not God. Because in the choice of that man and in the office that I gave him, in everything I acted with the circumspection, prudence, and providence that should and must be applied by a Prince

---

24. "One who does not forbid wrongdoing, when he has the power, commands it." In Seneca, *The Trojan Women*, line 291; in Seneca the Younger, *Hercules, Trojan Women, Phoenician Women, Medea, Phaedra*, trans. John G. Fitch (Cambridge, Mass.: Harvard University Press, 2002), p. 197.

25. Vieira's wordplay is built on the proximity between the Portuguese word for Adam, *Adão*, and the Portuguese word for thief, *ladrão*; the same thing applies to the terms *fruto*, fruit, and *furto*, theft.

26. Psalm 68:5, "Then did I pay that which I took not away."

who is most attentive to his obligations, most considerate, and most just. When I first did it, it was not with despotic imperiousness as other beings do, but upon mature counsel and through consultation with persons who are not human but divine, *Faciamus hominem ad imaginem, & similitudinem nostram, & præsit.*[27] The parts and qualities that were found in the chosen one were as adequate for the office as could be wished for or imagined; because he was the wisest of all men, just without vice, righteous without injustice, and master of all his passions, which he held subject and obedient to reason. He only lacked experience, and no other men competed for this choice; but neither of these things could exist then, since he was the first and only man. Well, if Your choice, Lord, was as just and justified as it had to be by simply being Yours, why should You pay for the theft that he committed when all the fault was his? Because I want to give this example and testament to Princes; and because such a bad and pernicious consequence should not remain in the world, something that would happen if Princes were to persuade themselves in any case that they were not obliged to pay and to make satisfaction for what their Ministers stole.

VII

But I see how with this very example of God Kings excuse, or can excuse, themselves. Because if things went so badly for God with Adam, even though God knew very well what he was to become, why should it be a great surprise that the same should happen to Kings with men whom they choose for offices, if they neither know, nor can know, what these men will do afterward? This is an apparent excuse, but one that is just as false as it is poorly founded. Because God does not make a choice of men for what He knows they will become, but for what they are at present. Christ knew well that Judas would become a thief; but at the moment He chose him for the office in which he became that, not only was he no thief, but he was very worthy of being trusted with the care of guarding and distributing the alms of the poor. Let Kings choose people this way and let them assign the offices this way, and God will release them on this score from the obligation of making restitution. However, choices and assignments are not usually made this way. Do Kings want to know whether those to whom they assign offices are thieves or not? Let them observe Christ's rule, *Qui*

---

27. Genesis 1:26, "Let us make man to our image and likeness, and let him have dominion." Here Vieira refers to angels as God's consultors.

non intrat per ostium, fur est, & latro, The only door through which one legitimately enters an office is merit.[28] And Christ calls every person who does not enter through the door not only a thief, but a thief and a thief, *Fur est, & latro.*[29] And why is this person twice a thief? Once because he steals the office, and again because of what he will steal with it. He who enters through the door may become a thief; but those who do not enter through it already are thieves. Some enter through kinship, others through friendship, others through pull, others through bribes, and all through negotiation. And those who negotiate need no further proof; it is clear that they do not stand to lose. They may be hidden thieves now, but afterward they will be exposed, for that is, as Saint Jerome says, the difference between *fur* and *latro.*[30]

It is certainly a wonderful thing to see some people so inserted and so far inside who have not entered, nor were able to enter, through the door. If they entered through the windows, like those thieves mentioned by Joel, *Per fenestras intrabunt quasi fur,* it is a great misfortune that, although windows are made to let light and air enter, darkness and disasters should enter through them.[31] If they entered by undermining the home of the head of the household, like the thief in Christ's parable, *Si sciret paterfamilias, quâ horâ fur veniret, non sineret perfodi domum suam,* it would be an even greater misfortune if the master of the house's sleepiness or lethargy was so heavy that, while his walls were being undermined, the blows did not wake him.[32] But what is exceedingly surprising is that there are those who, finding the door closed, endeavor to enter through the rooftops and succeed; succeed, moreover, without feet or hands, let alone wings. Christ Our Lord was miraculously healing the sick inside a house, and such was the crowd that when those who carried a paralytic could not enter through the door, they climbed with him to the roof and inserted him through the rooftop. The consideration of the subject is more surprising still than the manner and place of the insertion. Who would not think that a man who entered through the rooftop was a man fallen down from Heaven, *Tertius è*

---

28. John 10:1, "He that entereth not by the door . . . the same is a thief and a robber."

29. The original Portuguese edition contains the same repetition that the translation renders here, *ladram, & ladram.*

30. Book 2 of Jerome's *Commentary on Hosea* draws a distinction between *fures* and *latrones.*

31. Joel 2:9, "They shall come in at the windows as a thief."

32. Luke 12:39, "If the householder did know at what hour the thief would come . . . he would not suffer his house to be broken open."

Cælo cecidit Cato?[33] And that man was a paralytic who had no feet, or hands, or feeling, or movement; but he had the wherewithal to pay four men who carried him on their backs and raised him so high. And since those who carry such men on their backs are so well paid by them, why should it be any wonder that they say and testify (even though such men are so incapable) that his merits reach to the rooftops? Since they cannot invoke the deeds of one who has no hands, they mention virtues and goodness. They say that, by his actions, he captivates all; and why should he not captivate them, if he bought them? They say that, when he carries out his obligations, everyone is left owing him money; and why should they not owe it to him, if they took it from him? I leave aside those who ascend to posts by hair, and not by Samson's strength but by Delilah's favors.[34] I leave aside those who, with the recognizable voice of Jacob, receive Esau's blessing while not wearing gloves but by giving or promising them.[35] I leave aside those who, more leprous than Namaan the Syrian, cleansed themselves of leprosy, and not with the waters of the Jordan but with those of the Río de la Plata.[36] Is this, and all the rest that could be said about this, to enter through the door? Of course not. Well, if none of this is done *Sicut fur in nocte*, but facing the Sun and in the light of noon, how can he who at least confirms the assignments excuse himself by saying that he did not know that those who gained preferment by these means were thieves? In the end, he either knew them or he did not. If he did not know them, how could he assign offices to them without knowing them? And if he did know them, how could he, knowing them, assign them offices? But let us turn to those to whom offices were assigned with express knowledge of their qualities.

VIII

Sir So-and-So (says well-intentioned piety) is a poor nobleman, let us give him something to govern. And how many impieties, forewarned or not,

---

33. "A third Cato has tumbled from the sky!" In Juvenal, Satire 2, line 40; in *Juvenal and Persius*, trans. Susanna Morton Braund (Cambridge, Mass.: Harvard University Press, 2004), p. 153.

34. The story of Samson and Delilah is told in Judges 16.

35. Vieira uses *luvas*, which in Portuguese means both gloves, as the gloves referred to in the story of Jacob and Esau in Genesis 27, and bribes, pertaining to his argument.

36. Vieira plays with the Portuguese meaning of *Prata* (as in *Rio da Prata*, Rio de la Plata), silver. The story of Namaan the Syrian is found in 4 Kings 5.

are contained in this piety? If he is poor, give him honorable alms under the name of an endowment, and let him have enough to live on. But something to govern, just because he is poor? So that he will cease being poor at the expense of those he will govern? And so that he will make very many poor by making himself very rich? This is what they want, those who choose him for this reason. Let us turn to the ones who are rewarded, as well as to the ones who are punished. A certain older Captain has many years of service; give him a Fortress in the Conquests. But if these years of service belong to a man who took the uniforms and rations of his own soldiers as his first spoils of war, leaving them stripped and starving, what will he do in Sofala or in Muscat?[37] A certain graduate in Laws lectured to great applause in the Palace. However, in two Districts and one Circuit he did not give a good account of himself; so let him be deported to India with a magistrate's cloak. And if the hands of this Doctor became sticky in Beira and Alentejo, where there are no diamonds or rubies, how will it be at the High Court of Goa?[38]

King Dom João the Third commissioned Saint Francis Xavier to inform him about the Estado da Índia through his companion who was the Prince's Tutor. And what the Saint wrote from there, without naming offices or people, was that in India the Verb *Rapio* was conjugated in all modes.[39] In such a serious affair the sentence seems playful, but the servant of God spoke like God, who in one word says everything. Commenting on the words of Daniel, *Nabucodonosor Rex misit ad congregandos Satrapas, Magistratus, & Judices*, Nicholas of Lyra expounds on the Etymology of Satraps, who were the Governors of the Provinces, by saying that this noun was composed of *Sat* and *Rapio*.[40] *Dicuntur Satrapæ quasi*

---

37. Sofala and Muscat were Portuguese colonial ports in East Africa and Arabia, respectively. Curiously, the Portuguese garrison at Muscat had surrendered to Omani forces in 1650, five years before the time Vieira gave this sermon. The reference thus clearly suggests some imperial backwater.

38. Beira and Alentejo are two provinces in continental Portugal.

39. *Rapio* is Latin for "I steal." The original letter in which Francis Xavier (1506–1552) made this claim to Simão Rodrigues (1510–1579), his companion at the court of João III in Lisbon, was signed Cochin, January 27, 1545; a version of the quote was later included in the major biography of Xavier by João de Lucena. See *Monumenta Xaveriana*, 2 vols. (Madrid: Augustin Avrial, 1899–1912), vol. 1, p. 375, and Lucena, *Historia da Vida do Padre Francisco de Xavier, e do que fizerão na Índia os mais Religiosos da Companhia de Iesu* (Lisbon: Pedro Craesbeeck, 1600), p. 245.

40. Daniel 3:2, "Nabuchodonosor the king sent to call together the nobles, the magistrates, and the judges."

satis rapientes, quia solent bona inferiorum rapere:[41] They are called Satraps because they typically steal plenty. And this plenty is what Saint Francis Xavier specified better, saying that they conjugate the verb *Rapio* in all modes. What I can add, from my experience, is that not only beyond the Cape of Good Hope, but also in the parts on this side, the same conjugation is likewise employed. They conjugate the Verb *Rapio* in all modes, because they steal in all modes of the art, not to mention other new and exquisite ones that neither Donatus nor Despauterius knew.[42] As soon as they arrive there, they start stealing in the Indicative mode, because the first information that they ask from the experts is that they point out and show to them the ways to grasp everything. They steal in the Imperative mode, because, since they have *imperium merum* and *imperium mixtum*, they apply all their power despotically in carrying out rapine.[43] They steal in the Mandative mode, because they accept all that is remanded to them and, so that all remand, those who do not remand are not well accepted. They steal in the Optative mode, because they desire all that seems good to them and, by praising the things they desire to their owners, through involuntary courtesy they make these things their own. They steal in the Conjunctive mode, because they join the little money that they have with that of those who deal with a lot of it, and it is enough for them to add their favor to gain at least half the outcome of this greed. They steal in the Potential mode, because, without pretext or ceremony, they employ potency. They steal in the Permissive mode, because they permit others to steal, and these purchase their permissions. They steal in the Infinitive mode, because the stealing does not end with the end of their governing, and they always leave roots there that allow the thefts to continue. They conjugate in these same modes in all Persons, because the first person of the Verb is theirs, the second their servants', and the third pertains to whoever has industry and conscience

---

41. "They are called Satraps, as ones who steal enough, because they are accustomed to stealing the goods of their inferiors." The comment by Nicholas of Lyra (c. 1270–1349) is found in early modern editions of the Bible at Daniel 3:2; for example, *Bibliorum Sacrorum . . . cum Glossa ordinaria, & Nicolai Lyrani expositionibus, Additionibus & Replicis,* 6 vols. (Lyon: 1545), vol. 4, p. 299v.

42. Vieira's usage of the word *arte* invokes both the common grammar books of his day and the famous text, first published in 1652, called the *Arte de Furtar,* the Art of Stealing. Ælius Donatus was a late Roman author known for his *Ars Minor,* an introduction to grammar, and Johannes Despauterius (c. 1480–1520) was the author of one of the most widely used Latin grammars of the early modern period.

43. *Imperium merum* refers to a lord's total jurisdiction, while *imperium mixtum* refers to partial jurisdiction, such as that of ministers or officials.

for it. They steal in all tenses together. From the Present (which is their tense) they gather as much as their triennium yields; in order to include the Preterit and the Future in the present, they dig up from the Preterit crimes for which they sell pardons and forgotten debts which they collect in full; and from the Future they pawn the rents and anticipate contracts, making all that is due and not due fall into their hands as their due. Finally, in the same tenses, neither the Imperfect nor the Perfect, the Pluperfect, or any others escape them, because they steal, they stole, they used to steal, they would steal, and they were to steal more, were there more to steal. In sum, the summary of all this rampant conjugation amounts to the supine of the same Verb: Stealing to Steal. And when they have thus conjugated all the active voice, and the wretched Provinces have borne all the passive voice, they return home, as if they had performed great services, rich and loaded with spoils, and the Provinces stay behind, robbed and consumed.

This is certainly not what Kings want; rather they command precisely the opposite in their orders. But since the Patents are given to Grammarians so expert in these conjugations, or so experienced in them, what other effects can be expected from their governing? Each one of these Patents on its own terms amounts to a general license *in scriptis*, or a Passport for stealing. In Holland, where there are so many shipowners of Corsairs, they spread out along the Shores of Africa, Asia, and America for a limited time, and none of them can go out to steal without a Passport that they call a Letter of Marque. The same purpose is served by the Letter of Assignment, when given to those who would be more deserving of a Mark than of a Letter.[44] The inhabitants of the Conquests suffer the piracy of the foreign Corsairs at sea, which is contingent; on land, they suffer that of their countrymen, which is certain and ineluctable. And if anyone doubts which of these is worse, he should take note of the difference between the two. The sea pirate does not steal from those of his Republic; those on land steal from the Vassals of the same King in whose hands they swore homage. I can defend myself from the Corsair of the sea; I cannot resist those of the land. I can flee from the Corsair of the sea; I cannot hide from the ones of the land. The Corsair of the sea depends on the winds; those of the land always have the monsoon behind them. In short, the Corsair of the sea can only do what he can, those of the land can do everything they want, and because of that no prey escapes them. If there was an omnipotent

---

44. The Portuguese *Marca* refers to a brand mark placed as a punishment on the face of a thief.

thief, what do you think greed would do combined with omnipotence? Well, that is what these Corsairs do.

IX

We do have some examples, though only a few, of those who work in the opposite manner, with singular integrity of justice and purity of interest. But I would enjoy knowing how many examples there are, I dare not say of those who, being such notorious thieves, were executed, but of those who were deprived of their offices for their thefts. Well, if they steal through their offices and are given consent and are kept in the same offices, how are they not to take those whose consent they enjoy to Hell along with them? My Saint Thomas says it, and asserts with the Text of Saint Paul, *Digni sunt morte, non solùm qui faciunt, sed etiam qui consentiunt facientibus.*[45] And because the rigor of this Text is not to be understood as applying to anyone who consents, but only to those who, by reason of their office or status, have the obligation to impede, the Holy Doctor therefore makes this very specification and names Princes as an example, *Sed solùm quando incumbit alicui ex officio sicut Principibus terræ.*[46] Truly I do not know how Princes do not take great notice in a matter of such importance, and how they are not made to take notice by those who, in the exterior realm or in that of the Soul, have the charge of unburdening their consciences. Let the ones and the others see how Christ taught everyone that the thief who steals through his office shall not for a moment be given consent or kept in his post.

There was a wealthy Lord, says the Divine Master, who had a servant who, in the office of *Oikonomos*, or administrator, governed his estates (*Oikonomos* is the name in the Original Greek that corresponds to the *Villicus* in the Vulgate). The said Administrator was infamous for profiting from his administration and stealing. As soon as the first news reached the Lord, he was immediately ordered to appear before his master and told to give a reckoning, because he was no longer to perform that office. The resolution was even stricter than this, because he was not simply told that

---

45. Romans 1:32, "[They] are worthy of death; and not only they that do [such things], but they also that consent to them that do them."

46. "But only when he is obliged, in virtue of his office, to do so: as in the case of earthly princes." In Thomas Aquinas, *Summa Theologica* 2a2æ, 62: 7, "On Restitution"; translated in the edition of the Fathers of the English Dominican Province, Part 2, vol. 2, no. 2 (vol. 10), p. 183.

he would not, but that he could not do so, *Jam enim non poteris villicare.*[47] This Parable has not one word that is not full of remarkable doctrines befitting our purpose. First it says that this Lord was a wealthy man, *Homo quidam erat dives.*[48] Because he who has no resolution shall not be a man; neither, for all the estates he has, shall he be rich who is not careful, and very careful, about not consenting to having thieves govern them for him. Further it says that, to deprive this thief of his office, reputation alone sufficed without other inquiries, *Et hic diffamatus est apud illum.*[49] Because if in such cases information is to be sought from India or Brazil, before it arrives and a remedy is applied there will be no Brazil or India. It is not said or known, however, who the Authors or delators of this reputation were; because about these people the Lord shall keep an inviolable secret, lest there be no one who will dare warn him, justly fearing the wrath of the powerful. Further it says that he had the one who was delated come before him, *Et vocavit eum*, because if such inquiries are delegated to others and not performed by the Lord himself on his own, the result is that the thief, by sharing part of what he stole, ensures his innocence.[50] Finally, the Lord undeceives him and notifies him that he shall never, nor may he ever, exercise the office, *Jam enim non poteris villicare*, because neither should the known thief continue in the office in which he was a thief, nor can the Lord, even if he wanted to, consent and keep him in it if he does not want to condemn himself.

In spite of all this, I still have some pleas to enter on behalf of this thief, before the Lord and Author of the same Parable, Christ. Would that I could make the case that neither the theft for its quantity, nor the person for his talent, would seem to warrant privation of office forever. This man, Lord, even though he committed this error, is someone of great talent, of great industry, of great understanding, and of prudence, as You Yourself confessed. What is more, You even praised him, *Laudavit Dominus villicum iniquitatis, quia prudenter fecisset.*[51] Well, if he is a man of so much worth and if he has capacity and talents enough for You to make use of him again, why should You exclude him from your service forever, *Jam enim*

---

47. Luke 16:2, "For now thou canst be steward no longer."

48. Luke 16:1, "There was a certain rich man."

49. Ibid., "And the same was accused unto him."

50. Luke 16:2, "And he called him."

51. Luke 16:8, "The Lord commended the unjust steward, forasmuch as he had done wisely."

non poteris villicare? Suspend him now for some months, as is usual, and afterward return him again to service, so that neither You lose him, nor he be lost. No, says Christ. Since he is a known thief, not only shall he be suspended or deprived of his office *ad tempus* but forever, never ever to enter, or to be able to enter, *Jam enim non poteris.* Because the use or abuse of such actions, even if they seem piteous, is a manifest injustice. So, instead of the thief's returning what he stole in office, the thief is returned to office, so that he will steal even more? Those actions are not the restitutions for which the sin is forgiven, but are the actions for which the returned ones are condemned, as well as those who return them. Better to lose a man already lost than to lose the many who can be lost and are lost by their trust in such examples.

Assuming that this first article of my pleas has not held up, let us move to another. The thefts of this man were so light and their quantity so limited that the same Text does not call them absolute thefts, but quasi-thefts, *Quasi dissipasset bona ipsius.*[52] So in a world, Lord, and in a time in which we see so many thieves tolerated in their offices and, what is more, the *plusquam*-thieves rewarded in them, is it right that a man who only amounted to a quasi-thief should be deprived and forever deprived of his office? Yes, says Christ again, in order to amend the said times and so that the said world will know how wrong it is. Just as in matters of the sixth Commandment theologically there are no minimums, so there should be none politically in matters of the seventh.[53] Because whoever stole and dishonored himself with little will do it much more easily with a lot. Take, for instance, that same quasi-thief. As soon as he found himself notified that he was not to serve in his office, he still plotted to serve himself from it and to steal more than he had stolen. He sends for the tenants in a great rush, he tears up the debt contracts, he makes up others anew with earlier due dates, some he shortens by half and others by a fifth, and by stealing in this way days from time, truth from the contracts, and money from his master, he who had been only a quasi-thief while certified in his office became more than a thief afterward, when all he had was the reputation of holding the office. Here I just understood the emphasis with which the Shepherdess of the Canticles said *Tulerunt pallium meum mihi:*[54] They

---

52. Luke 16:1, "That he has wasted his goods."

53. According to Catholic tradition, the sixth commandment is against adultery and the seventh is against theft.

54. Canticles, 5:7, "[They] took away my veil from me."

took my cape away from me.[55] Because it is possible to steal a cape from a man by taking it not from him, but from another. This is what this thief's shrewdness accomplished, stealing the money from his master by taking it not from him but from those who owed it to him. So he who before was one thief became afterward many thieves, not content with being only himself a thief, but turning others into thieves. But let him go to Hell, and the others with him, and let Princes notwithstanding imitate the Master who freed himself from going also by depriving the thief so promptly of his office.

X

Since this general doctrine is Christ's, there is surely no Christian understanding that does not venerate it. There may be, however, someone Political who is so speculative that he may want to limit it to a certain kind of men, and who will found the exceptions on the Text itself. The man against whom this execution is carried out is called *Villico* by the Text; therefore it is right that this and other such rigors should be carried out against base people or people of inferior condition, and not against others of different stature, with whom, because of their quality and other constraints, it is licit and convenient for Kings to dissemble.[56] Oh how full Hell is with those who, in order to adulate the great and the supreme with these and other interpretations, do not take heed to condemn them! But, so that you will not believe in adulators, believe in God and listen. God revealed to Joshua that a theft had been committed from the spoils of Jericho, after having made it painfully clear to him through the misfortune of his army; and He commanded that, once discovered, the thief should be burned. Meticulous measures were taken and it was found that a certain Achan had stolen a scarlet cape, a bar of gold, and some silver coins, all together worth less than one hundred Cruzados.[57] But who was this Achan? Was he perchance some base man, or some little soldier of fortune, unknown and born of the weeds? He was nothing less than of the Royal blood of Judah and, on the masculine side, fourth grandson of the

---

55. Vieira says *Tomarãome a minha capa a mim*, which includes three references to the speaker instead of the two that the expression contains in English.

56. The term *Villicus* is linked by Vieira here to the word *vilis*, of little worth. The same Latin root produces the English term vile.

57. The story of Joshua and Achan is recounted in Joshua 7.

King. So is a person of such high quality, when no one in all Israel was illustrious other than through kinship with him, to die burned as a thief? And for a theft that today would be venial, is such an illustrious House to be forever affronted? You will say that it would be right to dissemble; but God, who understands it better than you do, judged otherwise. In the matter of stealing there is no exception for anyone, and whoever has lowered himself to such baseness has lost all privileges. The Law was in fact carried out, Achan was executed and burned, the people were instructed by his example, and he was fortunate in that punishment because, as grave Authors remark, God commuted the fire that he was to suffer in Hell to that temporal one: a happiness that those who dissemble with thieves prevent them from attaining.

And as for the dissemblance that they say Kings should employ toward people of great stature, on whom the conservation of the public good may depend and who are very necessary for their service, I answer by making a distinction. When the crime warrants death, the punishment can be dissembled and such people granted their lives; but when it is a case of theft, the occasion must not be dissembled, rather they should be deprived of their post right then and there. Both these circumstances concur in Adam's crime. God imposed the precept on him that he should not eat from the forbidden tree, on pain of dying that very day, *In quocumque die comederis, morte morieris.*[58] Adam did not observe the precept, he stole the fruit, and was subject, ipso facto, to the death penalty. But what did God do in this case? He immediately cast him out of Paradise, and granted him life for many years. Well, if God cast him out of Paradise for a theft that he had committed, why did He not also carry out on him the death penalty to which he was subject? Because upon Adam's life depended the conservation and propagation of the world; and when people are of such importance and so necessary to the public good, it is fair that, even if they deserve death, life be permitted and granted to them. However, if they are also thieves, by no means can it be consented or dissembled that they continue in the post and place where they were thieves, lest they continue to steal. So God did and so God said. He placed a Cherub with a sword of fire at the door of Paradise with the order that he should by no means let Adam enter. And why? So that, just as he had stolen from the tree of Science, he would not also steal from the tree of Life, *Ne forte mittat manum suam,*

---

58. Genesis 2:17, "For in what day soever thou shalt eat . . . , thou shalt die the death."

& sumat etiam de ligno vitæ.[59] The Law presumes that whoever was evil once will be evil again and will be so forever. Let Adam therefore exit the place where he stole and not enter it again so that he will not have the occasion to commit other thefts as he committed the first one. And notice how Adam, after being deprived of Paradise, lived nine hundred and thirty years. So, were a hundred years of privation of the post not enough for a man punished and repentant? Might two hundred or three hundred years not be enough? No. Even if he shall live nine hundred years, and should he live nine thousand, since he stole and is known as a thief he must never again be returned to, nor shall he enter, the same post.

XI

Thus did God with the first man in the world, and so should those who are in God's stead proceed with all. But how would it be if we were to see thieves not only kept in the places where they steal but, after stealing, promoted to other, greater ones? Here I run out of Scriptures, because there is no such example in them. Of Kings who commanded the conquest of enemies, yes; but of Kings who commanded the governing of vassals, no such thing can be read. The Ahasueruses, the Nebuchadnezzars, the Cyruses, who dilated their empires through arms, rewarded their captains this way: by promoting to posts those who most distinguished themselves in the destruction of Cities and in the accumulation of spoils. Hence the Nabuzaradans, the Holoferneses, and the others were turned into scourges of the world. However, as to the Kings who treat vassals as their own and States, though distant, as their own wealth and not as wealth belonging to others, read the Gospel and you will see who the men are to whom they commission their governing, and how useful they are.

A King, says Christ our Lord, taking leave of his Kingdom to conquer another, commissioned the administration of his wealth to three servants. The first one added to it and made it ten times greater than it was; and the King, after praising him, promoted him to the government of ten Cities, *Euge, bone serve, quia in modico fuisti fidelis, eris potestatem habens super decem civitates.*[60] The second one also added to the part that fell to him and made it five times greater; and, in the same measure, the King made

---

59. Genesis 3:22, "Lest perhaps he put forth his hand, and take also of the tree of life."

60. Luke 19:17, "Well done, thou good servant, because thou hast been faithful in a little, thou shalt have power over ten cities."

him Governor of five Cities, *Et tu esto super quinque civitates.*[61] So those whom the King promotes and should promote in governing are, according to Christ's doctrine, those who promote that King's wealth and not their own. But let us move on to the third servant. This one delivered back to the King as much as the King had commissioned to him, without any reduction, but also without improvement; and at that point, without further retort, he was deprived of his administration, *Auferte ab illo mnam.*[62] Oh how blessed our times would be if the faults for which this servant was deprived of his office were the services and merits for which servants now are promoted! If one who has not taken a Real for himself and has left things in the state in which they were delivered to him deserves deprivation of his charge, then those who leave them destroyed and lost, and so reduced and squandered that they no longer bear any resemblance to what they were, what do they deserve? They deserve to be confirmed, promoted, and put in charge of other greater things, so that they will consume them, too, and all will come to an end. I thought that, just as Christ introduced in His parable two servants who promoted the King's wealth and one who did not, so He would introduce another who was to steal it, making the division without remainder. But the Divine Master did not introduce such a servant, because He was speaking of a prudent and just King, and those who have these qualities (as they should, on pain of not being Kings) neither admit to their service, nor entrust their wealth to men who may steal it from them. To a man who does not promote it, perhaps, but to one man alone. However, to men who steal it either from him or from his vassals (whose wealth should not be distinguished from his own), he who consents to such a thing is neither just nor a King. And how would it be if these men, after robbing one City, were promoted to the government of five and, after robbing five, to the government of ten?

What else should a Christian Prince do if he were like those infidel Princes of whom Isaiah speaks? *Principes tui infideles socii furum:*[63] The Princes of Jerusalem are not faithful, rather they are infidels because they are companions of thieves. Well, let the Prophet know that there are Faithful and Christian Princes who are still more wretched and unhappy than these. Because a Prince who entered the company of thieves, *Socii*

---

61. Luke 19:19, "Be thou also over five cities."

62. Luke 19:24, "Take the pound away from him."

63. Isaiah 1:23, "Thy princes are faithless, companions of thieves."

furum, would also have his part of what was stolen; but these are so far from having their part of what is stolen that they are the first ones, and the most, robbed. Well, if these Princes are the robbed ones, how are they, or how can they be, companions of those thieves, *Principes tui socii furum?* Is it perchance because those who accompany and assist Princes are thieves? If it were so, it would be no new thing. In the old days, those who assisted at the side of Princes were called *Laterones*. And afterward, while this vocable was corrupted, as Marcus Varro affirms, they came to be called *Latrones*.[64] And how would it be if, just as the vocable was corrupted, those signified by that same vocable were corrupted as well? But I neither say nor think such a thing. All I say and know, because it is certain Theology, is that, in any part of the world, what Isaiah says of the Princes of Jerusalem can be verified, *Principes tui socii furum*: Your Princes are companions of thieves. And why? They are companions of thieves because they dissemble them; they are companions of thieves because they consent to them; they are companions of thieves because they give them the posts and the powers; they are companions of thieves because perhaps they defend them; and, finally, they are their companions because they accompany them and shall accompany them to Hell, whither the same thieves take them along with them.

Listen to God's threat and sentence against such people: *Si videbas furem, currebas cum eo.*[65] In the Hebrew we read *concurrebas*, and all it means is that there are Princes who go with thieves, and who go along with them.[66] They go with them because they treat them with familiarity and grace; and they go along with them because, by giving them authority and jurisdiction, they go along with their thefts.[67] And the most important circumstance of this most grave fault consists of *Si videbas*. If these thieves were unknown, and he who goes with them and along with them did not

---

64. The explanation of the similarity between *laterones*, those in a lateral position to the king, and *latrones*, thieves, is found in Varro, *On the Latin Language*, book 7: 52.

65. Psalm 49:18, "If thou didst see a thief thou didst run with him."

66. Vieira appears to cite the interpretation of Psalm 49:18 by the Jesuit exegete Jean de Lorin. Lorin, however, calls attention to several Latin different renderings of the Hebrew terms, noting how Cyprian, Pacian, and Augustine used *concurrebas* while Jerome, Tertullian, and Chrysostom employed other translations. Clearly these several variants are not reflected in Vieira's succinct reference to "the Hebrew." See Lorin, *Commentariorum in librum Psalmorum*, 3 vols. (Lyon: Horace Cardon, 1612–1616), vol. 1, p. 1027.

67. Vieira plays with two related expressions, *correr com*, "to run with," and *concorrer*, "to concur."

know them, he would have some excuse; but if they are public and known thieves, if they steal without disguise and with uncovered faces, if all see them stealing, and even he who consents to them and supports them sees it, *Si videbas furem*, what excuse can he have before God and the world? *Existimasti inique quod ero tui similis*: Do you think, O unjust one, says God, that I shall be like you and, just as you dissemble with these thieves, I shall dissemble with you?[68] You are wrong: *Arguam te, & statuam contra faciem tuam*. With those very thefts that you see and consent to, I shall make a mirror in which you may see yourself; and when you see that you are as much the culprit in all those thefts as the thieves themselves, since you do not prevent them, and even more than the thieves themselves because you have the sworn obligation to prevent them; then you will know that I condemn you as much as them, and more justly than them, to Hell. So declares the Chaldean Paraphrase of that Text, with a final and fearful sentence: *Arguam te in hoc sæculo, & ordinabo judicium Gehennæ in futuro coram te*, in this world I will argue with your conscience, as I am arguing now; and in the other world I will condemn your Soul to Hell, as will be seen on the Day of Judgment.[69]

XII

A great pity it will be, Gentlemen, to see how on that day thieves take many Kings along with them to Hell. And so that this fate is changed for both, let us now see how Kings can, if they wish, take thieves along with them to Paradise. After what has been said, some may think this will be a very difficult thing, one not to be achieved without great expense, but I affirm to you and will soon demonstrate that it is a very easy thing, and that without spending any of their wealth, but rather increasing it, Kings can do it. And how? With one word; but the word of a King. By ordering those

---

68. Psalm 49:21, "But I will reprove thee, and set before thy face."

69. "I shall accuse you in this world, and in the future I will order the judgment of Hell for you." Vieira's reference to the Chaldean Paraphrase refers to early modern Latin renderings of the Targum, a translation of the Hebrew text of the Bible into Aramaic. It is possible that this reference the commentary on Psalm 49:21 comes from Jesuit biblical commentator Jacobus Tirinus (1580–1636), who cites this Latin passage in his *Commentariorium in Sacram Scripturam*, 3 vols. (Antwerp: Martin Nuyts, 1632), vol. 2, p. 45. A modern translation of this passage from Psalm 50:21 (according to the Masoretic, rather than the Septuagint, numbering) is: "I shall reprove you in this world, and I will arrange Gehenna before you in the world to come." See David Stec, trans. and ed., *The Targum of Psalms* (Collegeville, Minn.: Liturgical Press, 2004), p. 106.

thieves, the ones who usually make no restitution, to indeed return all
that they have stolen. By carrying the order out in this way, the thieves will
save themselves and the Kings will save themselves. The thieves will save
themselves because they will return what they have stolen; and the Kings
will save themselves, too, because, by having the thieves make restitution,
they will not have the obligation to do so. Can there be an action more just,
more useful, and more necessary for all? Only those who have no Faith, or
conscience, or judgment can deny it.

And so that the thieves do not feel that they shall in this way lose the
fruit of their industry, consider how, even if they are as bad as the Bad
Thief, they should not only embrace and desire this order, but ask their
Kings for it. The Good Thief asked Christ, as King, to remember him in
his Kingdom; and the Bad Thief, what did he ask Him? *Si tu es Christus,
salvum fac temetipsum, & nos*: If You are the promised King, as my companion believes, save Yourself and save us.[70] This is what the Bad Thief asked
of Christ, and the same should all thieves ask of their King, even if they are
as bad as the Bad Thief. Neither Your Majesty, Lord, can be saved, nor can
we save ourselves, without making restitution. We do not have the heart
or the worth to make restitution, since no one makes it, whether in life or
in death; therefore, let Your Majesty order it coercively and, in this way,
even if it is violent for us, Your Majesty will save yourself and, moreover,
will save us, *Salvum fac temetipsum, & nos*. I believe there is no Christian
conscience who will not approve of this means. And so that I will not limit
myself to generalities, that is, to airy statements, let us come down to its
practice and see how this shall be done. God willing it shall be done!

What the thieves we speak of usually steal in these offices and by their
governing is either the Royal wealth or that of private individuals. And as
far as the one and the other are concerned, not only are the thieves who
did the actual stealing obliged to make restitution after the theft, so are
the Kings, either because they dissembled and consented to the thefts
when they were committed, or simply (since this is enough) because they
were aware of them after they were committed. And here there should be
a warning about a remarkable difference (one often overlooked) between
the wealth of Kings and that of private individuals. If their wealth is stolen, private individuals are not only not obliged to demand restitution,
but they will even gain great merit if they bear the theft with patience and

---

70. Luke 23:39, "If thou be Christ, save thyself and us."

are able to forgive whoever robbed them. Kings, in this matter, are in a much worse situation, because, after having been robbed, they have the obligation to return their own stolen wealth; they can neither relinquish it nor forgive those who stole it. The reason for the difference is that the wealth of a private individual is his; that of the King does not belong to him, but to the Republic. And just as the trustee or tutor cannot allow the wealth entrusted to him to be alienated, and would have the obligation to return it, so the King has the same obligation, as a tutor, trustee of the property, and keeper of the Purse of the Republic that he would be obliged to burden with new taxes if he allowed the alienation or loss of his ordinary revenues.

The way for restitutions of Royal wealth to be thus easily made was taught to Kings by a Monk who, just as he knew how to steal, also knew how to make restitution. Majolus, Crantzius, and others refer to this case.[71] The Monk was called Friar Theodoric and, since he was a man of great intelligence and industry, Emperor Charles the Fourth entrusted him with some important negotiations in which he profited in such a way that he could compete in riches with the great Lords. Having been warned, the Emperor called him into his presence and told him to prepare to give a reckoning. What was the poor, or rich, Monk to do? He answered without being frightened that he was already prepared, that he would give it that very moment, and this is what he said: I, Caesar, entered Your Majesty's service with this Habit and with ten or twelve pennies in my purse, from the alms from my Masses; allow me, Your Majesty, to keep my Habit and my pennies, and let Your Majesty collect everything else that I own, since it is yours, and this is my reckoning. The Monk made his restitution this easily and he was left in possession of his vows and the Emperor of his wealth. Ill-served Kings and Princes, if you want to save your Soul and recuperate your wealth, introduce, without exceptions for anyone, the restitutions of Friar Theodoric as a model. Let it be known with how much each one entered, let the rest be returned to whence it came, and let all be saved.

---

71. The story of Friar Theodoric, otherwise known as Dietrich Kagelwit (c. 1300–1367), and Emperor Charles IV is recounted by Albert Krantz (c. 1450–1517) in Book 8 of his *Vandalia* and repeated by Simeone Maiolo (1520–1597) in the Fifth Colloquy, called *Aula et Caula* ("Court and Sheepfold"), of vol. 2 of his *Dies Caniculares*. See Krantz, *Wandalia* (Frankfurt: Andreas Wechel, 1575), pp. 196–197, and Maiolo, *Dierum Canicularium tomi septem* (Frankfurt: Johann Gottfried Schönwetter, 1642), pp. 564–565.

XIII

The restitution that should likewise be made to private individuals cannot be as prompt or as exact, it appears, because wealth has been taken from many people and from whole Provinces. But since these fishermen of the high seas used trawling nets, let these be used on them as well. If they bring back much, as they ordinarily do, it is obvious that it was acquired against the Law of God or against the Royal Laws and Regiments and, according to either or both, unjustly. In this way five hundred thousand Cruzados are taken from India, two hundred from Angola, three hundred from Brazil, and even from poor Maranhão more than the whole of its worth. And what shall be done with this wealth? The King shall use it for his Soul and for the Souls of those who stole it, so that all these Souls will be saved. Of the Governors whom the Emperor Maximinus sent to several Provinces, it was said with an elegant and very appropriate simile that they were sponges.[72] The cunning or shrewdness with which he used these instruments was all channeled toward satisfying the thirst of his greed. Because they, as sponges, sucked all that they could from the Provinces they governed; and the Emperor, when they returned, squeezed the sponges and took for the Royal Fisc all they had stolen. With this, he was enriched and they were punished. One thing this Emperor did badly, another well, and he lacked the best thing. In sending men who were sponges to govern the Provinces, he did badly; in squeezing the sponges when they returned and confiscating what they brought back, he did well and justly; but he lacked the best thing, unjust tyrant that he was, because all that he squeezed from the sponges he should not have taken for himself but returned to the same Provinces from which it had been stolen. This is what Kings who wish to save themselves are, in conscience, obliged to do, and they should not think that they satisfy the zeal and obligation of justice by having the one who stole the City, the Province, the State locked up in a Castle. What does it matter that for some days or months he is given this shadow of a punishment, if after that time he will enjoy what he brought back stolen while those who suffered the damage do not see restitution?

---

72. Vieira here ascribes a story about Emperor Vespasian to Emperor Maximinus Thrax, who was also known for his exactions from the rich. The reference to "sponges," however, is found in Suetonius's biography of Vespasian in his *Lives of the Caesars*, book 8.1: 16. Herodian gives a substantial description of Maximinus Thrax's impositions on the wealthy in his *History of the Empire*, book 7: 3.

In this apparent justice there is a most grave mistake by which neither the punished nor he who punishes frees himself from eternal condemnation; and so that this mistake will, or can be, understood, it is necessary that it be declared. Whoever took something belonging to another is subject to two satisfactions: to the penalty of the Law and to the restitution of what he took. As for the penalty, the King as Legislator can dispense with it; as for the restitution, he cannot, because it is indispensable. And the opposite is done to such an extent, even when justice is done or thought to be done, that only the penalty or some part of it is carried out, whereas restitution is overlooked or dismissed. Let us conclude with Saint Thomas. The Holy Doctor raises the question *Utrùm sufficiat restituere simplum, quod injustè ablatum est?*, whether, in order to satisfy the restitution, it is enough to return as much as was taken.[73] And after deciding that it is enough, because restitution is an act of justice and justice consists in equality, he argues against that decision, invoking the Law in Chapter twenty-two of Exodus, in which God ordered that whoever stole a bull was to return five.[74] Therefore, either it is not enough to return in equal measure and instead it is necessary to return much more than what was stolen or, if it is enough, as was decided, then how shall this Law be understood? It shall be understood, says the Saint, as having two distinct parts: One, as Natural Law, pertaining to restitution; and another, as Positive Law, pertaining to the penalty. To maintain equality of damages, Natural Law orders only restitution of so much as was taken. To punish the crime of theft, Positive Law added four times as much to the penalty and therefore orders the payment of five for one. A warning, however, should be made, adds the Holy Doctor. There is a great difference between the restitution and the penalty, because the criminal is not obliged to satisfy the penalty before the sentence; however, he is always obliged to return what he stole, even if judges do not sentence or oblige him to do so. This clearly shows the manifest mistake in even the little justice that only infrequently is used: The person who stole is arrested and set free. But what follows? As soon as he was freed from the penalty of the crime, the man who was arrested feels very happy; the King thinks that he satisfied the obligation of justice. And yet nothing has been done: Because both are obliged to make complete restitution of what

---

73. "Whether it suffices to restore the exact amount taken?" In Thomas Aquinas, *Summa Theologica* 2a2æ, 62:3, "On Restitution"; translated in the edition of the Fathers of the English Dominican Province, Part 2, vol. 2, no. 2 (vol. 10), p. 172.

74. This legal demand is found in Exodus 22:1.

was stolen on pain of not attaining salvation. The Culprit, because he does not make restitution; and the King, because he does not make him make restitution. Let the King therefore use his executive power to take away the wealth from all those who stole it, and let him make the restitutions himself, since they do not, or shall not, make them. And this way (and there can be no other way), instead of thieves taking Kings along with them to Hell, as they do, Kings shall take thieves to Paradise, as Christ did: *Hodie mecum eris in Paradiso.*

XIV

I have finished my speech, Gentlemen, and it seems to me that I have demonstrated what I promised, and regarding that I have no regrets. If it seemed to anyone that I dared say what with more reverence I should have kept silent about, I answer with Saint Hilary, *Quæ loqui non audemus, silere non possumus*: That which we cannot in good conscience keep silent about we must say, though it be with disgust.[75] The listener to whom the Baptist said *Non licet tibi*[76] bore a crown, and so did the one, though he was no listener, to whom Christ sent the message *Dicite vulpi illi*.[77] Jeremiah, too, spoke with heart, because he was sent as a Preacher, *Regibus Juda, & Principibus ejus*.[78] And if Isaiah had done so, he would not have regretted it afterward, when he said *Væ mihi quia tacui*.[79] Physicians of Kings should prescribe them what is important to their health and life, with as much and greater liberty than those who perform cures in Hospitals. With private individuals, one man is cured; with Kings, the whole Republic is.

So, summing up what I have said, neither Kings, nor thieves, nor those who are robbed can feel bothered by the doctrine I preached, because it is good for them all. It is good for those who are robbed, because they will have what they had lost returned to them; it is good for Kings, because, without loss and instead with increase of their wealth, they will unburden their Souls. And finally, the very thieves who seem most harmed are

---

75. "We cannot remain silent about those matters of which we do not dare speak." In Hilary of Poitiers, *On the Trinity*; translated in the edition of this work by Stephen McKenna (Washington, D.C.: Catholic University of America Press, 1953), p. 223.

76. Mark 6:18, "It is not lawful for thee."

77. Luke 13:32, "Tell that fox."

78. Jeremiah 1:18, "To the Kings of Juda, and to the Princes thereof."

79. Isaiah 6:5, "Woe is me, because I have held my peace."

the ones who have the greatest interest in this. Either they stole with the intent of making restitution, or they did not. If with the intent of making restitution, that is what I tell them to do, and let them do it in time. If they did it without that intent, then they counted on going to Hell, and they cannot be so blind that they would not rather go to Paradise. The only thing that can scare them is to be plundered of what they plundered from others, but just as their victims were forced to have patience, let them have it, too, with merit. If almsgivers buy Heaven with what is their own, why should thieves not be content with buying it with what belongs to others? The wealth that belongs to others as well as one's own, all is thrown overboard into the sea without pain, in times of tempest. And is there anyone who, saving himself from a shipwreck by swimming, stripped bare, will not have an image of his good fortune painted and offered up on Altars with thanksgiving?[80] The man of good will, says the Holy Spirit, will give all of his wealth to save his life; and how much more willingly should he give the wealth that is not his, in order to save not his temporal but his eternal life? Would one sentenced to death and to the pyre not consider himself very fortunate if, in exchange, the confiscation of only his property were accepted? Let each one of you imagine yourself at the hour of death and with the fire of Hell in sight, and you will see if the exchange that I propose to you is a good one. If your hands and your feet are the cause of your condemnation, cut them off; and if it is your eyes, pull them out, says Christ, because it is better for you to go to Paradise lame, crippled, and blind than to go with all your limbs whole to Hell.[81] Is this true or not? Let us at last have Faith, let us at last believe there is a Hell, let us at last understand that, without making restitution, no one can be saved. See, see even with human eyes what you lose and why. With this restitution, made perforce or by force, that you do not want to make, what do you give up and what do you leave behind? What you give up is what you did not have; what you leave behind is what you cannot take with you and is your perdition. Naked I came into this world, and naked I shall leave it, said Job. And this is how the Good and the Bad Thieves left. Well, if this is how it shall be, like it or not, since you cannot avoid being stripped, is it not better to go with the Good Thief to Paradise than with the Bad Thief to Hell?

---

80. Vieira here refers to the practice of offering ex-voto paintings at saints' shrines after miraculous healings or other divine interventions.

81. Vieira here paraphrases Matthew 5:29–30.

King of Kings and Lord of Lords, You who died between thieves to pay for the theft of the first thief; and You who first promised Paradise to another thief, so that thieves and Kings could be saved; teach all Kings by Your example and inspire them with Your grace, so that they, by not choosing, or dissembling, or consenting, or increasing the number of thieves, may in such a way prevent future thefts and have past thieves make restitution that, instead of thieves taking them as they do to Hell, they will take the thieves along with them to Paradise, as You did today: *Hodie mecum eris in Paradiso.*

SERMAM
XXVII.
COM O SANTISSIMO
SACRAMENTO EXPOSTO.

Iosias autem genuit Iechoniam, & fratres ejus in transmigratione Babylonis. Et post transmigrationem Babylonis, Iechonias genuit Salathiel. Matth.1.

I.

434 UMA das grandes cousas, que se vé hoje no mūdo, & nós pelo costume de cada dia naõ admiramos, he a transmigraçaõ immensa de Gentes, & Naçoes Ethiopes, que da Africa continuamente estaõ passando a esta America. A Armada de Eneas, disse o Principe dos Poetas, que levava Troya a Italia :

Ilium in Italiam portans : Æ: & das naos, que dos Portos *neid. 1.* do Mar Atlantico estaõ successivamente entrando nestes nossos, com maior razão podemos dizer, que trazem a Ethiopia ao Brasil. Entra por esta Barra hũ cardume monstruoso de Balèas, salvando com tiros, & fumos de agua as nossas Fortalezas, & cadahũa pare hum Baléato : entra hũa nao de Angôla,& desóva no mesmo dia quinhentos, seiscentos,& tal vez, mil Escravos,

Frontispiece of Sermon XXVII in António Vieira's *Maria Rosa Mística . . . II Parte* (Lisbon: Officina Craesbeeckiana, 1688). Biblioteca da Ajuda, Lisbon, shelfmark C-X-9.

5

Sermon XXVII of the Series Called Maria Rosa Mística

With the Most Holy Sacrament Exposed.

Iosias autem genuit Iechoniam, & fratres ejus in transmigratione Babylonis. Et post transmigrationem Babylonis, Iechonias genuit Salathiel.

MATTHEW I[1]

I

One of the momentous things seen in the world today, and one that we, because of its everyday occurrence, find unsurprising is the immense transmigration of Ethiopian peoples and nations who are continually crossing over from Africa to this America. The Prince of Poets said that Aeneas's fleet carried Troy to Italy, *Ilium in Italiam portans*, and we can say with all the more reason that the ships from the Atlantic Sea Ports that are successively entering ours bring Ethiopia to Brazil.[2] A monstrous pod of Whales enters this harbor Bar, saluting our Fortresses with shots and sprays of water, and each one gives birth to a Calf; a carrack from Angola enters, and on the same day it spawns five hundred, six hundred, and perhaps a thousand Slaves. The Israelites traversed the Red Sea and crossed from Africa to Asia, fleeing captivity; these traverse the Ocean Sea at its greatest width and cross from that same Africa to America to live and die as captives. *Infelix genus hominum* (as Maffei so rightly says of them) *& ad*

---

1. Matthew 1:11–12, "Josias begot Jechonias and his brethren in the transmigration of Babylon. And after the transmigration of Babylon, Jechonias begot Salathiel."

2. "Transporting Ilium to Italy." In Virgil, *Aeneid*, Book 1, line 68. Vieira pares the original phrase to its bare minimum; Virgil's verse refers to Juno's speech to Æolus about the gods that the exiled Trojans carried with them across the Mediterranean: "A people hateful to me sails the Tyrrhene sea, carrying into Italy Ilium's vanquished gods." See Virgil, *Eclogues, Georgics, Aeneid: Books 1–6*, trans. H. L. Fairclough, ed. G. P. Goold (Cambridge, Mass.: Harvard University Press, 1916), p. 267.

servitutem natum.[3] Others are born to live, these to serve. In other lands, from what men plow and women spin and weave commerce is done; in that one, they whom fathers beget and mothers nurse at their breast are what is bought and sold. Oh inhuman trade, in which the traffic is in men! Oh diabolical traffic, in which profits are drawn from the Souls of others and the risks are borne by the traders' own!

Now if we look at these miserable creatures after they arrive, and at those who call themselves their Masters, what was seen in Job's two states is what fortune presents here again by bringing together happiness and misery on the same stage. The Masters few, the Slaves many; the Masters breaking out their finery, the Slaves stripped and naked; the Masters feasting, the Slaves perishing of hunger; the Masters swimming in gold and silver, the Slaves weighed down with irons; the Masters treating them as beasts, the Slaves adoring and fearing them as Gods; the Masters standing and pointing to the lash, like Statues of pride and tyranny, the Slaves prostrate with their hands tied behind them like the vilest Images of servitude and Spectacles of extreme misery. Oh God! How we must give thanks for the Faith that You gave us, for it alone captivates our understanding so that at the sight of these inequalities we may nevertheless recognize Your justice and providence! Are these men not children of the same Adam and of the same Eve? Were these Souls not ransomed by the Blood of the same Christ? Are these bodies not born, and do they not die, like ours? Do they not breathe the same air? Are they not covered by the same Sky? Are they not warmed by the same Sun? What star is it, then, that rules them, so sad, so unfriendly, so cruel?

And if the influences of their star are so hostile and harmful, how are they not transmitted, at least, to the labor of their hands and, like Adam's curse, to the land that they till? Who would think that plants watered with so much innocent blood were to flourish and grow, and produce anything but thorns and thistles? But the blessings of sweetness that Heaven pours over them are so copious that the plants themselves are the fruit, and the fruit is so precious, abundant, and pleasant that great Fleets are loaded with it alone, and it enriches Brazil with treasures and fills the world with delights.[4] Some great mystery lies therefore in this transmigration, and even more so when we notice how singularly favored and assisted it is by

---

3. "Unhappy sort of men, and born into servitude." In Giovanni Pietro Maffei, *Historiarum Indicarum Libri XVI* (Florence, 1588), Book 1, p. 5.

4. The plants and fruit of Brazil here are sugarcane and sugar.

God; for although no navigation across the whole Ocean is without danger or contrary winds, that which rips these people from their homelands and brings them to the experience of captivity is the only one that always runs before the wind and without need of changing sails.[5]

All this I ponder, and so should everyone, about the hidden judgments behind such a remarkable transmigration and its effects. There is not a slave in Brazil who for me is not matter for profound meditation, and it is all the more so when I see the most miserable ones. I compare the present with the future, time with eternity, what I see with what I believe, and I cannot understand how God, who created these men as much in His image and likeness as all others, would predestine them for two Hells, one in this life, another in the other. But when I see them today so devout and merry before the Altars of Our Lady of the Rosary, all siblings together like that Lady's Children, then I am persuaded beyond doubt that the captivity of the first transmigration is ordained by His mercy for the freedom of the second one.

Our Gospel mentions two transmigrations: one in which the children of Israel were carried from their homeland to captivity in Babylon, *In transmigratione Babylonis*; and another in which they were brought from captivity in Babylon to their homeland, *Et post transmigrationem Babylonis*. The first transmigration, that of the captivity, lasted seventy years; the second, that of freedom, had no end, because it lasted until Christ's coming. And how did God link the first transmigration to the second? Just as He ordered that, from Josiah, Jeconiah should be born, *Iosias autem genuit Iechoniam, & fratres ejus*. Throughout this Gospel, the narration of how one Patriarch begat another Patriarch conveys how, in the mystical sense, from the meaning of the name of the father came the meaning of the name of the son. Let David, the first one who is named in this Gospel, suffice as an example. David, says the series of generations, begat Solomon, *David autem Rex genuit Salomonem*.[6] And what does it mean to say that David begat Solomon? David means the Warrior, Solomon means the Peaceful one; and that Solomon was born of David means that, from war, peace would be born, and so it was. In the same way, the Gospel says that Josiah begat Jeconiah in the Babylonian captivity, *Iosias autem genuit Iechoniam*

---

5. Vieira refers to the trade winds in the South Atlantic which blow from east to west, from Angola to Brazil.

6. Matthew 1:6, "And David the king begot Solomon."

in transmigratione Babylonis. Let us now learn the meaning of these two names, that of the father Josiah, and that of the son Jeconiah. Josiah means *Ignis Domini*, fire of God; Jeconiah means *Præparatio Domini*, preparation of God. The text thus says, or means, that in the Babylonian transmigration the fire of God begat the preparation of God. Why? Because fire burns and illuminates; and, in the Babylonian captivity, God not only burned and punished the Israelites, but He also illuminated them. And because He punished and illuminated them in the captivity of the first transmigration, *In transmigratione Babylonis*, through this, and with this, He readied and prepared them for the freedom of the second one, *Et post transmigrationem Babylonis.*

Behold, Black Brothers of the Rosary (for only in you are these meanings confirmed), behold your present state, and the hope that it gives you for the future: *Iosias autem genuit Iechoniam, & fratres ejus.* You are the Brothers of the preparation of God, and the Children of the fire of God. Children of the fire of God in the present transmigration of the captivity, because the fire of God in this state stamped upon you the mark of Captives; and though it is a mark of oppression, as fire it has also illuminated you, because it has brought you to the light of the Faith and to the knowledge of the Mysteries of Christ, the ones that you profess in the Rosary. But in this very state of the first transmigration, the one of the temporal captivity, God and his most Holy Mother are readying and preparing you for the second transmigration, that of eternal freedom. This is what I shall preach to you today for your consolation. And reduced to a few words, this shall be my Subject: That your Brotherhood of Our Lady of the Rosary promises you all a Letter of Manumission with which you will not only be able to enjoy eternal freedom in the second transmigration of the life to come but also be delivered in this life from the greatest captivity of the first one.[7] Instead of the reward that I should ask you for these good tidings, I ask you that you help me attain the Grace with which I can persuade you of their truth. *Ave Maria, etc.*

---

7. Vieira refers to *cartas de alforria*, actual letters which granted freedom to slaves. These legal documents were the physical proof of manumission and were carried by their holders as defense against re-enslavement. For an analysis of such letters in the specific social context in which this sermon was preached, see Stuart B. Schwartz, "The Manumission of Slaves in Colonial Brazil: Bahia, 1684–1745", *Hispanic American Historical Review*, 54.4 (November 1974): pp. 603–635.

II

As exiled children of Eve, we all have, or we all await, a universal transmigration, from Babylon to Jerusalem, and from the Exile of this world to the Homeland of Heaven. You, however, came, or were brought, from your homelands to this exile; beyond the second and universal transmigration, you have another, the Babylonian transmigration in which you continue your more or less severe captivity. And so that you know how you should behave while in it, and so that you yourselves will not be the ones who compound it, I want first of all to explain to you what it is and what it consists of. I will seek to do it with such clarity that you will all understand me. But in case that is not the outcome (because the matter demands greater capacity than all of you may have), I will if nothing else, as Saint Augustine said in your Africa, be content if your Masters and Mistresses understand me, so that they may more slowly teach you what for you, and also for them, is very important to know.[8]

Know then, all of you who are called Slaves, that not all that you are is a Slave. Every man is composed of body and Soul; but that which is and is called a Slave is not the whole man, but only half of him. Even the Heathens who had little knowledge of Souls knew this truth and made this distinction. Homer, cited by Clement of Alexandria, says this: *Altitonans Iupiter viro, quem alij servire necesse est, aufert dimidium.*[9] He means that those men whom Jupiter made Slaves he split in half, leaving but one half to them as their own, because the other half belongs to the Master whom they serve. And what is this enslaved half which has a Master whom it is obliged to serve? There is no doubt that it is the less valuable half, the body. Seneca says most excellently, *Errat, si quis existimat servitutem in totum hominem descendere: pars melior ejus excepta est:*[10] He who thinks that what is called a

---

8. Augustine was Bishop of Hippo in Roman Africa. This reference likely refers to his treatise *On Catechizing the Uninstructed*. That text contains an elaboration on the Egyptian and Babylonian migrations in chapters 20 and 21. For a translation of this text by S. Salmond, see Philip Schaff, ed., *A Select Library of Nicene and Post-Nicene Fathers of the Christian Church*, 14 vols. (New York: Christian Book Company, 1898–1909), vol. 3, pp. 283–314.

9. "The half of virtue the far-seeing Zeus / takes from man, when he reduces him to a state of slavery." In Clement of Alexandria, *Stromata* [*The Miscellanies*], Book 4; William Wilson, ed. and trans., *The Writings of Clement of Alexandria*, 2 vols. (Edinburgh: T. & T. Clark, 1867–1872), vol. 2, p. 144.

10. "It is a mistake for anyone to believe that the condition of slavery penetrates into the whole being of a man. The better part of him is exempt." In Seneca, *De Beneficiis*, Book 3, chapter 20; in Seneca the Younger, *Moral Essays: Volume III*, trans. John W. Bashore (Cambridge, Mass.: Harvard University Press, 1935), p. 165.

Slave is the whole man is wrong and does not know what he says; the best part of a man, which is the Soul, is exempt from all outside rule and cannot be made captive. The body, and the body alone, yes: *Corpus itaque est, quod domino fortuna tradidit. Hoc emit, hoc vendit; interior illa pars mancipio dari non potest.*[11] The body of the Slave alone (says the great Philosopher) is what fortune gave to his Master; this he bought and this he can sell. And he remarks most wisely that the rule exercised by the Master over the body was given to him not by nature but by fortune, *Quod domino fortuna tradidit*, because nature, as Mother, from the King down to the Slave, made all equal, all free. Speaking of Slaves, and with Slaves, Saint Paul says that they should obey their Masters in the flesh, *Obedite dominis carnalibus.*[12] And what Masters in the flesh are these? All Interpreters declare that they are the temporal Masters, like yours, whom you serve for a whole lifetime; and the Apostle calls them Masters in the flesh because the Slave, like any other man, is composed of flesh and spirit, and the Master's rule over the Slave only has jurisdiction over the flesh, which is the body, and does not extend to the spirit, which is the Soul.

This is the reason why, among the Greeks, Slaves were called bodies. Saint Epiphanius recounts this, and how their usual way of speaking among themselves was to say not that such-and-such Master had so many Slaves, but rather that he had so many bodies.[13] Seneca says that the Romans had the same custom. And erudition is what he teaches to his disciple Lucilius, because, even though all have knowledge of words, to know their origin is only for those who know things as well as their causes, *Quandoquidem dominium corporibus dominatur, & non animis, propterea servos corpora vocaverunt, ut usum corporum ostenderent.*[14] Do you know,

---

11. "It is, therefore, the body that Fortune hands over to a master; it is this that he buys, it is this that he sells; that inner part cannot be delivered into bondage." Ibid.

12. Ephesians 6:5, "Be obedient to them that are your lords according to the flesh."

13. Epiphanius of Cyprus makes this claim in his *Ancoratus*, chapter 59.3. The observation comes within the context of a discussion of Old Testament genealogies of the same type that Vieira takes as his theme here.

14. "Since the power of a master rules over the bodies of men but not their souls, because of this [custom] reasonably called slaves 'bodies' (with souls), in order that it might show the use of the bodies." In Epiphanius of Cyprus, *Ancoratus*, 59.3, trans. Young Richard Kim (Washington, D.C.: Catholic University of America Press, 2014), p. 144. Vieira confuses Epiphanius and Seneca here. The editio princeps version of this sermon contains a marginal note to Seneca's Epistle 47 ("On Master and Slave") instead of the source of the quote, although the spirit of Seneca's letter is similar to what is said. Closer still to what Vieira describes as Seneca's lesson is found in the section of Book 3 of *De Beneficiis* cited above.

Lucilius, why our Ancestors called Slaves bodies? Because one man's rule over another can only extend to the body and not to the Soul. But it is not necessary to go as far back as Rome and Greece. I ask: Even in this Brazil of yours, when you want to say that so-and-so has many or few Slaves, why do you say that he has this or that many Pieces? Because the first to give them this name meant to say, in a wise and Christian manner, that the Slave's submission to the Master, and the Master's rule over the Slave, consists only of the body. Men are not made of one piece alone, like angels and beasts. Angels and beasts (to put it this way) are integral: in the Angel all is spirit; in the beast all is body. Not man. Man is made of two pieces, Soul and body. And because the Slave's Master is Master only of one of these pieces, the one capable of being ruled, that is, the body, for that reason you call your Slaves Pieces. And if this derivation does not content you, let us say that you call your Slaves Pieces just as we say a piece of gold, a piece of silver, a piece of silk, or of any other of those things which do not have a Soul. And, in this way, it is even more clearly proven that the name Piece does not comprehend the Slave's Soul, and it can only be understood and extended to mean the body. This alone is made captive, this alone bought and sold, this alone held under fortune's jurisdiction, and this, finally, what the transmigration of the children of Israel took from Jerusalem to Babylon, and what the transmigration of those who here are called Slaves and who here continue their captivity brings from Ethiopia to Brazil.

III

So, Black Brothers, the captivity you suffer, hard and harsh as it is or as it seems to you, is not a total captivity or a captivity of all that you are, rather it is a half captivity. You are Captives in that external and less valuable half of yourselves that is the body. However, in that other, internal and most noble half that is the Soul, principally in what pertains to it, you are not Captives, but free. And this first point being posited, it now follows that you should know the second and much more important one, and that I should declare to you whether that part, or free half, which is the Soul, can also in any way be made captive, and, if so, by whom. I say then that your Soul, too, like everyone else's, can be made captive; and it is not your Masters who can make it captive, or even the King, or any other human power, but you yourselves and by your free will. Blessed be those among you who so resign themselves to the fate of their half captivity that they serve themselves by their own servitude and know how to take advantage of what in it and through it can help them gain what they deserve! But the harm and the misery that will totally make you miserable comes when, even though your fortune makes you Captive only in the body, you, much by your own will, make captive your Soul, too. Two remarkable cases were seen in the Babylonian transmigration. Some of those Captives and exiles, having had permission and freedom to return to their homeland, wanted instead to remain in their captivity. Others, almost all of them, living in a captivity of the body only, were not content with being half captives, but, in order to be wholly and totally so, made their Souls captive, too. There are solid grounds to pose the question whether, for human nature to submit to and fall into vice, freedom or captivity is the greater temptation. It is certain that on this occasion captivity showed by experience that it had not only greater strength to tempt, but also to conquer. Because among all the Captives, who were many thousands, only a certain Tobias was found who would not make his Soul captive. Thus says Sacred Scripture, celebrating him as a great wonder: *In captivitate tamen positus, viam veritatis non deseruit.*[15] So ordinary and universal a misery it is that Half captives are not only half captive but wholly so, captive in one half and in the other: Captives in the body, and Captives in the Soul as well.

And if you ask me, as you should ask me, in what way souls are made captive, who those are who sell them, and to whom they sell them, and for what price, I answer about those who sell them that each one sells his own; about whom they sell them to that it is the Devil; about the price for which they sell them that it is sin. And because the Soul is invisible and the Devil is invisible, too, and these sales are not seen—in order that you do not think that these are exaggerations and ways of speaking, instead of truths of Faith—know that it is defined in this way by God and repeated many times in all the Sacred Scriptures. Saint Paul, that great Apostle who was taken in life to Heaven and who then returned from Heaven to earth, to teach men what he had seen and learned there, says this when speaking of this sale of the Soul: *Lex spiritualis est: Ego autem carnalis sum, venundatus sub peccato.*[16] Do you know, says Saint Paul, how men sell their Souls? Listen to me attentively, I will tell you *Lex spiritualis est,* the Law is of the spirit, *Ego autem carnalis sum,* and man is of the flesh. The Law is of the spirit because it ordains what is beneficial to the spirit and the Soul; man is of the flesh because he naturally craves what the flesh and the body ask

---

15. Tobias 1:2, "Even in his captivity, [he] forsook not the way of truth."

16. Romans 7:14, "The law is spiritual; but I am carnal, sold under sin."

for. As far as the Law is concerned, God is commanding that He be obeyed and promising that to those who observe it He will later give Heaven. As far as the flesh is concerned, the Devil is advising that the Law not be observed and promising man that he will give him promptly and straight away the pleasure or the interest for which his appetite asks. So, with the Soul placed as if at auction between God and the Devil, between Law and sin, what does volition, what does the free will do, being the Master of all our actions and resolutions? Instead of taking God's bid, it accepts the Devil's; and so much did it consent to sin that the Soul was made captive and the sale closed, *Venundatus sub peccato*. This is what Saint Augustine says in his exposition of this same text: *Unusquisque peccando, animam suam Diabolo vendit, accepta, tanquam pretio, dulcedine temporalis voluptatis.*[17] The first sale, and the first auction of Souls, made in this world happened in the earthly Paradise. On one side was God, commanding that the forbidden fruit not be eaten; on the other side was the Serpent urging that it be eaten.[18] And what happened? Eve, who represented the flesh, inclined towards the Devil's side; and because Adam, who played the part of the will, instead of obeying God's precept followed the appetites of the flesh, right there the two first Souls were sold to the Devil and that was the origin of the sale of all the others.

Tell me, Whites and Blacks, do we not all condemn Adam and Eve? Do we not know that they were ignorant and more than ignorant, mad and more than mad, blind and more than blind? Are we not the ones who curse and execrate them for what they did? So why do we do the same and sell our Souls as they sold theirs? Let the Whites listen first to an example, so that they see their deformity, and then we will show another to the Blacks in which they will see theirs. The Sacred History affirms that King Ahab was the most evil King among all those of Israel, because by sinning, and in order to sin, he sold himself: *Non fuit alter talis sicut Achab,*

---

17. "Everyone, by sinning, sells his own soul to the Devil because he received as his price the sweetness of temporal pleasure." In Augustine, "Propositions from the Epistle to the Romans," point 42, in Paula Fredriksen Landes, ed. and trans., *Augustine on Romans: Propositions from the Epistle to the Romans, Unfinished Commentary on the Epistle to the Romans* (Chico, Calif.: Scholars Press, 1982), p. 17.

18. The editio princeps contains marginal references to Genesis 2:16, "And he commanded him, saying: Of every tree of paradise thou shalt eat," and Genesis 3:1, "Now the serpent was more subtle than any of the beasts of the earth which the Lord God had made. And he said to the woman: Why hath God commanded you, that you should not eat of every tree of paradise?"

qui venudatus est, ut faceret malum.[19] The Prophet Elijah told him as much to his face. The King asked him, *Num invenisti me inimicum tibi?*:[20] Elijah, did you perchance find anything in me for which you should consider me your enemy? Yes, I did, answered the Prophet, because I found that you are such, that you sell yourself to offend God: *Inveni, eò quòd venundatus sis, ut faceres malum in conspectu Domini.*[21] Elijah did not complain of the wrongs that Ahab had done against him, but of those that he did against God; nor did he complain that the King was not a friend of His Prophet, but that he, though a King, sold himself and made himself a Slave: *Eò quòd venundatus sis, ut faceres malum.*

And what evils and sins were those by which Ahab sold himself? Scripture mentions two principally: A general one, with which he obliged his subjects to adore the golden Idols of Jeroboam, forbidding them to go to the Temple of the true God;[22] and another, specific one, when on a certain occasion he had Naboth falsely condemned to death in order to confiscate and take his vineyard.[23] See if this is a good example for the Princes of our Recôncavo![24] Is it possible that, to add another length of land to the Cane fields and half a parcel more to the Mill each week, you shall sell your Soul to the Devil? Well, your Soul, since it is yours, go ahead, sell it or resell it to him. Those of your Slaves, however, why should you sell them to him as well, putting before their salvation the golden idols of your cursed and ever ill-fated interests? That is why your Slaves have no doctrine; that is why they live and die without the Sacraments; and that is why, even if you do not forbid them the Church, with a greed so artful that only the Devil could invent it (to use a popular phrase), you do not want them to go near the door of a Church. You allow the male and female Slaves to live in sin, and you do not permit them to marry, because you say that, when married,

---

19. 3 Kings 21:25, "There was not such another as Achab, who was sold to do evil."

20. 3 Kings 21:20, "Hast thou found me thy enemy?"

21. Ibid., "I have found thee, because thou art sold, to do evil in the sight of the Lord."

22. A reference to 3 Kings 21:26 appears in the margin of the editio princeps, "And he became abominable, insomuch that he followed the idols which the Amorrhites had made, whom the Lord destroyed before the face of the children of Israel."

23. A reference to 3 Kings 21:18–19 appears in the margin of the editio princeps, "Achab, king of Israel, who is in Samaria; behold he is going down to the vineyard of Naboth, to take possession of it. . . . Thus saith the Lord: Thou has slain, moreover also thou hast taken possession."

24. The Recôncavo is the region around the Bay of All Saints where the majority of Brazilian sugar plantations were located.

they do not serve so well. What a reason (if this were one), befitting your understanding as much as your Christianity! Let my service prevail over the service of God and, provided my slaves serve me better, let them live and die in the service of the Devil! I have hope in God that He will have mercy on their misery and on their Souls; but on your Souls, and on your misery—for it, too, is misery—I have no grounds for such good hopes.

Let us move on to an example more proper to the Slaves, who in no circumstance should sell their Souls, even if it were to cost them their lives. After King Antiochus, surnamed the Illustrious, leaving Greece with a powerful army, ruled Jerusalem and with it all its relics that had escaped the Babylonian transmigration (for men do not always take captivity with them to exile; sometimes captivity comes to find them at home), the barbarian and insolent King commanded that in all Judea the Law of God not be observed, rather his laws alone, and that the Gods to whom sacrifices were to be offered should be those of Heathendom whom he adored.[25] What do you think such miserable Captives would do in this tight situation? I was wrong in calling them all indiscriminately miserable. Some were miserable, weak, and vile, others strong, constant, and glorious. The Text says that the miserable, weak, and vile ones, in order to be in their Masters' graces, obeyed and, making themselves Heathens, sold their Souls: *Et juncti sunt Nationibus, & venundati sunt, ut facerent malum.*[26] On the contrary, the ones who were strong, constant, and glorious, in order to not sell their Souls, lost their lives valorously, since being in their Masters' graces meant nothing to them. We saw clearly here that the bodies alone are captives, not the Souls. The Masters were so tyrannical that they cut off their fingers and toes, they ripped out their eyes and tongues, they fried and roasted them alive in burning pans, and with other exquisite torments they took their innocent lives. But they would rather suffer and die than sell their Souls. Now it is for you to judge, you who find yourselves with the same fortune, as Slaves, which of these did better: Whether those who sold their Souls to please their Masters or those who would rather lose their lives than make their Souls captive. Are you not all saying that the valor and constancy of the latter is worthy

---

25. A marginal note in the editio princeps indicates 1 Maccabees 1:11, "And there came out of them a wicked root, Antiochus the Illustrious, the son of king Antiochus, who had been a hostage at Rome; and he reigned in the hundred and thirty-seventh year of the kingdom of the Greeks."

26. 1 Maccabees 1:16, "And joined themselves to the heathens, and were sold to do evil."

of eternal praise? Yes. Then I tell you to imitate them. By the grace and great favor of God, even if you are Slaves and Captives, you are not in a land where your Masters will oblige you to leave the Faith. But it is true that, without losing or risking the Faith, one can still lose and sell one's Soul. And in such a case (one that can happen many times), keep well in mind the example that you have just heard, so that you will not fail to meet your obligations. If the Master were to command a male Slave, or want from the female Slave, something that would gravely offend the Soul and the conscience, just as he may not want or command it, so the Slave is obliged not to obey. Say constantly that you shall not offend God. And if, because of that, they threaten and punish you, suffer in a valorous and Christian manner, even if it be for your whole life, because those punishments are martyrdoms.

IV

We have seen that, just as man is composed of two parts or two halves, that is, the body and the Soul, so captivity is divided into two: One, the captivity of the body, in which bodies are involuntarily made captives and slaves of men; another, the captivity of the Soul, in which Souls, by their own will, are sold and made captives and slaves of the Devil. And since I promised you that the Virgin, Our Lady of the Rosary, shall liberate you or, as you say, manumit you from the greater captivity, it is important that you first know and understand which of these two captivities is the greater, so that you know just how much you should esteem this manumission. The Soul is better than the body, and the Devil is a worse Master than man, as tyrannical as man may be. The captivity of men is temporal, that of the Devil eternal. Therefore there can be no understanding so crude and so blind as not to recognize that the greatest and worst captivity is that of the Soul. But since the Soul, the Devil, and this captivity are things that cannot be seen with the eyes, as I said before, where shall I find a means proportional to your capacity by which I can make this demonstration visible to you? Let us found it on your very captivity, the thing that is most readily perceived by you. I ask: If at this very moment God were to release you all from the captivity in which you find yourselves and you were all suddenly to see yourselves free and manumitted, would this not be a strange and admirable favor granted to you by God? Well, a much greater one, of much greater and higher value, is the favor that Our Lady of the Rosary will grant you by releasing your souls from the captivity of the Devil and of sin. We have it in our Gospel passage.

The Gospel makes repeated mention of the Babylonian captivity, and it does not record the memory of the Egyptian captivity. The Babylonian captivity happened in the time of Jeconiah, the Egyptian one in the time of Judah. Well, just as the Evangelist says, *Iechoniam, & fratres ejus in transmigratione Babylonis*, why does he not say also, *Iudam, & fratres ejus in captivitate Ægypti?* The reflection, and the answer, is given by Saint Chrysostom with these words: *Cur sicut captivitatis Babylonicæ meminit, non autem descensus in Ægyptum? Quia illùc non propter peccata abducti fuerant; hùc verò ob scelera translati sunt.*[27] At the time of these Patriarchs, who are mentioned in the genealogy of Christ, the Egyptian captivity occurred and also the Babylonian. And if you want to know why in that genealogy the Evangelist makes mention of the Babylonian captivity and is silent about the Egyptian captivity, the reason is, Chrysostom says, that those who were taken to the Babylonian captivity were taken there because of their sins, as a punishment for the great wrongs they had committed in their homeland; whereas those taken to the Egyptian captivity did not go to Egypt because of their sins, rather they were called by their brother Joseph, and later made captive by Pharaoh's tyranny. The Egyptian captivity was only temporal, of the bodies alone, and they were captives not because of their own sins but because of another's tyranny; on the contrary, the Babylonian captivity was a spiritual captivity, one of Souls whose sins had made them slaves of sin itself and of the Devil. This is the reason why this captivity alone is referred to in the genealogy of Christ, who did not come to liberate men from the temporal captivity of the body, but from the spiritual one of the Soul. This was certainly an excellent reflection and answer.

And if we search for the fundamental principle why Christ, being the Redeemer of humankind, came only to redeem and liberate men from their Souls' captivity and not from their bodies' servitude, the clear and manifest foundation is that, to liberate from the captivity of men, men sufficed; to liberate from the captivity of the Devil and of sin, the whole power of God is necessary. These children of Israel of whom we speak were often Captives of various Nations: Captives right from birth of the Egyptians;

---

27. "By why can it be, that as he mentioned the captivity of Babylon, he did not mention also the descent into Egypt? . . . And to the one they were carried down for no sins, but to the other, transgressions were the cause of their being removed." In John Chrysostom, Homily 4 on Matthew; in *Homilies of S. John Chrysostom, Archbishop of Constantinople, on the Gospel of St. Matthew*, trans. George Prevost, 3 vols. (Oxford: J. H. Parker, 1843–1851), vol. 1, pp. 45–46.

Captives later of the Mesopotamians; Captives of the Ammonites; Captives of the Canaanites; Captives of the Midians; Captives of the Philistines.[28] And from all these captivities God always liberated them through men. From the captivity of the Egyptians, through Moses; from the captivity of the Mesopotamians, through Othniel; from the captivity of the Ammonites, through Ehud; from the captivity of the Canaanites, through Barak; from the captivity of the Midians, through Gideon; from the captivity of the Philistines, through Jephthah.[29] So, to liberate from the captivity of men, men suffice. And if you insist that the Captives of the Babylonian trans-migration were not only Captives of the Babylonians, but also Captives of the Devil and of sin, as we have just seen, and that nevertheless it was a man, Cyrus the King, who liberated them, then you will now understand the mystery, perchance not understood until now, of Isaiah's words, as he spoke of this very captivity and of this very freedom: *Verè tu es Deus abscon-ditus, Deus Israel Salvator*, In you, O King Cyrus, is God truly hidden, and not only hidden as God, but as Savior and Liberator of Israel.[30]

Well, if Isaiah speaks of the liberation from the Babylonian captivity and Cyrus as King of that very Babylon was the one who liberated the child-ren of Israel from this captivity, why does he say that God, as Liberator of

---

28. The editio princeps includes a series of references in the margin of the text to the rele-vant passages for these captivities. They are: Exodus 1:10, "Come, let us wisely oppress them, lest they multiply: and if any war shall rise against us, join with our enemies, and having overcome us, depart out of the land"; Judges 3:8, "And the Lord being angry with Israel, delivered them into the hands of the Chusan Rasathaim king of Mesopotamia, and they served him eight years"; Judges 3:14, "And the children of Israel served Eglon king of Moab eighteen years"; Judges 4:2, "And the Lord delivered them up into the hands of Jaban king of Chanaan, who reigned in Asor"; Judges 6:1, "And the children of Israel again did evil in the sight of the Lord: and he delivered them into the hand of Madian seven years"; Judges 10:7, "And the Lord being angry with them, delivered them into the hands of the Philistines and of the children of Ammon."

29. The editio princeps includes a series of references in the margin of the text to the rele-vant passages for these deliverances. They are: Psalm 76:21, "Thou hast conducted thy peo-ple like sheep, but the hand of Moses and Aaron"; Judges 3:9, "And they cried to the Lord, who raised them up a saviour, and delivered them, to wit, Othoniel the son of Cenez, the younger brother of Caleb"; Judges 3:15, "And afterwards they cried to the Lord, who raised them up a saviour called Aod, the son of Gera, the son of Jemini, who used the left hand as well as the right"; Judges 4:6, "And she sent and called Barac the son of Abinoem out of Cedes in Nephtali"; Judges 7:20, "Standing every man in his place round about the enemies' camp. So all the camp was troubled, and crying out and howling they fled away"; Judges 11:32, "And he smote them from Aroer till you come to Mennith, twenty cities, and as far as Abel, which is set with vineyards, with a very great slaughter; and the children of Ammon were humbled by the children of Israel."

30. Isaiah 45:15, "Verily thou art a hidden God, the God of Israel the saviour."

Israel, was hidden in this Cyrus? Because in the Babylonian captivity there were two captivities together, and so those children of Israel were twice Slaves: a temporal captivity of their bodies, in which they were Captives of King Cyrus, and another, a spiritual one of their Souls, in which they were Captives of the Devil and of sin. From the captivity of the bodies, the King, a man, liberated them, since as a man he sufficed to liberate them and as King he could. From the captivity of the Devil and of sin, since no man could liberate them, it was necessary that God, too, should concur as Liberator—*Deus Israel Salvador*—because only God could liberate them from that captivity. And why does the Prophet add that God was hidden in Cyrus, *Verè tu es Deus absconditus?* Because, just as one captivity was hidden and the other public, so were the two Liberators, one public and the other hidden. The captivity of the bodies was public and, since it was public, Cyrus liberated the captives publicly. However, the captivity of the Souls, and of the Devil, was hidden and invisible, and so God, hidden and invisible, liberated them also in a hidden and invisible manner: *Verè tu es Deus absconditus, Deus Israel Salvator.*

In sum, such and so immensely greater than all unhappiness is the captivity of the Souls enslaved by the Devil and by sin that only God by Himself was able to ransom and liberate them from such a captivity. And as Saint Augustine, Saint Jerome, Saint Hilary, and the other Fathers say, this is what Isaiah meant to teach as history about the Babylonian captivity, and as prophecy about the captivity of all humankind, ransomed and liberated by none other than the very Son of God in Person, when at the infinite price of His Blood He redeemed us on the Cross.[31] The Disciples of Emmaus and the other more primitive followers of Christ thought that His coming into the world had been to liberate the children of Israel from the subjugation and captivity of the Romans: *Nos autem sperabamus, quia ipse esset redempturus Israel.*[32] But that is why they deserved to be called foolish men, and of slow and lowly hearts, *O stulti, & tardi corde.*[33] In order to liberate the children of Israel from the Roman yoke, did God perchance lack a staff of Moses, a jawbone of Samson, a sling of David, a sword of Maccabee? But these weapons and these arms suffice only to liberate from

---

31. Jerome addresses this theme in Book 1 of his *Commentary on Matthew*, as does Augustine in the first of his *Sermons on the New Testament*, as well as Hilary of Poitiers in his commentary on Psalm 136.

32. Luke 24:21, "But we hoped, that it was he that should have redeemed Israel."

33. Luke 24:25, "O foolish, and slow of heart."

the captivity of bodies. However, for the captivity of Souls and to liberate them from the yoke of the Devil and of sin, God alone has strength and power, and that with both arms stretched on a Cross. See, see well, how much is spent from captivity to captivity, from ransom to ransom, and from price to price.

Saint Peter pondered this with admirable energy as if he were speaking with you who are sold and bought for money: *Scientes, quòd non corruptibilibus, auro, vel argento redempti estis: sed pretioso Sanguine quasi agni immaculati Christi.*[34] The Apostle exhorts all to take care of the salvation of their Souls, to preserve them in grace; and for that he says that we should consider how we were not ransomed for gold or silver, but for the infinite price of the Blood of the Son of God. In these words it is very worthwhile pondering how Saint Peter not only orders us to consider the price for which we were ransomed, but also the price for which we were not ransomed. The price for which we were not ransomed is gold and silver, *Non corruptibilibus, auro, vel argento*, and the price for which we were ransomed is the Blood of the Son of God, *Sed pretioso Sanguine quasi agni immaculati Christi*. Well, if for us to be very careful and vigilant about the Salvation of our Souls, the only and greatest reason to consider is that God ransomed them with the Blood of His own Son, then why does the Apostle add in the same reflection the price for which they were not ransomed, that of gold and silver? Because his main purpose in these two prices that he ordered us to consider was to allow us, through the difference between the ransoms, to know the difference between the captivities. In order to ransom a Slave from the captivity of the body, it is enough to pay in gold or silver as much as the Slave cost at sale. But to ransom someone from the captivity of the Soul, how much gold or silver shall suffice? Shall a Million suffice? Shall two Million suffice? Shall all the gold of Sofala and all the silver of Potosí suffice?[35] Oh the vileness and ignorance of human understanding! If the whole sea were transformed into silver and all the land into gold, if God were to create another world and a thousand worlds out of a substance more precious than gold and greater in carats than diamonds, all this price would not be enough to liberate a single Soul, for a single moment, from the captivity of the Devil and of sin. That is why it was necessary for the

---

34. 1 Peter 1:18–19, "Knowing that you were not redeemed with corruptible things as gold or silver . . . But with the precious blood of Christ, as of a lamb unspotted."

35. Sofala, a port in East Africa, was the site of a Portuguese colony and was known for its gold trade. Potosí, in Bolivia, was known as the richest silver mine in the Americas.

Son of God to be made Man and to die on a Cross, so that with the infinite price of His Blood He would be able to ransom, as He did ransom, the Souls from the captivity of the Devil and of sin. And it is from such a difficult, such a fearsome, and such an immense captivity that I promise you a Letter of Manumission, through the devotion to the Rosary of the Mother of this God.

V

By way of putting this Letter of Manumission to the proof, you may rightly ask me, and so may those more lettered than you: How can this be? I answer: In the same way that this Lady's Son, Christ, liberated all of humankind from that captivity of the Devil and of sin. And if you still insist that I should tell you more assertively what this way is, I will tell you that it is not by having the Lady give the Contract of Freedom to the Slaves, rather it is by having her take the Contract of captivity from the Devil's hands. Listen to a Text as great as its very Subject: *Delens quod adversus nos erat chirographum decreti, quod erat contrarium nobis, & ipsum tulit de medio, affigens illud Cruci: & expolians principatus, & potestates.*[36] These are words of Saint Paul, in which he says that, when Christ died on the Cross, He stripped the Demons, taking the Contract that they had against us from their hands, and that, after erasing all that was written on it, He nailed it to the same Cross. Now it remains to be learned what Contract this was. And even though the Holy Fathers and Interpreters offer various literal readings of it, they all uniformly say that it was the Contract of sale by which man, through sin, delivers his Soul to the Devil, being condemned by it to the eternal punishments that Divine Justice has decreed against him. And just as the Contract that the creditor had in his hand has no force or vigor once the debt is paid, so Christ, dying on the Cross with the same Blood with which He paid the debt of sin, also erased the Contract by which man had sold his Soul to the Devil and had made himself his Slave: *Delens quod adversus nos erat chirographum.* And so, for Christ to liberate man from the captivity of the Devil, He did not give man a new Contract of freedom, but He took from the Devil the Contract of Captivity by which that man had

---

36. Colossians 2:14–15, "Blotting out the handwriting of the decree that was against us, which was contrary to us. And he hath taken the same out of the way, fastening it to the cross: And despoiling the principalities and powers."

sold himself to him. And this is what Our Lady the Virgin does, as we now shall see.

The sins by which men sell themselves to the Devil, as Saint John remarked, are three that comprise all: Pride, Greed, Sensuality.[37] And in all three we have the evidence of the Contracts of captivity that the Mother of God, like her Son, takes from the hands of the Devil, to set free those who sold their Souls to him. The case of a man named Theophilus is famous and celebrated by all the Ancient Fathers. Seeing himself insulted by a false witness and not finding a legal way to restore his lost reputation and honor, he sought help from the Devil through the intervention of a Sorcerer and, after denying God and the Virgin Mary, handed him a letter in his own hand and under his own seal in which he delivered himself over to him as a perpetual Slave. How powerful among the proud is the vain estimation of their own honor![38] Another person, referred to by the Blessed Alanus, seeing himself in great misery on account of poverty, unable to become rich by his own industry, as he insanely wished, also appealed to the Devil and after the same sort of heretical and blasphemous ceremony in which he denied God and His Mother, in the same way turned in to him a letter of perpetual servitude.[39] To what sacrileges will the abominable hunger of greed not precipitate mortal spirits! Finally, another, mentioned by Torsellino, after ineffectively employing and deploying for the conquest of an honest and constant woman all those extreme measures to which in such follies the blindness and madness of profane love usually turns, sought as a last resort or as a last precipice the powers of the Devil, to whom under the same clauses of his Infernal Formulary he sold himself and became captive forever.[40] He would have done even more, if a Slave of sensuality could have asked more from the Devil.

---

37. 1 John 2:16, "For all that is in the world, is the concupiscence of the flesh, and the concupiscence of the eyes, and the pride of life, which is not of the Father, but is of the world."

38. The story of Theophilus can be found, for example, in the *Legenda Aurea* by Jacobus de Voragine (c. 1230–1298) in the discussion of the Birth of the Virgin. See Voragine, *The Golden Legend: Readings on the Saints*, trans. William Granger Ryan, 2 vols. (Princeton, N.J.: Princeton University Press, 1993), vol. 2, p. 157.

39. Alain de la Roche (c. 1428–1475), also known as Alanus de Rupe, was a French Dominican friar known for his preaching of the Rosary. A version of this story by the Jesuit João Rebelo (1541–1602) is found in Dialogue 7 of his *História dos Milagres do Rosário da Virgem Nossa Senhora* (Lisbon: Pedro Craesbeeck, 1617), pp. 26v–28r.

40. The Jesuit Orazio Torsellino (1545–1599) includes this story at the end of Book 2 of his account of the Holy House at Loreto. See his *De L'Historia Lauretana Libri Cinque* (Milan: Herd. Pacifico Pontio, 1600), pp. 160–162.

All these Slaves of the Devil, as confirmation of the pact by which they had sold themselves, achieved what the Devil himself had promised them: the Proud one, the lost credit; the Greedy one, the desired wealth; the Sensual one, the rebuffed turpitude. But after the burning appetite was satisfied in all of them, and when it was therefore less blind, what were these sad Souls to do, seeing themselves sold? The strength of regret was now greater than the fury of that appetite had been. And since the Devil did not neglect to show each one his signature and his letter, little remained for all of them to fall from that most unhappy state into the ultimate despair. By the extraordinary light and favor of Heaven, however, they all appealed with moans, tears, penances, and continual prayers to the sole patronage of the Mother of Mercy. It would have been fair if they had found the doors of mercy closed in God and in the Mother of God, they who had denied them both. But what do you think was to be the outcome, not of one but of all three cases, so difficult and horrendous? Of the two Thieves on the Cross, one was saved as an example of Mercy and the other condemned as an example of Justice. However, where your sovereign hand enters, O most merciful Virgin, there are no exceptions or half mercies. To all three the most powerful Lady returned their Contracts, taking them by force from the hands of the Devil and delivering them once again to those who had written them, so that they would throw in the fire and extinguish the letters by which they had condemned themselves to that fire which cannot be extinguished. This is what Christ does on the Cross: *Delens quod adversus nos erat chirographum.* And it is the proportion that the ancient Geometer found between Christ and His Mother, when he elegantly called that Lady *Spongiam nequitiæ nostræ adversus Diaboli Scripturam.*[41]

This is how the Virgin Our Lady, imitating her Son, not making but unmaking Contracts, gave Letters of freedom to these three Slaves of the Devil. And what did they do? They employed all the rest of their lives in praise and in thanksgiving to the Sovereign Author of such a singular and extraordinary benefaction. The Slave of Greed, who lived at the time of Saint Dominic, prayed the Rosary; the Slave of Pride, who lived long before the Rosary existed, without its order but in perpetual repetition saluted Our Lady with the Hail Mary; the Slave of Sensuality, who received

---

41. "The Sponge of our iniquity against the writing of the Devil." In John Kyriotes, or Geometres, Hymn 4 to the Blessed Virgin. Vieira's version is a loose adaptation of the original passage. See John the Geometer, *Hymni V in B. Deiparam* (Paris: Claude Morel, 1621), p. 10.

his letter in that sacred house (today called Loreto) where the Angel began his embassy by saying *Ave gratia plena*, repeated the same words infinite times. And so all three prayed the Rosary, with one difference only: That in the first case it was a strung Rosary, in the others an unstrung one. And Blacks should take this example for when the weight of their occupation or labor does not permit them to string their Hail Marys in the order of the Mysteries, though they always invoke the same Lady to help them in their labor. And is there anything else to imitate? Yes, and it is the main thing. According to the Letter of freedom received by the three Slaves of the Devil, they were not to see themselves as Freed, but as Captives of the one who liberated them. So they did, as indeed they should have, because this is not only the perfection, but the obligation of all those whom God delivers from the captivity of the Devil and of sin.

When Christ died on the Cross, He erased, as we saw, the Contracts of all those who since Adam and after him had sold themselves to the Devil. Now take note that, after being resurrected, when He ascended triumphant to Heaven, in the manner of the Roman Triumphers, He took before Him all those whom He had until then taken from the dungeons of that captivity. So sings David, but in such a way that he seems to deny what he celebrates and to contradict what he wants to say. In the Text of the Vulgate he says that, when Christ ascended to Heaven, he made captivity captive, *Ascendisti in altum, cepisti captivitatem.*[42] In Saint Paul's version, he says that He took the Captives captive, *Ascendens in altum, captivam duxit captivitatem.*[43] Well, if the Lord in His triumph did not take anyone but those whom He had liberated, and if because He had liberated them, they were all the spoils of His victories, they the greatest pomp, ostentation, and majesty of that triumph, how can David say that he then made captivity captive and took before him the Captives, not free but captive? Because the very freedom with which Christ liberated them was a new captivity, with which He made them captive once again; and because He took them liberated and free, He took them captive once again. Freedom is a state of exemption which, once lost, is never again restored. Whoever was once Captive, remained forever Captive, because he is either liberated from captivity or he is not: If he is not liberated, he remains a Captive of the Tyrant; if he is liberated, he becomes a Captive of the liberator. And this is what happened to all those whom Christ liberated on the Cross, the Contracts

42. Psalm 67:19, "Thou hast ascended on high, though hast led captivity captive."

43. Ephesians 4:8, "Ascending on high, he led captivity captive."

of their captivity erased. Before freedom, Captives; and after freedom, Captives as well. Before freedom, Captives of the Devil, to whom they had sold themselves; after freedom, Captives of Christ, who ransomed them. Before freedom, Captives of sin; after freedom, Captives of God, as the Apostle says, *Liberati à peccato, servi autem facti Deo.*[44]

This way those three captives showed their gratitude for their Letter of Manumission, making themselves captive once again and turning themselves into Slaves of the very Lady who had liberated them. And all those who still find themselves in the Babylonian captivity and want to leave it should do the same. Make yourselves captive in order to liberate yourselves; and turn yourselves into Slaves of Our Lady of the Rosary, in order not to be Slaves of the Devil, if you are still so, or in order to stay free, if you are already outside this captivity. Erase the mark of the Devil, the mark of Captives, and in its place put the mark of the Rosary, the mark of the free. And if you want to know the shape of this mark, I will tell you it is a Rose. It is recounted in the Second Book of Maccabees that the Tyrant had the Captives of Jerusalem marked with an Ivy leaf, so that they would profess themselves Slaves of the God Bacchus, to whom that plant was dedicated.[45] And what mark more befitting the Slaves of the Rosary than a Rose, not only as the glorious brand of their new captivity, but as a public sign and seal of their Letter of Manumission? Those of you who are, or who were, marked, bear one mark on your chest and another on your arm. In the same way Our Lady of the Rosary wants you to bear her mark: *Pone me ut signaculum super cor tuum, ut signaculum super brachium tuum.*[46] Let the strings of Beads that you carry wrapped around your wrists and around your necks (I speak to the Black women) be all made of Rosary Beads. Those around your neck, falling over your chests, shall be the mark of the chest, *Pone me ut signaculum super cor tuum,* and those around your wrists like bracelets shall be the mark of the arm, *Ut signaculum super brachium tuum.* And the one and the other mark, in your heart as in your works, shall be a testimony and public revelation for all that your Souls are already free from the captivity of the Devil and of sin, never again to serve him: *Et post transmigrationem Babylonis.*

---

44. Romans 6:22, "made free from sin, and become servants to God."

45. 2 Maccabees 6:7, "when the feast of Bacchus was kept, they were compelled to go about crowned with ivy in honour of Bacchus."

46. Canticles 8:6, "Put me as a seal upon thy heart, as a seal upon thy arm."

VI

Free in this way from the greatest and heaviest captivity, which is that of the Souls, you still remain Slaves of the second, that of the bodies. But you should not imagine on that account that the favor Our Lady of the Rosary grants you is less complete. That Our Lady of the Rosary has the power to liberate from the captivity of the body is seen in the countless examples of people who, Captives in the land of the Infidels, found themselves free through the devotion of the Rosary, and after offering at the Altars of that Lady the shackles and broken chains of their captivity as trophies of her power and mercy, hung them in the Temples. When God descended to liberate His People from the Egyptian captivity, why do you think he appeared to Moses in the Bush?[47] Because the Bush, as all the Saints say, was an image of Our Lady the Virgin; and God already then wished to make manifest to the world that this Most Holy Virgin was not only the most commensurate and effective instrument of Divine Omnipotence for liberating men from the captivity of Souls (and for that He chose her as Mother, when He came to redeem humankind), but also for liberating them from the captivity of bodies, which was that suffered by the People in Egypt under Pharaoh's yoke. So the Mother of the Redeemer would have the power to liberate you also from this second and lesser captivity. But it is a particular providence of God, and of her, that you live at present as Slaves and Captives, so that, through this temporal captivity, you will very easily achieve eternal freedom.

We have arrived at the second part of the manumission that I promised you, and at a point where you only lack the knowledge and good use of your present state in order to be in it the most fortunate men in the world. About this matter I shall only argue with you by drawing upon the two Princes of the Apostles, Saint Peter and Saint Paul, who very opportunely dealt with it in various places, speaking with Slaves as seriously as if they were speaking with the Emperors of Rome, and so loftily and profoundly as if they were speaking with the Wise Men of Greece; and this I shall do so that those who despise Slaves do not think that this Subject (above all in a land where there are so many) does not merit all the force of Eloquence and all the effectiveness of Spirit of the greatest Preachers of the Gospel. So, the Apostle Saint Paul speaks with Slaves and in two places says thus,

---

47. The editio princeps contains a marginal note to Exodus 3:2, "And Moses said: I will go and see this great sight, why the bush is not burnt."

Servi, obedite per omnia Dominis carnalibus, non ad oculum servientes, quasi hominibus placentes, sed in simplicitate cordis timentes Deum. Quodcumque facitis, ex animo operamini sicut Domino, & non hominibus: scientes quòd à Domino accipietis retributionem hæreditatis. Domino Christo servite:[48] Slaves (says Saint Paul), obey your Masters in all, not only serving them before their eyes, and when they see you, as one who serves men, but with much heart, and when you are not seen, as one who serves God. Let all you do be not by force but by will, keeping in mind once again that you serve God, who shall pay you for your labor, making you His heirs. In short, serve Christ: *Domino Christo servite.*

Leaving this last word for later, now I want to ponder these, *Scientes quòd à Domino accipietis retributionem hæreditatis.* Two things God promises to Slaves for the service they render their Masters, both not just in disuse but unheard of: pay and inheritance, *Retributionem hæreditatis.* Pay close attention to this. When you serve your Masters, you are not their heirs, nor do they pay for your labor. You are not their heirs because the inheritance belongs to their children and not to their Slaves. And they do not pay for your labor, because Slaves serve under an obligation and not for a stipend. What a sad and miserable state, to serve without hope of reward throughout life, and to work without hope of any rest except in the grave! But there is a good remedy, says the Apostle (and this is not exaggeration, but Catholic Faith). The remedy is for you, while serving your Masters, to serve them not as one who serves men, but as one who serves God, *Sicut Domino, & non hominibus,* because then you will not be serving as Captives, but as free men; you will not be obeying as Slaves, but as children. You will not be serving as Captives, but as free men, because God shall pay you for your labor, *Scientes quòd accipietis retributionem;* and you will not obey as Slaves, but as children, because God, to whom you conform yourselves in that fortune that He gave to you, shall make you His heirs, *Retributionem hæreditatis.* Tell me: If you were to serve your Masters for a daily wage, and

---

48. Colossians 3:22–24, "Servants, obey in all things your masters according to the flesh, not serving to the eye, as pleasing men, but in simplicity of heart, fearing God. Whatsoever you do, do it from the heart, as to the Lord, and not to men: Knowing that you shall receive of the Lord the reward of inheritance. Serve ye the Lord Christ." The editio princeps also includes a marginal note to Ephesians 6:5–8, "Servants, be obedient to them that are your lords according to the flesh, with fear and trembling, in the simplicity of your heart, as to Christ: Not serving to the eye, as it were pleasing men, but, as the servants of Christ doing the will of God from the heart, With a good will serving, as to the Lord, and not to men. Knowing that whatsoever good thing any man shall do, the same shall he receive from the Lord, whether he be bond, or free."

if you were to become heirs to their estates, would you not serve them with great willingness? Well, serve the one whom you call Master, serve that man as if you were serving God; and in that very labor, which is forced, the voluntary application of this "as"—*Sicut Domino*, as God—will suffice for God to pay you as free men and to make you heirs as His children, *Scientes quòd accipietis retributionem hæreditatis.*

This is what Saint Paul says. And Saint Peter, what does he say? He raises the issue and stresses it more. And after speaking to Christians of all states in general, he expands further on this with the Slaves and, with all this majesty of reasons, encourages them to endure their fortune, *Servi, subditi stote in omni timore Dominis, non tantùm bonis, & modestis, sed etiam dyscolis:*[49] Slaves, be submissive and obedient in all to your Masters, not only to the good and modest ones, but also to the mean and unjust. This is the summa of the precept and advice that the Prince of the Apostles gives them, and right away he adds the reasons that are worth giving to the most noble and generous Spirits. The first one: Because the glory of patience is to suffer without blame, *Quæ enim est gloria: si peccantes, & colaphizati suffertis?*[50] The second one: Because that is the grace with which men make themselves more acceptable to God, *Sed si benè facientes patienter sustinetis: hæc est gratia apud Deum.*[51] The third and truly stupendous one: Because in that state in which God placed you, your vocation is similar to that of His Son, who suffered for us, leaving you the example that you shall imitate, *In hoc enim vocati estis: quia & Christus passus est pro nobis, vobis relinquens exemplum, ut sequamini vestigia ejus.*[52] It is with utmost justification that I called this reason stupendous, because is there anyone who will not be amazed at the sight of the lowliness of those to whom Saint Peter speaks and of the height of the most high comparison to which he raises them? He does not compare the Slaves' vocation to any other rank or state in the Church, but to Christ Himself, *In hoc enim vocati estis, quia & Christus passus est.* But there is more. The Apostle does not stop here but adds another new, and greater, prerogative of the Slaves,

---

49. 1 Peter 2:18, "Servants, be subject to your masters with all fear, not only to the good and gentle, but also to the froward."

50. 1 Peter 2:20, "For what glory is it, if committing sin, and being buffeted for it, you endure?"

51. Ibid., "But if doing well you suffer patiently; this is thankworthy before God."

52. 1 Peter 2:21, "For unto this are you called: because Christ also suffered for us, leaving you an example that you should follow his steps."

declaring for whom Christ suffered and for what, *Quia & Christus passus est pro nobis, vobis relinquens exemplum.* I have always taken great notice of the difference between that *Nobis* and that *Vobis*. The Passion of Christ had two purposes: the remedy and the example. The remedy was universal for all of us, *Passus est pro nobis,* but Saint Peter affirms without a doubt that the example was particularly for the Slaves with whom he spoke, *Vobis relinquens exemplum.* And why? Because, among all, there is no state better prepared, by what it naturally suffers, to imitate the patience of Christ and to follow in the footsteps of His example: *Vobis relinquens exemplum, ut sequamini vestigia ejus.*

Oh blessed be you, again and a thousand times, as I said, if, just as God gave you the grace of your state, He gives you the knowledge and good use of it as well! Do you know what the state of your captivity is, if you use well the means that it carries with it, without adding any other? Not only is it a state of Religious life, but it is one of the most austere forms of Religious life in the whole Church.[53] It is Religious life according to the Apostolic and Divine Institute, because, if you do that which you are obliged to do, you serve not men but God, and namely with the title of Servants of Christ, *Ut servi Christi, facientes voluntatem Dei ex animo, cum bona voluntate servientes, sicut Domino, & non hominibus.*[54] Take good notice of that phrase, *Cum bona voluntate servientes.* If you serve by force and with ill will, you are apostates from your Religious order. But if you serve with good will, conforming your will to the divine one, you are true Servants of Christ, *Domino Christo servite.* Just as in the Church there are two Religious orders of the Redemption of Captives, so is yours one of Captives without Redemption,[55] so that it would not lack the perpetuity that is the perfection of this state. Some Religious orders are Discalced, others Calced; yours is Discalced and Disrobed.[56] Your Habit is of your very color, because you are not dressed in sheep or camel skins, like Elijah, but in those with which nature covered or uncovered you, exposed to the heat of the Sun and the

---

53. Vieira the Jesuit here compares the condition of slaves to that of professed religious, considering the "institutes," or rules and spirit, of various orders known for their austerity.

54. Ephesians 6:6–7, "As the servants of Christ doing the will of God from the heart, with a good will serving, as to the Lord, and not to men."

55. The two orders Vieira invokes are the Order of the Most Holy Trinity for the Redemption of Captives (the Trinitarians) and the Order of Our Lady of Mercy and the Redemption of Captives (the Mercedarians).

56. Most famously, the Calced (shod) and Discalced (unshod) Carmelites.

cold of the rains.[57] Your poverty is poorer than that of the Minorites and your obedience more submissive than that of those we call Minims.[58] Your abstinences are more properly called hunger than fasts, and your vigils do not last one hour at midnight, but the whole night without a break in the middle. You have one Rule or many, because it is the will, and the wills, of your Masters. You are bound to them, because you cannot leave their captivity, and they are not bound to you, because they can sell you to another when they want. Only in your Religious order is a contract like this one to be found, making it singular in this regard, too. I will not speak of the names by which you are called, because they do not express Reverence or Charity, but Contempt and Offense. In short, every Religious order has a particular purpose, vocation, and grace. The grace of yours consists of Lashes and Punishments, *Hæc est gratia apud Deum*. Your vocation is the imitation of the patience of Christ, *In hoc vocati estis, quia & Christus passus est*. And your purpose is eternal inheritance as reward, *Scientes quòd accipietis retributionem hæreditatis. Domino Christo servite*. And since the State, or Religious order, of your captivity, with no more asperities or penances other than those that it carries with it, secures, by the promise of God Himself, not only the reward of the Blessed, but also the inheritance of Children, it is the Virgin Mary's very particular favor and providence that you shall preserve yourselves in the same state and its great merits, so that through the temporal captivity you will achieve, as I promised you, Eternal Freedom or Manumission.

VII

Believe, believe everything I have said to you, since everything, as I have alerted you before, is a matter of Faith, and upon this Faith raise your hopes, not only to Heaven, but also to that which, as you will now hear, is prepared for you there. Oh what change of fortune yours will be then, and what amazement and confusion for those who today have so little humanity that they despise it and so little understanding that they do not envy it! Tell me: If, just as you serve your Masters in this life, they were to serve you in the other life, would this not be a very remarkable change and an unimagined glory for you? Well, know that it shall not be so, because

---

57. Elijah's rough clothing is mentioned in 4 Kings 1:8.

58. Minorites is another name for Franciscans; Minims are friars who follow the rule of Saint Francis of Paola (1416–1507) and are known for their continual "Lenten" austerity.

this would be too little. Does God not tell you that, when you serve your Masters, you should not serve as one who serves men, but as one who serves God, *Sicut Domino, & non hominibus?* Therefore this great change of fortune that I speak of shall not be between you and them, but between you and God. Your current Masters are not the ones who shall serve you in Heaven, since many will very likely not go there, but God Himself shall serve you in Person. God is the one who shall serve you in Heaven, because you have served Him on earth. Listen now attentively.

Among the Gods of the Heathens in the old days, there was one named Saturn who was the God of Slaves. And when the time came for the feasts of Saturn, called Saturnalias for that reason, one of the Solemnities on those days went as follows: the Slaves were the Masters who were seated, and the Masters were the Slaves who stood by to serve them.[59] But when the Feast was over, so was the performance of that Comedy, and each one reverted to what he was before. In Heaven it is not so, because there everything is eternal and feasts have no end. And what shall the Feasts of Slaves be in Heaven? Far better than the Saturnalias. Because all those Slaves who in this world serve their Masters as if serving God shall not be served in Heaven by their earthly Masters; rather, God Himself shall serve them in Person. Who would dare say or imagine such a thing, if Christ Himself had not said it? *Beati servi illi, quos, cùm venerit Dominus, invenerit vigilantes:*[60] Blessed be those Slaves whom, at the end of their lives, the Master finds to have been vigilant in fulfilling their obligation. And how will that Master pay them? He Himself says it, and affirms it with an oath, *Amen dico vobis, quòd præcinget se, & faciet illos discumbere, & transiens ministrabit illis:*[61] He will have the Slaves sit at His table and He, as Slave, will tie on His apron and serve them. Through this exceeding honor, Christ declares how much God shall honor slaves in Heaven if they serve their Masters as if they were serving God. Did you serve your Masters on earth as you would Me?

---

59. Macrobius, *Saturnalia*, Book 1, section 7 includes a remark on the liberties granted to slaves during the Saturnalia feast. But there is much longer discourse on slaves and slavery in Book 1, section 11, which cites extensively from Seneca's Epistle 47. See Macrobius, *Saturnalia*, trans. Robert Kaster, 3 vols. (Cambridge, Mass.: Harvard University Press, 2011), vol. 1, p. 77, pp. 111–135.

60. Luke 12:37, "Blessed are those servants, whom the Lord when he cometh, shall find watching."

61. Ibid., "Amen I say to you, that he will gird himself, and make them sit down to meat, and passing will minister unto them."

Then I, who am the Master of your Masters, will serve you in Heaven, as you served them. Saint Peter Chrysologus: *En pavenda conversio servitutis: quia parumper Servus astitit in Domini sui expectatione succinctus: &c. cui ut Talionem redderet, dissimulat se in ipsa Divinitate Divinitas!*[62] Oh change of servitude (says Chrysologus), not only admirable and stupendous, but tremendous! That, just because for a little while the Slave served and had hope in God, Divinity should disguise itself and God Himself should serve the Slave in Heaven! And God does this (says the Saint, elegantly and discreetly) because just as on earth there is the Law of Talion for crimes, so in Heaven God has a Law of Talion for rewards, *Ut Talionem redderet*.

But lest it appear to exceed the terms of rigorous Theology to say that in Heaven God as a Slave will serve the Slaves who served God on earth, listen to the Prince of Theologians, Saint Thomas, on this same text from the Gospel, *Deus Omnipotens Sanctis omnibus in tantum se subjicit, quasi sit Servus emptitius singulorum, quilibet verò ipsorum sit Deus suus:*[63] Omnipotent God subjects Himself in such a way to all those who served him in a saintly manner, that it is as if God were a Slave purchased by each one, and as if each one who had served Him this way were God of God Himself. See, see if it is better for you to serve your Masters as you would God, or to serve them as men. After you have served them as men all your life, the most you can expect from them on earth is a mat of Bulrushes for a shroud. And if you serve them as you would God, what you shall receive from Him in Heaven is His service and honor to you for all Eternity, as if you, a miserable Slave here, were His God and He your purchased Slave: *Quasi sit servus emptitius singulorum, quilibet vero ipsorum sit Deus suus.*

And so that from what you experience and enjoy on earth you can judge how Heaven will be, lay your eyes on that Altar. Is it too much that the same most benign Master who seats you, while in exile and captivity, at His

---

62. "What a tremendous reversal of servitude! For a short time the servant stood girded in expectation of his Lord . . . so that the Lord might repay him in the same fashion, divinity conceals itself in its very divinity!" In Peter Chrysologus, Sermon 24; in his *Selected Sermons*, trans. William Palardy, 2 vols. (Washington, D.C.: Catholic University of America Press, 2004), vol. 2, p. 104.

63. "God Almighty submits Himself to the saints in such a way that it is if He was the purchased slave to each one, as if each of them was His God." Vieira cites a work called *De Beatitudine*, which early modern editors attributed to Thomas Aquinas. Modern scholars describe the text as Thomistic, but not by Thomas himself. Moreover, Vieira changes the original Latin slightly to remove reference to Angels. See, for example, Opusculum 63 in Aquinas, *Opuscula Omnia* (Venice: Heirs of Girolamo Scotti, 1587), p. 648.

table should serve you at it in Heaven? This question was raised among ancient Philosophers: Whether it be just and decent for Masters to admit and seat their Slaves at table with them. The Stoics, who were the most rational Sect and, among Heathens, the most Christian one, used to teach that Masters should admit Slaves to their table; and they used to praise the humanity of those who did this and laugh at the pride of those who found it repugnant: *Servi sunt* (said the greatest Teacher of that Sect), *Servi sunt? Imò homines. Servi sunt? Imò contubernales. Servi sunt? Imò humiles amici. Servi sunt? Imò conservi. Ideoque rideo istos, qui turpe existimant cum Servo suo cœnare.*[64] All Seneca's reasons can be reduced to one, namely that Slaves are men, too. If fortune made them Slaves, nature made them men. And why should inequality of fortune do more for contempt than equality of nature does for esteem? When I despise them, I despise myself more, because I despise in them what they are by misfortune, and in myself what I am by nature. To this reason, which is indisputable everywhere, another is added in Brazil, one that compounds injustice and exaggerates ingratitude. Who sustains you in Brazil if not your Slaves? Well, if they are the ones who feed you, why should you deny them a table that is more theirs than yours? Nevertheless, the majesty or inhumanity of the opposite opinion is what prevails, and not only are Slaves not admitted at table, but they are not even given its crumbs; the fortune of dogs is better than theirs, even though they are called by the same name. Does it matter, however, that the Masters will not admit them to their table, if God invites them and regales them at His? *O res mirabilis* (Saint Thomas exclaims, and with him the whole Church), *O res mirabilis, manducat Dominum pauper, servus, & humilis!*:[65] The poor and humble Slave not only eats at table with his Master, but eats the Master! Now compare table with table and Master with Master, and laugh with Seneca at those who even in this respect will not lower themselves from their authority as Masters, *Rideo istos, qui turpe existimant cum Servo suo cœnare.*

---

64. " 'They are slaves,' people declare. Nay rather they are men. 'Slaves!' No, comrades. 'Slaves!' No, they are unpretentious friends. 'Slaves!' No, they are our fellow-slaves. . . . That is why I smile at those who think it degrading for a man to dine with his slave." In Seneca, Epistle 47; in his *Epistles*, trans. Richard Gummere, 3 vols. (Cambridge, Mass.: Harvard University Press, 1917), vol. 1, pp. 301, 303.

65. "O what a wondrous thing! / The poor, the humble, the lowly / consume the Master and King." From the hymn Sacris Solemniis by Thomas Aquinas for the Feast of Corpus Christi. Translated in Paul Murray, *Aquinas at Prayer: The Bible, Mysticism and Poetry* (London: Bloomsbury, 2013), p. 203.

And if God seats you, while Slaves, at His table on earth, is it too much that He, having promised it and with you finally free from captivity, should serve you at the table in Heaven, when the table is none other than the same? All the doubts that this wonder could elicit have already been put to rest by Christ in the Institution of this Sacrament. Before Christ instituted the Sovereign Mystery of the Most Holy Sacrament, He prepared Himself and He prepared the Disciples. And what preparations were these? There were two in one action alone which was the Washing of the feet: His own, serving them as a Slave; and that of the Disciples, obliging them to let themselves be served as Masters. And if Christ served men as a Slave because He was going to seat them at His table on earth, is it too much that He should serve the already freed Slaves when He has them at His table in Heaven, *Faciet illos discumbere, & transiens ministrabit illis*? This is the change, stupendous beyond all wonder, with which you will then see your fortune switched: serving men here, and being served by God Himself there. But what matters now is that you not fail in any way to meet the obligation which alone promises this happy change to the present misery of your fortune. And what is it, in case you do not remember well? It is for you, too, to change your intention and to switch the purposes of your very labor, turning it from forced to voluntary and serving your Masters as you would Christ, and under men as under God: *Sicut Domino, & non hominibus. Domino Christo servite*. This way you will be twice manumitted and free: free from the captivity of the Devil through the freedom of the Souls; and free from temporal captivity through eternal freedom. These are the two captivities of the first Babylonian transmigration and the two freedoms of the second: *In transmigratione Babylonis. Et post transmigrationem Babylonis.*

VIII

I have finished my Speech and it seems to me that I have not broken my promise to you. And since this is the last time that I shall speak to you, I want to finish with a testimony taken from the same words, one that, while very necessary for you, is still much more so for your Masters: *Iechoniam, & fratres ejus in transmigratione Babylonis.* This Jeconiah and these brothers of his, who were they? They were all Kings and sons of Kings, and Kings of the Kingdom of Judah, the most famous in the world, founded by God Himself. None of this stopped them from being taken to Babylon as captives and treated there like the most vile of

Slaves: one weighed down with chains, another with shackles on his feet, another with his eyes gouged out after using them to see his own children killed in his presence. As a sign of the impending captivity, the Prophet Jeremiah walked the streets and squares of Jerusalem with a thick chain around his neck.[66] To this one he later added five others, which he sent to the neighboring Kingdoms and Kings through their Ambassadors resident at that court. One to the King of Edom, another to the King of Moab, another to the King of Ammon, another to the King of Tyre, another to the King of Sidon; because they would all be made captive at the same time, as they were, by the armies of the Chaldeans. Well, if Scepters and Crowns did not spare so many Kings from captivity, and if after being adored by their vassals they saw themselves Slaves of the foreigners, these remarkable turns of the wheel of fortune should comfort you, too, in yours. If this happens to Lions and Elephants, what reason can Ants have to complain? If they, born in golden Palaces and rocked in silver cradles, found themselves Captives weighed down with irons, then consider, you who were born and raised in the Ethiopian thickets, the great reasons you have to resign yourselves to your fortune, which is so much lighter, and to take its setbacks with a good heart. What you should do is comfort yourselves greatly with these examples; suffer with great patience the travails of your state; give many thanks to God for moderating the captivity to which He brought you; and, above all, profit from it in order to exchange it for the freedom and happiness of the other life, one that unlike this one does not pass but shall last forever.

This was the testimony for the Slaves. And will the Masters also have something to take away from this Babylonian Captivity? It seems that they will not. I (each one is saying to himself), I by the grace of God am White and not Black; I am free and not Captive; I am a Master and not a Slave; rather, I own many Slaves. And were those who found themselves Captive in Babylon Black or White? Were they Captive or free? Were they Slaves or Masters? They were not inferior to you in color, freedom, or ownership. Well, if they saw themselves reduced to captivity, for which they had to come down so many rungs, why do you, who by moving one foot can see yourselves in that state, not fear that you are in danger? If you are young,

---

66. The editio princeps includes a marginal note to Jeremiah 27:2–3, "Thus saith the Lord to me: Make thee bands, and chains; and thou shalt put them on thy neck. And thou shalt send them to the king of Edom, and to the king of Moab, and to the kind of the children of Ammon, and to the king of Tyre, and to the king of Sidon: by the hand of the messengers that are come to Jerusalem to Sedecias the king of Juda."

you have many years to experience this change; and if you are old, a few will do. Macrobius introduces two interlocutors in a dialogue, one called Prætextatus, a great despiser of Slaves, and another called Evangelus, who defended them. So this one, who was just shy of being called Evangelium,[67] spoke thus to Prætextatus, *Si cogitaveris tantumdem in utrosque licére fortunæ, tam tu illum vidére liberum potes, quàm ille te servum:*[68] If you consider, O Prætextatus, how fortune has as much power over Slaves as over free men, you will find that this man whom you see a Slave today you may see free tomorrow; and he who sees you free today may see you a Slave tomorrow. And, if not, tell me: How old were Hecuba, Crœsus, and Darius's Mother, and Diogenes, and Plato, when they saw themselves Captive? *Nescis qua ætate Hecuba servire cœpit, qua Crœsus, qua Darij Mater, qua Diogenes, qua Plato ipse?*[69]

Masters, since you are called so today, consider how, in order to pass from freedom to captivity, the Babylonian transmigration is not necessary; this change can happen in your own land, and there is none in the world that deserves it more and that cries out more for it to Divine Justice. Hear a cry for that Divine Justice in the mouth of Saint John the Evangelist, *Si quis habet aurem audiat:*[70] Let him hear, he who has ears and is not deaf to God's warnings. And what shall he hear? Few words, but tremendous ones, *Qui in captivitatem duxerit, in captivitatem vadet:*[71] All those who make captives will be made Captives. Look at Brazil's two poles, the Northern and the Southern, and see if there has ever been a Babylon or an Egypt in the world in which so many thousands of Captivities were made, those whom Nature made free turned into captives without any Right other than violence, or any cause other than greed, and sold as Slaves.[72]

---

67. Vieira's *Evangelo* is one letter short of *Evangelho*, meaning "gospel."

68. "If you reflect that chance has the same power over us both. You can look on him as a free man as easily as he can see you as a slave." In Macrobius, *Saturnalia*, Book 1, section 11; in his *Saturnalia*, vol. 1, p. 115.

69. "Are you unaware how late in life Hecuba was enslaved, or Crœsus, or Darius' mother, or Diogenes, or Plato himself?" Ibid.

70. Revelation 13:9, "If any man have an ear, let him hear."

71. Revelation 13:10, "He that shall lead into captivity, shall go into captivity."

72. Vieira here again invokes his years in Maranhão, far to the north of Bahia where he gave this sermon. There he witnessed the enslavement of the indigenous peoples, while in Bahia he condemns that of Africans.

Joseph's Brothers made captive only one free man when they sold him to the Ishmaelites to be taken to Egypt, and, as a penalty for this one captivity, God made captive the whole generation of those who made him captive and their descendants, who numbered Six hundred thousand, in Egypt, for a span of four hundred years. But why should we look for examples outside our house, and so far away, when we have them in all of our Conquests? For the captivities of Africa, God made captive Mina, São Tomé, Angola, and Benguela; for the captivities of Asia, God made captive Malacca, Ceylon, Ormuz, Muscat, and Cochin; for the captivities of America, God made captive Bahia, Maranhão, and, under the name of Pernambuco, four hundred leagues of Coastline for twenty-four years.[73] And because our captivities began where Africa begins, God allowed there for the loss of King Dom Sebastião, followed by Sixty years of captivity of our very Kingdom.[74]

I know well that some of these captives are taken justly, within the limits of the laws, and that such is believed to be the case of those bought and sold in Brazil, not the natives, but the ones brought from elsewhere. But what Theology is there or can there be that justifies the inhumanity and brutality of the exorbitant punishments with which these Slaves are mistreated? I said mistreated, but this word is too short for the meaning that it contains or conceals. I should rather say tyrannized or martyrized, because when these miserable people are scalded with burning lard or sealing wax, cut, bludgeoned, and subjected to other great excesses that I omit, these deserve to be called martyrdoms more than punishments. So be sure not to fear any less the injustice of these oppressions than the captivities themselves when they are unjust; rather, I tell you, you should fear them far more, since God regrets them far more. While the Egyptians only held the children of Israel captive, God pretended not to see this captivity. But, in the end, Divine Justice could not suffer its own dissimulation; and after the

---

73. These Portuguese colonies were all taken by the Dutch in the second quarter of the seventeenth century. Some were surrendered back to the Portuguese; others were lost. The cities and lands listed fell to the Dutch (although some where later recovered) in the following years: São Jorge da Mina, 1638; São Tomé, Angola, and Benguela, 1640; Malacca, 1641; Ceylon (Sri Lanka), 1658; Muscat, 1650; Cochin, 1662; Bahia, 1624; Maranhão, 1641; and Pernambuco, 1630. Ormuz fell to a joint Anglo-Persian fleet in 1622.

74. Here Vieira refers to the death of King Sebastião I at the Battle of Alcácer-Quibir in Morocco (at the northwestern corner of Africa, closest to Portugal) in 1578, and the subsequent integration of Portugal into the Habsburg Monarchy from 1580 until 1640.

ten plagues with which those Egyptians were lashed, it finished them off once and for all, destroying and devastating them totally. And why? God Himself said it, *Vidi afflictionem populi mei in Ægypto, & clamorem ejus audivi propter duritiam eorum, qui præsunt operibus:*[75] See, says God, my people's affliction, and hear their cries for the harshness of the oppressions that they bear, and for the rigors with which they are punished by those who preside over the works in which they labor. Take note of two things. The first is that God does not complain of Pharaoh, but of his overseers, *Propter duritiam eorum, qui præsunt operibus,* because the overseers often are the ones who most cruelly oppress the slaves. The second is that God does not give captivity as a motive for His justice but rather the oppressions and rigors against the Captives, which afflicted Him, *Vidi afflictionem populi mei.* And the Lord adds that He heard their cries, *Et clamorem ejus audivi,* which for me is a remark that causes great pity, and which, for God, must be a circumstance that greatly provokes His wrath. They are cruelly lashing the miserable Slave, and he is crying out at each lash, Jesus, Mary, Jesus, Mary, but the reverence of these two names is not enough to move to pity a man who calls himself Christian. And how do you want these two names to hear you at the hour of death, when you cry out for them? But these cries that you do not hear, know that God hears. And even if they are worth nothing to your heart, no doubt they will be irremediably worth something toward your punishment.

Oh how I fear the Ocean will be a Red Sea for you, your houses like that of Pharaoh, and all Brazil like Egypt! The final punishment for the Egyptians was preceded by the plagues, and we already see the plagues repeating themselves so, one after the other, and some so new and unusual as were never seen in the clemency of this Climate. If they are enough to soften our hearts, we will have reason to hope for mercy as we make amends. But if hearts, like Pharaoh's, will further harden, that is too bad, because on top of the plagues the final punishment will not fail to come. I pray to God that I am mistaken in this sad thought, since here and at our Court those who are the most cheerful are the most believed. Know, however, that it is certain (and let this stay in your memory) that if Jeconiah and

---

75. Exodus 3:7, "I have seen the affliction of my people in Egypt, and I have heard their cry because of the rigour of them that are over the works."

his Brothers had believed Jeremiah, they would not have been Captives.[76] But because they gave more credit to the false Prophets who adulated them, he as well as his Brothers thus all ended up in the Babylonian captivity: *Iechoniam, & fratres ejus in transmigratione Babylonis.*

FINIS.

---

76. The editio princeps contains a marginal note to Jeremiah 37:2 and 18, "But neither he, nor his servants, nor the people of the land did obey the words of the Lord, that he spoke in the hand of Jeremias the prophet," and "Where are your prophets that prophesied to you, and said: The king of Babylon shall not come against you, and against this land?"

SERMAM
NONO.
BRAÇO.

Po∫uit pedem ∫uum dextrum ∫uper mare, ∫ini∫trum autem ∫uper terram. Apocalyp∫is 10.

I.

 Crueldade mais hôro∫a, ou a hôra mais cruel, q̃ nunca vio o mundo, he hum tremendo e∫pectaculo, que primeiro a∫∫ombrou a terra, & depois o mar, o qual eu re∫ervei de propo∫ito para e∫ta ultima clau∫ula da no∫∫a Novena.

II.

Morreo em fim Sam Franci∫co Xavier, & como naõ ha duas cou∫as taõ parecidas como a morte, & a vida, ∫endo taõ miraculo∫a a ∫ua vida, naõ podiaõ faltar milagres na ∫ua morte. Depois della naõ foy embal∫emado ∫eu corpo, como era antigo co∫tume, ou rito funeral do Oriente; mas como o me∫mo corpo

Frontispiece of the Ninth Sermon, Arm, in António Vieira's *Xavier Dormindo e Xavier Acordado* (Lisbon: Miguel Deslandes, 1694). Biblioteca da Ajuda, Lisbon, shelfmark C-X-21.

6

Arm, Sermon IX of the Series Called Xavier Acordado

Posuit pedem suum dextrum super mare, sinistrum autem super terram.

REVELATION 10[1]

I

The most honorable cruelty, or the cruelest honor, that the world has ever seen is a tremendous spectacle that first astounded the land and then the sea, and which I deliberately reserved for this last part of our Novena.

II

In the end Saint Francis Xavier died; and because there are no two things so alike as death and life, with his life being so miraculous, there could be no lack of miracles in his death. After it occurred, his body was not embalmed according to the ancient custom or funeral rite of the Orient. But since that body was inhabited for fifty-five years by that Most Holy Soul, full of so many virtues, these virtues were the balsam, the myrrh, the nard, the aloes, and the other celestial aromatic species that preserved it incorrupt, odorous, and as whole as if alive.[2] *Inest quædam ejusmodi virtus incorporibus Sanctorum propter tot annos inhabitatas in illis Animas justas quorum ministerio usæ sunt,* says Saint Cyril of Jerusalem.[3] This is a rare

---

1. Revelation 10:2, "He set his right foot upon the sea, and his left foot upon the earth." The same verse is used for the first nine sermons of the series Xavier Acordado.

2. Vieira here invokes the garden described in Canticles 4:13–14, "Thy plants are a paradise of pomegranates with the fruits of the orchard. Cypress with spikenard. Spikenard and saffron, sweet cane and cinnamon, with all the trees of Libanus, myrrh and aloes with all the chief perfumes."

3. "There is a mysterious power in the body of the saints, because of the just soul which dwelt in it so many years and used its ministry." In Cyril of Jerusalem, *Catecheses* (or Lenten

privilege, and only conceded by God to those Saints who particularly merited being called His own: *Non dabis Sanctum tuum videre corruptionem.*[4] And who is more a Saint of God, *Sanctum tuum*, and wholly of God, and in everything and for everything, than Xavier?

Death is the daughter of sin, *Per peccatum mors.*[5] And in Adam's sin, where she had her beginning, she also gained the power not only to kill men, but to corrupt their bodies and reduce them to dust: *Pulvis es, & in pulverem reverteris.*[6] This is the resentment, or horror, that David had, not just of death, but of the very dust into which she would render him in the grave: *Et in pulverem mortis deduxisti me.*[7] Well, if these are your powers, O death, why did you not use them on Xavier? Do not say that you lacked the most efficient instruments for this second rigor of yours, because the holy cadaver was twice covered with quicklime, the strongest and most caustic lime used to corrode and render into dust all the varied materials that make up the fabric of a body, until it strips and disjoints the bones. But such was the respect with which the lime's natural voracity reverenced those mortal remains in the dead figure of Xavier, that it dared not touch the smallest thread of his clothes and so, by this miracle, the lime itself deserved to be venerated as a relic.

More. That final accident freezes the blood, dries out the flesh, hardens the nerves, changes and fades the colors. Yet, all of these effects, or consequences of death in that dead body, or in that living miracle, were halted or stunned to such an extent that the blood ran liquid, the flesh yielded supple, the nerves bent flexible, and the color, freshness, and grace of the face was so constant and so much the same, that those who dealt with the Saint alive believed him to be dead only because he did not speak. Sight was deceived, touch was deceived, smell was deceived, and even taste was deceived, because there was devotion so daring—or so famished—that it thievishly cut off part of his toe with its teeth. And as if Xavier's death were a mystery of faith, only hearing believed, and confessed that he was not alive.[8] What did you do then, O death, or why did you not do what you usually do?

Lectures) 18: 16, in his *Works*, trans. Leo P. McCauley, and Anthony A. Stephenson, 2 vols. (Washington, D.C.: Catholic University of America Press, 1970), vol. 2, p. 129.

4. Acts 2:27, "Thou shalt not suffer thy Holy One to see corruption."

5. Romans 5:12, "And by sin death."

6. Genesis 3:19, "For dust thou art, and into dust thou shalt return."

7. Psalm 21:16, "And thou hast brought me down into the dust of death."

8. Vieira refers to Romans 10:17, "Faith then cometh by hearing; and hearing by the word of Christ."

Death did not do in Xavier's body what she usually does in others, because she died killing. She killed Xavier, and Xavier killed her. She was like the Bee, who dies stinging; or, less sweetly and more nobly, like Samson, who died killing. The appropriateness of this likeness is more than a little cast into relief by the Angel's two columns, represented by Xavier.[9] When death kills and lives, after separating the Soul she corrupts the body; but when she dies killing, she loses her strength completely, becoming the cadaver of death, and the cadaver of the one she killed stays whole and incorrupt with all the other signs of life. Xavier thus anticipated in himself, as Precursor of Christ in this regard, what He, as victor over Death, will universally do at the end of the world. Let us listen to Saint Paul: *Oportet corruptibile hoc induere incorruptionem, & mortale hoc induere immortalitatem: cum autem mortale hoc induerit immortalitatem, tunc fiet sermo, qui scriptus est: Absorpta est mors in victoria.*[10] The time will come, says the Apostle, when this corruptible and mortal body will be dressed in immortality and become incorruptible, and then what is written will be fulfilled, that death will be smothered in her victory. Note carefully that *tunc* (meaning then), because that dressing of the corruptible body in incorruptibility, which is what will happen at the end of the world, is exactly what happened ahead of time at the death of Xavier, and in the same way, that is, by smothering death in her own victory: *Absorpta est mors in victoria*. Death defeated, smothered, and killed Xavier; but when she smothered him, she was smothered; when she defeated him, she was defeated; and when she killed him, she was killed. Death was like Eleazar when he killed the Elephant, and Xavier like the Elephant of India who fell dead upon Eleazar and buried him underneath himself.[11]

I do not speak in metaphor; rather, I speak the literal truth as experienced and seen at the time through the eyes. The first journey that Xavier made after his death was from the beaches of Sanchão, where he

---

9. The verse which precedes Revelation 10:2, the passage found in the epigraph of this sermon, describes the Angel's feet as *columnæ ignis*, "pillars of fire."

10. 1 Corinthians 15:53–54, "For this corruptible must put on incorruption; and this mortal must put on immortality. And when this mortal hath put on immortality, then shall come to pass the saying that is written: Death is swallowed up in victory."

11. Vieira here refers to 1 Maccabees 6:43 and 46, "And Eleazar the son of Saura saw one of the beasts harnessed with the king's harness: and it was higher than the other beasts . . . And he went between the feet of the elephant, and put himself under it: and slew it, and it fell to the ground upon him, and he died there."

was buried, to the port of Malacca.[12] The City was aflame with a most ferocious plague, with death going about with its tremendously bloody scythe among Heathens and Christians, reaping countless lives.[13] And now I would like to make an apostrophe, directed not to the living or to the dying, but to Xavier's dead body; knowing that such a great Saint should not lack the quality of true sanctity that lies in persecutions, and in the inheritance that Christ bequeathed to the Apostles as an entail when He said to them, *Si me persecuti sunt, & vos persequentur.*[14] This is, Father Master Francisco, that ungrateful and unworthy, not to say infamous City, which owed you faith, doctrine, and so often liberty; a City so miraculously preserved and defended from its enemies by you. Yet it is one where, in obedience to and in adulation of the impiety of a Tyrant who governed it, you were so egregiously cursed and insulted in the public streets; and the authority and Apostolic bulls that you carried were disobeyed and despised, as if you had falsified them.[15] And to this rebel, damned, and excommunicate City you bid farewell by shaking its dust from your shoes according to Christ's advice, as a testament to Heaven and to earth of its complete obstinacy. So your unconquered patience suffered all, as if mute and unfeeling. But now Divine Justice has declared itself by punishing it and defending your innocence, putting the irreparable venom of corrupt air into its entrails so that the same breath that gives force and food for life will turn into the cord and garrote of death. Now, now is the time for you, too, to be on the side of

12. "Sanchão" is an early modern Portuguese rendering of the Chinese name for Shangchuan Island off the southern coast of China.

13. Different accounts of Xavier's postmortem travels give varying reports of what happened during their journey from China to India. Vieira here draws on a hagiography by the Spanish Jesuit Francisco Garcia (1641–1685) which adds details not found in earlier published lives but which are nevertheless present in a late sixteenth-century manuscript report to the Jesuit curia in Rome. See Francisco Garcia, *Vida y Milagros de San Francisco Xavier* (Madrid: Juan Garcia Infanzon, 1672), p. 313. The original source for this claim is found in the notes on the life of Xavier compiled by Manuel Teixeira (1536–1590); see Teixeira to Pedro de Ribadeneyra, Goa, December 8, 1584, in *Monumenta Xaveriana*, 2 vols. (Madrid: Agustin Avrial, 1899–1912), vol. 2, p. 900.

14. John 15:20, "If they have persecuted me, they will also persecute you."

15. Vieira refers to Xavier's final visit to Malacca in 1552, when its governor Álvaro de Ataíde refused to grant him assistance for his planned embassy to China. The rivalry between the two men is a standard topic for Xavier's early hagiographers, such as João de Lucena (c. 1549–1600). See, for example, João de Lucena, *História da Vida do Padre Francisco Xavier e do que fizerão na India os mais Religiosos da Companhia de Iesu* (Lisbon: Pedro Craesbeeck, 1600), pp. 840–851.

that Justice, and for that rough-hewn box in which you lay dead, like that other Ark of the Covenant where the Living God resided, to unleash the destruction and extermination in Malacca that the Ark, captive and insulted, wrought in all of the lands of the enemy Philistines where it passed.

This is what reason, truth, and justice should counsel and persuade Xavier to do. But how would he show that he was in death the same that he had been alive? The sacred deposit comes out and appears on land, and at that same point all those who were wounded and expiring from the plague suddenly rose up healthy. The air was purified, the contagion disappeared and fled without harming anymore or touching any Christian or Heathen. And death also wanted to flee, but Xavier, as her conqueror, put her and shut her in the very graves that were opened for the dying. Death and the enemies of Christ had kept watch over His sepulcher with troops of armed soldiers, *Cujus sepulchrum plurimo custode signabat lapis.*[16] But what were these measures worth against the conqueror of death? Festively and most wisely, the Church sang it: *Victor triumphat, & suo mortem sepulchro funerat:*[17] He buried in His grave the very death who had killed Him. So did Xavier, not in one grave only, the one where she had put him on the beaches of Sanchão, but in the many graves which that same death had opened in Malacca for those she went about killing. At the death of Christ many graves were opened, *Monumenta aperta sunt.*[18] And what happened shortly after? As many graves as were open, that many of the dead came out resurrected: *Et multa corpora Sanctorum, quæ dormierant, surrexerunt.*[19] Consider now whether there were any more or fewer who rose up alive and healthy in Malacca, and the many who did not go to the graves that death had opened up for them; and that these were not only Saints like those, *Multa corpora Sanctorum*, but Christians with faith and Heathens without it, all without exception or distinction.

---

16. "A numerous body of soldiers kept watch at the tomb; a stone is rolled against it and all is sealed." In the liturgical hymn Aurora Cœlum Purpurat one of the morning prayers used at Easter time. In Prosper Guéranger, *The Liturgical Year*, trans. Laurence Shepherd, 15 vols., 2nd ed. (Dublin: James Duffy, 1867–1890), vol. 7, p. 33.

17. "But Jesus triumphs over death and buries it in his own Grave." Ibid.

18. Matthew 27:52, "The graves were opened."

19. Ibid., "And many bodies of the saints that had slept arose."

III

So universal and plenary was the indulgence that Xavier's relics granted there merely on their way, their route being directly to Goa. But what eloquence will suffice to tell of the devotion, the affection, the applause, the magnificence, and triumph with which he was received when dead in that Imperial Metropolis of Asia, he who had deserved so much from it in life? I leave aside seven manifest shipwrecks from which, with as many miracles, the Saint delivered the carrack that carried him.[20] But I cannot pass over in silence something that I will now say. As soon as the happy news was known in Goa, the Father Provincial of the Society with three other Religious left in a cutter to meet the Sacred guest. They found the carrack in Baticalla, not anchored but under sail becalmed;[21] and, as soon as they passed the box in which the Holy body came over to the cutter, the carrack, having now done its job, went of its own accord, without wind, without touching the ground, and even though there was no danger, straight to the bottom.[22] Lest the Expositors get tired inquiring what happened to the Star of the Orient, after it stopped above Christ's manger, both one and the other went down, because the air, too, has a bottom.[23] In this way God wanted to honor Xavier, showing that it was only fitting and proper that the Star which He had created to serve his Son, and the ship that He had constructed to serve His servant, in ceasing to serve them, would end together and serve no one else. The cutter spent the night at the bar of Goa, where no one slept that night, nor did any other day take so long to dawn, leading someone to utter the poetic thought that Aurora took long to

20. Lucena mentions one near wreck; Garcia describes three dangerous moments for the ship. In either case, Vieira's total of seven is an exaggeration (although both authors describe at least seven miracles that occurred during the body's translation). See Lucena, *Historia da Vida*, p. 905, and Garcia *Vida y Milagros*, pp. 315–316.

21. Baticalla was the Portuguese name for the port of Bhatkal on the coast of Karnataka State in Western India.

22. This claim is found in both Garcia and Lucena's lives of Xavier. Lucena adds the detail that the carrack which had carried Xavier's body was decrepit when it made this journey from Malacca to Goa in 1553–1554 and that none of the merchants in Malacca were willing to ship their cargoes on it. After accomplishing its mission, when the ship was safely tied up in port in India, it sank straight to the bottom. See Lucena, *Historia da Vida*, p. 906, and Garcia, *Vida y Milagros*, p. 316.

23. Vieira here draws a parallel between the star that guided the Three Kings to Christ's manger and the ship that carried Xavier's body to Goa. Both, he suggests, dropped out of sight as soon as their mission was accomplished: The ship sank to the bottom of the sea, without an external cause, just as the star dove down to the "bottom" of the air.

adorn herself so that she would be more arrayed and more beautiful than ever to open the gates to the Sun of the Orient. At the first break of light, eighteen brigantines rowed with rapid strokes to find the cutter. On them sailed the principal nobility of what was then the second Court of Portugal, all with lit torches; after making their due reverence to the Saint, they returned in two rows accompanying the cutter to the City. And since the brigantines came bedecked with pennants and streamers of various colors and supplied with noisemakers of all sorts, the lights that reverberated and multiplied in the water and the consonance of the instruments with the slow stroke of the oars made such a harmony to the eyes and to the ears that they greatly furthered the hearts' joy.

The Viceroy waited on the shore, with all the Tribunes of the State and its Ministers, the Council with its banner, Judges, Aldermen, and all other officials of the Republic, and the whole City in an innumerable multitude of all the estates; and not only the healthy, but also the sick, either standing on their own, or in the arms of others, waiting to return to their homes in health. When the cutter was arriving, it was a sight to see the arms that raised and reached out from the middle of the crowd, as if embracing, as much as they could, the Saint's feet from afar. There were some who, lacking the patience to wait any longer, cast themselves, dressed as they were, into the sea. When the Saint was disembarked, all saluted him with knees on the ground and with cheers that reached Heaven. And uniting in full accord the funereal with the triumphal, so as to not exceed the Church's rites, the Procession, or train, was organized in the following manner. First went the children from doctrine class, through whom Xavier had worked so many miracles in those same streets and squares; they numbered ninety, all dressed in white, with crowns of flowers on their heads and green fronds in their hands, singing *Benedictus Dominus Deus Israel, quia visitavit, & fecit redemptionem plebis suae.*[24] Then followed the entire Brotherhood of the Misericórdia with its insignia. And after it came two long lines of the nobility that had waited on land, as well as those who had gone out to sea, all with lit torches and dressed in the best finery that befitted them. After them, the Canons of the Metropolitan Cathedral and the Clergy of all the Parishes. Between them went all the Religious of the Society, who also carried their Holy Priest on their shoulders in a richly decorated bier or float. The entire train was completed by the Viceroy, the

---

24. Luke 1:68, "Blessed be the Lord God of Israel; because he hath visited and wrought the redemption of his people."

City, and the Ambassadors from nearly all the Kingdoms and Nations of Asia; their diversity of colors and costumes made for a beautiful and pompous finale.[25]

The streets were carpeted with the finest, most precious, and skillfully made Ormuz.[26] The walls were richly adorned with tapestries of gold and silk. At intervals, triumphal arches and other items of devout and magnificent architecture were raised. From the windows and terraces flowers rained down upon the float and the Saint's body. When it went by the militiamen, who were aligned in a wing, they lowered their weapons and flags. And everywhere there burned, or boiled in odoriferous liquors, all the aromas of India, among which, with stupendous wonder, the redolent and celestial fragrance that the blessed cadaver exhaled could be distinguished from far away. While thus marched the most solemn triumph seen by that so oft-triumphant City, the applause accompanied resoundingly the continuous thunderclaps of the artillery from all of the fortresses, and the happy tolling of the bells from all the Churches. At those peals some of the sick were encouraged to come to their windows, others to the street, with the first signs of health that the Saint then confirmed. And here I recall the subtle murmuring of a Heretic, who, in mocking the relics of the Catholics, made sure to write that a Religious, after visiting the places of the Holy Land, brought back from there, in a little box, the sound of the bells of Jerusalem.[27] But what he said there for a laugh was verified on this day with true experiences.

When the Procession reached the Church of the Society of Jesus, the Sacred deposit was placed in the High Chapel. The rails, broken in many places by the press of the people, were unable to protect him against the impetus with which some threw themselves against others to kiss his feet. Three times was the Saint propped up and shown to the People, whose shock at that sight was equal to the tears that all shed; and three days,

---

25. Lucena and Garcia recount this event in detail. See Lucena, *Historia da Vida*, pp. 900–902; and Garcia, *Vida y Milagros*, pp. 316–319.

26. Ormuz, the former Portuguese colony in the Gulf, here serves as shorthand for Persian rugs.

27. It is possible that Vieira refers here to the tale of Fra' Cipolla from Boccaccio's *Decameron*, Story 10 on Day 6, in which a relic collector claims to have *alquanto del suono delle campane del tempio di Salamone*. Protestant polemicists, such as the famed scholar-printer Henri Estienne (c. 1528–1598), were especially keen to denounce the cult of relics and so repeated the story. See, for example, Estienne, *L'Introduction au Traité de la Conformité des Merveilles Anciennes avec les Modernes, ou Traité Preparatif à l'Apologie pour Herodote* (Lyon: H. Estienne, 1566), p. 561.

dressed in priestly vestments, was he thus exposed. There was no Sermon of honors at these glorious obsequies or a special panegyric of the dead victor over death, because everyone's tongues everywhere (not speaking for long of any other thing) were most eloquent orators of his praises. Some referred to prophecies, others to miracles, others to conversions, others to excellent virtues, testifying in themselves to the favors received at sea and on land, and others, the Heathens and foreigners, telling of their own. But even if all these were mute, others without memories of the past would suffice as present witnesses: the blind, the lame, the crippled, the lepers, and the other infirm of all types, who, flocking to the new Propitiatory of health, went away from his presence wholly healthy, because the body that God had conserved so incorrupt, and whole, could not make partial grants or miracles.[28]

IV

But before we move along, it will be not only just but necessary to know for what particular merit Divine Providence conceded to Saint Francis Xavier this privilege of incorruption and wholeness, something that not only was conceded to few Saints, but perhaps to no other with so many circumstances and signs of life in a dead body (according to what we read in the Ecclesiastical histories). The reason, or merit, was declared by Saint Augustine about this text: *Neque dabis Sanctum tuum videre corruptionem.*[29] The greatest light of the Church says that God does not concede this privilege to the Saints as sanctified ones, but only as sanctifiers; not because they are Saints in themselves, but because they sanctify others: *Neque sanctificatum corpus, per quod & alij sanctificandi sunt, corrumpi patieris.*[30] And since Saint Francis Xavier, among all the Saints and Apostolic Men of the Church, was not only the one who was to sanctify, *Sanctificandi sunt,* but the one who had sanctified in his life and cooperated with the salvation of so many thousands and thousands of Souls that the Authors

---

28. The Propitiatory, also called the "Mercy Seat," was the golden cover of the Ark of the Covenant mentioned in Exodus 25:17. Here it takes the more general meaning of a "throne," a place of power.

29. Psalm 15:10, "Nor wilt then give thy holy one to see corruption."

30. "You will not allow the sanctified body, through which others also are to be sanctified, to undergo decay." In Augustine, Exposition of Psalm 15, in his *Expositions of the Psalms,* ed. John Rotelle, trans. Maria Boulding, 6 vols. (Hyde Park, N.Y.: New City Press, 2000–2004), vol. 1, p. 184.

of greatest knowledge and the most well informed stretch to two million (something that is not known of any other Saint), how could God consent that the wholeness of such a body should suffer corruption, *Neque corrumpi patieris?* Comparing the crowns of those who are saved with those of the victors who are crowned in this world, Saint Paul calls these corruptible and those incorrupt: *Et illi quidem, ut corruptibilem coronam accipiant, nos autem incorruptam.*[31] Pondering the price for which the said crowns of Heaven were purchased, which was the most precious blood of the immaculáte Lamb, Saint Peter also considers what is incorrupt in them compared to what is corruptible: *Non corruptibilibus auro vel argento, sed pretioso sanguine, quasi agni immaculati Christi.*[32] And how could he who distributed such innumerable, incorruptible, and incorrupt crowns suffer corruption in himself? Finally, when Xavier arrived in the Orient, it could be said of all of Asia what was said of the world before the deluge, *Quia omnis caro corruperat viam suam.*[33] And, in the middle of that immensity, or deluge, of corruptions, what did the great Apostle do? In Heathens he cleaned and banished the corruption of Idolatry, in the Moors the corruption of the infamous Sect of Mohammed; in the ones and the others and the Christians themselves, the corruption of turpitude, of greed, of injustice, and of the other vices so rooted in so many diverse Nations, and in so many lands so remote. And those feet that walked so many thousand leagues, nearly always unshod; those arms that baptized so many thousand Souls, more than ten and twenty thousand in one day; that blood that so many times spilled from the veins with pious harshness to convert sinners; that tongue that never ceased to preach the Faith of the Gospel in all tongues; those eyes that kept watch day and night, and the heart that always burned with the zeal for preaching the name of Christ; and all that body so mortified and so alive, so abstinent and so strong, so tired and so tireless, so divided in a thousand pieces and so whole, why would there be any corruption to defy its wholeness? I leave aside the many pestilent ones whom he freed from the corruption of contagion, and the twenty dead whom, while he was alive, he also freed from the corruption of the tomb.

---

31. 1 Corinthians 9:25, "And they indeed that they may receive a corruptible crown; be we an incorruptible one."

32. 1 Peter 1:18 and 19, "Not with corruptible things as gold or silver . . . But with the precious blood of Christ, as of a lamb unspotted."

33. Genesis 6:12, "For all flesh had corrupted its way."

V

In this way the dead body of Saint Francis Xavier persevered whole for sixty-three years, until in the year sixteen hundred and fourteen, the climacteric for his wholeness, it was divided and his right arm cut off. And this is what, in the exordium of this discourse, I called the most honorable cruelty, or the cruelest honor. Beginning with the honor: When the Supreme Pontiff Paul V heard that the body of Father Francis Xavier was conserved whole, with such singular exceptions of nature and of death, he wished to have with him from that same body a relic of great significance, as the Church calls the principal parts which compose it.[34] And since the wishes of the supreme authority are the strictest ways of commanding, once His Holiness declared this wish to the Society, it became the stroke that obliged the Order to such a rigorous separation. But what greater honor can one imagine in Heaven, or pretend on earth, than that of seeing the very Vicar of Christ, and Vice-God, who has at his right hand in Rome Saint Peter with the keys against which the gates of hell cannot prevail and at his left hand Saint Paul with the sum of doctrine and Catholic Faith which the world has always feared, wanting to put together and to have by his side the arm of a man not yet canonized as a Saint, nor beatified?[35] Oh man more than man in life, and honor and exception to all men after death! Is not Rome that universal Sanctuary which distributes relics to the whole Christian world? Is that ground not holy, watered with the blood of infinite Martyrs, where there is not an inch that cannot and should not be venerated as a relic? Is it not by antonomasia the City from whose cemeteries whole bodies of Saints are continually disinterred with which the Altars of all of Christendom are enriched and dignified? How then can that same Rome ask with such determination for a relic of Xavier from so far away? If we saw the sea ask for water from a fountain, and the Sun light from a Star, how great would our admiration be? Yet this is the one unique honor with which the Head of the Church singularizes that part of the dead Xavier among all of the saints, receiving and embracing it with so much applause, or glorifying himself through Xavier's embrace.

---

34. The original term *reliquia insigne* means more than simply a "first-class relic," any part of the body of a saint. Its "great significance" derives from the fact that it is one of the body's principal parts: the head, the trunk, an arm, or a whole leg.

35. Xavier was beatified in 1619, five years after this papal request from Pope Paul V was received in Goa. He was canonized under Pope Gregory XV in 1622, although his bull of canonization was not promulgated until the following year owing to the pope's death.

But how is it too much, if the same Church had prophesied it in this way with great expectation and joy? *Læva ejus sub capite meo, & dextera illius amplexabitur me:*[36] His left arm has already come under my head, and his right arm will embrace me later. So did both of Xavier's arms, before and after. When he renounced his designs on the temporalities of the world to which he was so attached, and dedicated himself to the service of the Church in the Institute of Saint Ignatius with special subjection and obedience to the Pope who is its head, he then put his left arm under the head of the Church:[37] *Læva ejus sub capite meo.* And when, after having worked such marvels with his right arm, he brought it, or sent it to Rome, he then completed the embrace of the same Church, and perfected and made whole the arm: *Et dextera illius amplexabitur me.* She prophesied it, the Pontiff ordered it, Xavier fulfilled it, and Rome, by honoring it, did what was her duty and custom. When its Captains conquered Kingdoms and Provinces, they erected trophies there, but in Rome statues were placed in their honor and their triumphs decreed. And since Xavier had conquered for that same Rome a new world, even though the trophies of the victories had been erected over there, it was fitting that he would come to receive the honors of statues, triumphs, and Temples in Rome. Saint Ignatius and Saint Francis Xavier, in carrying out their Institute, were like the two points of the compass: Ignatius like the one in the center, ever fixed and immobile in Rome, and Xavier like the point of the circumference, going around the world. And the Pontiff with high council ordered that he come back to Rome, to perfect the circle, closing it at the same point from where he had left. So had this son of Saint Ignatius been taught by another Son of a better and greater Father, *Exivi à Patre, & veni in mundum, iterum relinquo mundum, & vado ad Patrem.*[38] Just like Christ, leaving the Father, came alive to the world and, after death, leaving the world, returned to the Father, so did Xavier, alive and dead. Alive, he left his Holy Father in Rome, and dead he came to seek him again at Rome,

---

36. Canticles 8:3, "His left hand under my head, and his right hand shall embrace me."

37. *Instituto,* as Vieira uses it here, denotes the rules and customs of the Society of Jesus. He also makes mention of the Fourth Vow of professed Jesuits, a special vow to accept whatever mission the pope may choose for them.

38. John 16:28, "I came forth from the Father, and am come into the world: again I leave the world, and I go to the Father."

where I am seeing both of them glorious in the Temple that Rome herself calls the *Gran Gesù*.[39] When Christ showed Himself to the Apostles
in the glory of Tabor, there appeared majestically with Him on His right
side Moses, and on His left Elijah.[40] At that moment, Saint Peter wanted
to build three tabernacles, but they were built by his successor, the
Supreme Pontiff, on this second Tabor: In the high Chapel, Christ with
the name of Jesus; on the right-hand side, Saint Ignatius as Moses and
as Legislator; and, on the left-hand side, Xavier as Elijah and as the most
zealous promotor of the Faith. About Achilles it was said, *Unus Pæleo
juveni non sufficit orbis*,[41] that for Achilles one world was not enough.
And for Xavier, as the Achilles of the Society, the old world alone was not
enough for his victories, so he conquered the new one. It became necessary, to enjoy the honors he earned during his life, that after death he
should be divided and shared between Goa and Rome, so that he would
be venerated and adored in the Orient by the head of Asia, and in the
West by the head of Europe, of Christendom, and of the world.

VI

Enough about the honorable. And with regard to what may appear cruel,
let Rome allow me to address her, and this will not be the first time that
she hears me.[42] For Rome to gain relics of Xavier, and relics of great significance, it appears that it was not necessary to imitate Longinus's thrust
of the lance or to bloody its iron. And I argue against Rome with Rome
herself. The custom and ancient style of the Roman Church, when great
Princes asked for any relic of the Saints, was for the Supreme Pontiffs to
send them not a part of the Saints' bodies but a veil called a *Brandeum*

---

39. The Church of the Gesù in the center of Rome was attached to the Society's Professed
House, where the Jesuit Curia resided. The tomb of Loyola and the altar which bears the arm
relic of Xavier are situated on either side of the church's crossing.

40. The story of the Transfiguration is told in Matthew 17:1–9, Mark 9:2–8, and Luke 9:28–36.

41. Vieira plays with the reference to two ancient heroes here. The original phrase, from
Juvenal's Satire 10, line 168, reads *Unus Pellæo juveni non sufficit orbis*, "One world is not
enough for the young man from Pella." Juvenal describes Alexander, born at Pella in
Macedonia, while Vieira describes Achilles, son of Peleus. Juvenal's Satire 10 is particularly
appropriate here for Vieira since it includes a lengthy discussion of the trophies of ancient
heroes. In *Juvenal and Persius*, trans. Susanna Morton Braund (Cambridge, Mass.: Harvard
University Press, 2004), p. 381.

42. Vieira here refers to the sermons he preached in Rome in the early 1670s.

which had touched them or their tombs.[43] So was one sent by Pope
Saint Gregory to Empress Constantina, as the third book of his Epistles
recounts;[44] and the same is found throughout all of Ecclesiastical history,
which can be seen in Baronius.[45] Those veils were of the finest and whit-
est linen, of which Prudentius sang: *Candore nitescere claro lintea.*[46] And
it may be that already Saint Peter had learned this lesson at the tomb of
Christ, where he noticed that the Lord had left as relics of his Sacred body
linteamina, & sudarium.[47] And since the devotion of some Princes was not
sufficiently satisfied with those relics which had been consecrated only by
the touch of the holy bodies or sepulchers, there was a Pontiff who, after
ordering that these veils be brought before their ambassadors, squeezed
them and they oozed blood. What a relic of great significance from Xavier
his poor, rough, and patched cassock therefore would be, under which the
Saint had so many times suffered the most frigid snows of Japan, the most
burning suns of the Meliapor sands, and which, during the few hours of
sleep, between the fatigued body and the bare ground, served as his bed?
In the midst of a terrible storm, the Pilots and Sailors shouted that the
ship was sinking. Xavier was aboard and, quickly ripping a small stitch
of the hem of that same cassock, threw it into the sea; and the winds and
the waves calmed at that very moment. It is true that, if the great Anthony,
Patriarch of all Monks, dressed on Easter day with the cloak of Saint Paul,
the first Hermit, woven of palm leaves, then Xavier's cassock was worthy
of being worn by Roman Pontiffs under their pontifical vestments at the
greatest solemnities.[48]

---

43. The term has its origin in the city Brindisi, where the cloth for these secondary relics
came from.

44. The editio princeps includes a marginal note to Gregory the Great, *Epistles*, Book 3: 30,
which reflects the early modern numbering of the letters. Modern critical editions call the
same letter Book 4: 30. See Pope Gregory I, *The Letters of Gregory the Great*, trans. and ed. John
R. C. Martyn, 3 vols. (Toronto: Pontifical Institute of Medieval Studies), vol. 1, pp. 310–312.

45. Vieira refers to Cesare Baronio (1538–1607), the author of the monumental *Annales
Ecclesiastici*, originally published in 12 volumes (1588–1607).

46. "Linen cloths of gleaming whiteness." In Prudentius's *Cathemerinon*, Poem 10 (A Hymn
on the Burial of the Dead), lines 49–50: *Candore nitescere claro / praetendere lintea mos est*,
"Why it is our custom to spread over it linen cloths of gleaming whiteness." In *Prudentius*,
trans. H. J. Thomson (Cambridge, Mass.: Harvard University Press, 1949), p. 85.

47. The wrappings and the shroud left at the tomb are mentioned in Luke 24:12 and John 20:7.

48. This story about Paul the Hermit can be found in many medieval and early modern col-
lections of saints' lives. See, for example, Pedro de Ribadeneyra's *Flos Sanctorum, o Libro de
las Vidas de los Santos* (Madrid: Luis Sánchez, 1616), pp. 109–110.

More. In that very Rome, on the day of the Conversion of Saint Paul, in his church, is shown, as a special relic of the Apostle of the Gentiles, not the whole, but part of the staff upon which he leaned during his great pilgrimages, which were in truth much shorter than Xavier's. No miracles are mentioned of this relic; none are necessary, when in other ways they are spoken of as true. It is likewise said of Elisha's staff that it is the Prophet's own, even though it is also said that when it was placed upon the dead child, the expected miracle did not occur.[49] Therefore, far more attested a relic would be that of Xavier on which he often placed his hands, when he walked and when he did not, every day and every night, and which he always carried over his breast: his Rosary. When in his absence it was placed on possessed bodies by the children from his doctrine class, it cast out demons; and when on the sick, it cast out fevers and all other infirmities. Let this consequence serve as proof for another, greater argument. One of the Saint's great devotees, having to travel from Meliapor to Malacca, fearful of the dangers of so long a navigation and of such dangerous seas, asked upon saying goodbye to him and receiving his blessing if he might give him some small gift to console and animate him.[50] Xavier had nothing but his Rosary with him. He took it off his neck and, putting it in his hands, heartily instructed him to always keep it with him, trusting that it would save him from any danger. After a few days of the journey, the ship had suffered so much that, not able to withstand the fury of the winds, it was carried away by them and left to chance, as they say, until it ran aground on some boulders where it broke apart. Among those few sailors who escaped with their lives was the devotee of the Saint. On the hardness of the boulder there was neither green grass to eat nor a drop of water to drink, so that, half dead from hunger and thirst, they rigged a raft from the shipwreck's timbers, got on it, and delivered themselves again to the sea, more to delay death than with hope of living. And so it happened. Because neither they nor the raft appeared again; and only the devotee of Xavier, with his Rosary, found himself five days later on an unknown beach, which afterward he learned was close to Meliapor, from whence he had left and where he had his house. Asked who had brought him there and how he had spent those five days, he answered that he did not know, because during all that time he either imagined, enrapt, or dreamed, asleep, that he was conversing with his family. And so the Sacred

---

49. How Elisha's staff did not work miracles in the hands of Giezi is told in 4 Kings 4:29–35.

50. The story of Xavier's rosary is found in Garcia, *Vida y Milagros*, pp. 88–89.

relic not only saved him from death and from danger, but also from imagi-
nation and from fear. Doubly stupendous portent, and its instrument worthy of being hung by Rome in the Temple of Minerva before the Altar of
Our Lady, the inventor of the Rosary, as one of her most famous trophies.[51]

God promised Jeremiah to spare him not only from dangers, but also
from the fear of them: *Nec enim timere te faciam.*[52] And from this same
grace resulted that very deep sleep of Saint Peter on the night before the
day upon which he was to go out and be judged publicly, as the Syrian
more expressly ponders: *In illa ipsa nocte erat Petrus dormiens.*[53] The Angel
awakened him to free him from the prison of chains and from death, and
God put him beforehand in the prison of sleep to free him from worry
and from the fear of death. And if this double favor was granted to Saint
Peter by the prayers of the whole Church that pleaded for his life, what
great excellence is Xavier's that both graces were conceded to the rosary
with which he prayed, as we saw in the case that we have just mentioned.
But let us turn to the chains. Those of Saint Peter are among the most
famous relics of Rome, with a Temple and a feast day dedicated to them.[54]
The way of sharing this relic was not to give a part, or link of those same
chains, but only a small shaving from that sacred iron, sanctified by the
touch of the hands of the said Prince of the Apostles: *Ceciderunt catenæ
de manibus ejus.*[55] Thus Pope Saint Gregory sent one of these shavings to
Childebert, King of France. And Justinian, who later became Emperor,
begged another from Pope Hormisdas.[56] And if this was the style of the
Supreme Pontiffs, so praiseworthy and decorous toward those relics at
an age when the church was already so mature, Rome could just as well
have been satisfied with those chains of Xavier, so many times sanctified with his blood, as Rome orders to be sung in her lessons: *Ferreis in*

---

51. Vieira here refers to the Dominican church of Santa Maria sopra Minerva in Rome.

52. Jeremiah 1:17, "For I will make thee not to fear."

53. Acts 12:6, "The same night Peter was sleeping." Luke the Evangelist is here referred to by
his place of origin, Antioch in Syria.

54. Vieira refers to the church of San Pietro in Vincoli, and to the feast of Saint Peter ad
Vincula, celebrated on August 1.

55. Acts 12:7, "And the chains fell off from his hands."

56. The requests by Childebert and Justinian are both mentioned in Cesare Baronio's
martyrology in his discussion of the feast of Saint Peter in Chains. See Baronio, *Sacrum
Martyrologium Romanum* (Cologne: Johann Gymnik, 1610), p. 519.

se flagellis ita sævijt, ut saæpe copioso cruore difflueret.[57] These chains with sharp points served as cilice and scourge to the Saint, who with them took upon himself the sins of great and obstinate sinners and, disciplining himself cruelly in front of them, his back all washed in blood, converted them, astonished as they were by such a spectacle of charity. Such, and no less than these conversions, were the miracles of Xavier's chains, and it is the doctrine and the verdict of all the Saints, with all the rigor of Theology, that to convert a sinner is a greater miracle than to resurrect the dead, which Christ did three times, or to create worlds, which God did only once.

But for Rome to have relics of great significance, and of very great significance, of Xavier, neither iron nor blood was necessary; other ones were enough which, without touching the Saint's body or being touched by it, would work, as they did work, stupendous wonders. Let us go to Naples. In front of the Altar of Saint Francis Xavier in the Church of the Society of Jesus, one sees twenty-nine standards hanging, each one bearing the name of one of the twenty-nine neighborhoods into which that royal City is divided, and one inscription on all of them that says *Ob urbem à peste servatam*: For having defended this City from the plague.[58] The plague was so cruel that the dead numbered in the hundreds of thousands. And which was the relic that worked this universal wonder? An image of Xavier that healed one citizen first, then four, then many. And when the Republic learned that in the image was health, also contagious, it elected the Saint as its Protector, and on the afternoon of that same day he healed more than four hundred persons. And with the same rush the fire was put out, so that the whole City was free. Let us go to Calabria. We will see by authentic information, gathered under Apostolic authority, that in the Town of Potamo alone, in one year and a half, in addition to infinite other miracles, Saint Francis Xavier resurrected twenty-nine dead. This did not occur through another relic of his body, but through a simple image of himself which was so used to working similar resurrections that the dead were not buried two, three, and

---

57. "He scourged himself so severely with disciplines, to which were fastened pieces of iron, as to be frequently covered with blood." In the prayers for the Feast of Francis Xavier, December 3, in the Roman Breviary. In Guéranger, *Liturgical Year*, vol. 1, p. 327. The phrase refers to his mortifications as a young man in the company of Ignatius, before going to India.

58. Xavier's intercession during the plague in Naples is recounted in Garcia, *Vida y Milagros*, pp. 428–429.

four days after death, in the hope that the Saint would resurrect them, as some achieved from him, either before they were taken to the tomb or by jumping off their biers alive.[59] Finally, let us go to India, where its great Apostle had indoctrinated in the Faith a woman of Chinese origin whose name was Luzia Vilhançano, who was a hundred and twenty years old and was known for her virtue.[60] She suddenly healed all types of infirmities with an image of her Holy Master, applying it to the sick with only these words: In the name of Jesus Christ, and of Father Francis Xavier, may God restore you to health. Some of these miracles, with the name of the said woman, are mentioned in the Saint's Canonization Bull. And eyewitnesses under oath declare that at the very moment when the Holy image was applied, they saw suddenly healed the crippled, the lame, the blind, the deaf, mutes, lepers, consumptives, paralytics, and the cankerous with their flesh eaten away and rotten. And no illness was so old and incurable, no moribund so prostrate and almost expiring, some not having more than skin on bones and seeming more like cadavers than living men, that, when touched with that shadow of Xavier, they would not suddenly rise up with their vigor, with their strength, with their senses, with their color, and with the corpulence of their limbs returned. Since these images of Xavier, so absent and remote from his body, never having touched it, were relics so significant and powerful, Rome sent one of its famous Painters to Goa to depict him in a true effigy that would be the living image of the dead Xavier. It seems that, with this bloodless relic, Rome would be just as enriched without his arm, as the Saint would be whole with it.

VII

But it is about time we see the sacrifice; and prepare yourselves, hearts, with new spirit and valor for a never before seen spectacle. The site that was chosen was an interior Chapel to which the holy body was translated for the sake of greater decency. The time was the most secret hour of midnight and no word was spread inside or outside of what had been determined, *Ne tumultus fieret in populo*, because, if it were known, all of Goa and all of India would take up weapons to defend the arm that had so

---

59. For the account of Potomo, see ibid., p. 424.

60. For this story, see ibid., p. 432.

often defended her.[61] The assistants were the Visitor, the Provincial, the Superior, and three Consultors of the Province. The Executor was a lay Brother, since it did not seem decent that the Sacred hands that offer to God the bloodless sacrifice of his Son should be bloodied in that of Xavier. As they all kneeled, the Executor raised the Saint's arm, as natural and flexible as if it were from a living body asleep; and, as he moved to cut it, suddenly the earth, the Chapel, and all that were in it shook.[62] They tried the stroke a second time, and not only the paving stones but the walls, in a second tremor, appeared to want to collapse, with the stones dislodging themselves. Who would not be dispirited at the repetition of such a prodigy! Nevertheless insisting a third time on the same intent, the shake and the quake were so much greater that the roof and the whole edifice of that great house fell on those who were in the Chapel, so that, astonished, they all left the place. Who would not have said of each of these Priests in that case, had the execution not been upon Xavier's body but upon some statue of him, *Ter conatus erat casus effingere in auro, ter patriæ cecidere manus!*[63] They made a new consultation, and though it seems that the decision should have been to write again to Rome, to relate the manifest and prodigious signs with which God had showed that He would not have the holy body divided but preserved whole, so that its very wholeness would be a perpetual testimony to all of the Orient of the truth of the Faith that Xavier had preached to it, what was decided instead was that they should take the very saint as an intercessor against himself, and ask him for permission for the deed that they had been ordered to perform. They all entered the Chapel again and knelt, and one of the Prelates spoke thus: Blessed Saint, you know well that we come here not so much of our own will but out of obedience to our Father General. And since in life you were so obedient,

---

61. Matthew 26:5, or Mark 14:2, "Lest there should be a tumult among the people." Vieira leaves out the "perhaps," *forte*, in this citation. India, for Vieira, refers to Portuguese India, not the whole of the subcontinent.

62. The report of this tremor and the Jesuits' subsequent trepidation at their task is not found in eyewitness reports of this event such as the one by Sebastião Gonçalves (c. 1555–1619), but only in Francisco Garcia's retelling. See Garcia, *Vida y Milagros*, pp. 320–321. Cf. Gonçalves, *Primeira Parte da Historia dos Religiosos da Companhia de Jesus* (1614), ed. Josef Wicki, 3 vols. (Coimbra, Portugal: Atlântida, 1957–1962), vol. 1, p. 450.

63. "Thrice he essayed to fashion your fall in gold; thrice sank the father's hands." Vieira adapts the original *bis*, in Virgil's *Aeneid*, Book 6, lines 31–32, for *ter*, thrice, since the Jesuits attempted to cut the arm three times in this account. In Virgil, *Eclogues, Georgics, Aeneid: Books 1–6*, trans. H. L. Fairclough, ed. G. P. Goold (Cambridge, Mass.: Harvard University Press, 1916), p. 535.

now that you are dead give us permission to execute what is demanded of us, so that we may send this relic of your body requested by the Supreme Pontiff. This he said; and upon hearing the name of the Supreme Pontiff and of the Father General, and the word obedience, the Saint obeyed, the earth obeyed, the walls obeyed, everything obeyed, and the arm let itself be cut, with so much blood flowing from the wound that it filled a silver vase, and soaked a towel that had been readied for this effect, which many years later the Count of Linhares, Viceroy of India, took as a present to King Dom Philip IV.

In the end, after sixty-three years, we have the body of Saint Francis Xavier, as if in him the prophecy of the Priest Heli were fulfilled: *Ecce dies venient & præcidam brachium tuum.*[64] But even though he lacks the right arm, I hope and promise that the victories of his left will be so many that, changing the terms around, about the right one it can be said, *Cadent à latere tuo mille*; and of the left it be said, *Et decem millia à sinistris tuis.*[65] Yet if everything done in this case was more by Divine instinct, as I will later show, than by human reason, then we have all the more cause for wanting to know what the purpose of Divine Providence was in permitting in the incorrupt and whole body of Xavier that which we have not read of having been done in another of those that God has conserved until now without corruption. I understand, and I say, that the most sublime aims of so particular a Providence were two, one for the Society, another for Xavier. With regard to the Society, that in all of the circumstances of this case the most perfect example of the strict obedience professed by it be clearly shown. And with regard to Xavier, that after death God would grant him the martyrdom that he most ardently desired and always sought without being able to attain in life.

VIII

As for the first, three types of Superiors and Subordinates were involved: The Supreme Pontiff, Superior of the General, and the General, Subordinate of the Pontiff; the General, Superior to the Priests of India, and the Priests of India, Subordinates of the General; the Priests of India, Superiors of—in as much as they could be—Xavier's body, and Xavier's

---

64. 1 Kings 2:31, "Behold the days come: and I will cut off thy arm."

65. Psalms 90:7, "A thousand shall fall at thy side, . . . and ten thousand at thy left hand." Vieira changes the Vulgate's *dextris* to *sinistris*.

body, Subordinate of those same Priests. Let us now go over all the types of these Superiors and Subordinates, and we will see in their obedience all the excellences and peaks of perfection of this virtue in which Saint Ignatius was the most precise of the many Legislators who demanded it and of the many Writers who wrote about it.

Firstly Saint Ignatius orders in his Rules that all seek to observe and to distinguish themselves in obedience in such a way that for obeying there be no need for precepts or express orders from the Superior, but the signal of his will alone shall suffice: *Omnes obedientiam observare, & in ea excellere studeant, licet nihil aliud, quàm signum voluntatis Superioris sine ullo expresso præcepto videretur.*[66] And such was the perfection of obedience of the Father General, who was Claudio Aquaviva, to the Supreme Pontiff, Paul V. The Supreme Pontiff did not command him or impose a precept, he only made known the desire that he had to have in Rome a relic of great significance from the body of Saint Francis Xavier, or, better said, of Francis Xavier, who was not yet a Saint and whom he wanted to canonize. This signal of the will of the only Superior of the General of the Society, the Supreme Pontiff, sufficed for Claudio to command the Priests of India to execute what was done there. This high degree of obedience confirms what Saint Paul taught or insinuated to his disciple Timothy when he wrote him: *Quia Lex justo non est posita.*[67] Because to obey through Laws, or precepts, is ordinary obedience; but excellent obedience, as is found in the Institute of the Society *In obedientia excellere studeant*, has no necessity, nor waits for Laws or precepts, and the signal of the Superior's will alone suffices. So our most learned Portuguese Mendonça, as a disciple of the school and spirit of Saint Ignatius, comments upon this text of the Apostle, applying it to the obedience of Samuel. This exposition is not found in the ancient Doctors, even when they are Holy, to whom I usually only refer when it is necessary. *Perfectus obediens*, he says, *qualis erat Samuel, imperium non*

---

66. "All should strongly dispose themselves to observe obedience and to distinguish themselves in it . . . even though nothing else be perceived except an indication of the superior's will without an expressed command." Vieira cites Ignatius Loyola (1491–1556) here as the author of the Constitutions of the Society of Jesus. This particular phrase comes from Rule 33 in the *Summarium Constitutionum*, the compendium of rules drawn from the Constitutions, Part 6, chapter 1, translated in John Padberg, ed., *The Constitutions of the Society of Jesus and their Complementary Norms* (Saint Louis: Institute of Jesuit Sources, 1996), p. 220.

67. 1 Timothy 1:9, "The law is not made for the just man."

requirebat, quia solo nutu etiam absque ullo jussu ad voluntatem Prælati exequendam ferebatur.[68]

The second document of Saint Ignatius is that his sons must proceed in cases of obedience as in issues of Faith, closing their eyes to any difficulties and objections that arise about them, without examining them or inquiring, it being enough to believe the word of the Superior who gives the orders: *Ut ad credenda quae catholica Fides proponit, toto animo, assensuque vestro incumbetis; sic ad ea facienda quæcumque Superior dixerit, cæco quodam impetu voluntatis parendi cupidæ, sine ulla disquisitione feramini.*[69] And this was the perfect obedience of the Priests of India in obeying and not answering back to the Father General. There was the terrible objection of having to put iron into that holy and miraculous body, and to cut and divide the wholeness with which God had conserved it for so many years. It became more terrible still after the quakes grew more intense and fearsome, once, twice, and three times repeated. And still they obeyed, closing their eyes and restraining their understanding as if this was a decree of the Faith. The confirmation of this most important point is found in no less a source than the Prince of the Apostles, Saint Peter, who, in recounting the famous vision of what he had seen and heard on Mount Tabor, adds to the Christians to whom he writes that he has yet another, more solid testimony, that of the Prophets, whom they would do well to follow and to believe in with full attention: *Et hanc vocem nos audivimus à Cælo allatam, cum essemus cum ipso in monte sancto: Et habemus firmiorem propheticum sermonem, cui benefacitis attendentes.*[70] Well, if that same Saint Peter and the other two Apostles had seen and heard all the things so wondrous that were seen and heard on Mount Tabor, why does he say that he has another

---

68. "He should be perfect and obedient like Samuel, who did not require authority because he was brought to execute the will of the Prelate on a simple nod and without any order." In Francisco de Mendonça, *Commentariorum in IV Libros Regem*, 2 vols. (Lyon: Gabriel Boissat, 1627), vol. 2, p. 100. Francisco de Mendonça (1573–1626) was a Portuguese Jesuit famed for his preaching and exegesis.

69. "In the same way you devote yourself what the Catholic faith teaches with your whole heart and assent, you will hopefully be moved to carry out whatever the Superior has said, with a certain blind impulse of the will, eager to obey, without any inquiry." This passage comes from a letter from Ignatius Loyola to the Members of the Society of Jesus in Portugal, Rome, March 26, 1553. A different translation of the letter can be found in Ignatius of Loyola, *Letters and Instructions*, ed. John Padberg, trans. Martin Palmer, and John McCarthy (Saint Louis: Institute of Jesuit Sources, 2006), p. 419.

70. 2 Peter 1:18–19, "And this voice we heard brought from heaven, when we were with him in the holy mount. And we have the more firm prophetical word: whereunto you do well to attend."

testimony more solid than his own, that of the Prophets, to which they do well to attend, *Cui benefacitis attendentes?* Here, too, it falls to the commentator of the school and spirit of Saint Ignatius, the most Learned à Lapide, to say, further sharpening the argument in the voice of the Priest: *Licet enim vox Patris objective, puta in se, esset verissima, & certissima æque ac oracula Prophetarum, tamen subjective, quatenus in auribus S. Petri recipiebatur, & resonabat, non erat tam certa, & firma quàm visiones Prophetarum: auditus enim omnisque sensus falli potest; visio verò Prophetarum falli nequit, quia fit per lumen supernaturale, & Divinum.*[71] So that the reason for the difference is that the vision of the Apostles was through the natural knowledge of the senses, in which there can be mistakes. And that of the Prophets comes through supernatural and Divine light, in which there can be no failing. Therefore we believe what the Faith says, against what we see, hear, and touch; and so the truly obedient one must believe what the Superior says, whose voice is that of God, as Christ himself teaches: *Qui vos audit, me audit.*[72]

There remains the third consideration of the fine and perfect obedience, that of the dead body of Saint Francis Xavier to the Superiors of the house where he was so venerated. And on this so extraordinary point it appears that Saint Ignatius spoke not only as a Legislator, but as a Prophet. He says that those who live under obedience should let themselves be guided and ruled by Divine Providence through their Superiors, as if they were a dead body that lets itself be carried wherever they carry it and be treated in any way they wish to treat it: *Qui sub obedientia vivunt, se ferri, ac regi à Divina Providentia per Superiores suos finere debent, perinde, ac si cadaver essent, quod quoquo versus ferri, & quacunque ratione tractari se sinit.*[73] Could there be anything more fitting or more natural, or more supernatural, for our case? The dead body of Saint Francis Xavier, not *ac si cadaver*

71. "Indeed, even though the voice of the Father was, objectively speaking, most true, in itself, for instance, and equally as certain as the oracles of the prophets, yet in the subjective sense, such as it was received by Saint Peter's ears and resounded in them, it was not as certain and firm as the visions of the prophets. Indeed, hearing as well as all the senses can be deceived; the vision of the Prophets, however, cannot be deceived because it is produced by the Supernatural and Divine light." In Cornelius Cornelii à Lapide's commentary on 2 Peter in his *Commenataria in Epistolas Canonicas* (Lyon: Jacques et Mathieu Prost, 1627), p. 345.

72. Luke 10:16, "He that heareth you, heareth me."

73. "Everyone of those who live under obedience should let himself be carried and directed by Divine Providence through the agency of the superior as if he were a lifeless body, which allows itself to be carried to any place and to be treated in any way." In the Constitutions of the Society of Jesus, Part 6, chapter 1; translated in Padberg, *Constitutions*, p. 222.

esset, but indeed as the cadaver that he was, let himself be taken where they wished, because he let himself be taken from Asia to Europe, and from Goa to Rome, where the Pontiff wanted him to be. And as the cadaver that he was, he let himself be treated by them as they wished, because they wanted to wound him, cruelly even if without cruelty, to the point of rendering his wholeness in pieces and cutting off nothing less than his right arm. Only in one thing did Xavier not show that he was completely dead, in the copious blood that flowed from the veins. From the Side of the dead body of Christ blood flowed, but to that body another living and immortal nature was united. And as if Xavier's obedience was second nature to him, the body was dead but the obedience lived. Saint Ignatius wanted the living obedient ones to be like dead bodies, and Saint Francis Xavier made his dead body like one obedient and alive. Obeying Christ, Lazarus, who was dead, came out of the tomb alive. A greater miracle would be if, dead as he was, he came out and obeyed. Because this obedience would then not be of all of Lazarus, but only of half of him: *Ad unam vocem Domini totus Lazarus vivus processit, qui totus ibi non fuerat.*[74] Lazarus, says Saint Augustine, was not whole in the tomb, but only half, that of his body, but at the voice of Christ he came out alive and whole. So that, for Lazarus to obey, it was necessary for him to first live, and to first have the part that he was missing restored, his Soul, and thus he obeyed alive and whole: *totus Lazarus vivus processit.* Yet the dead body of Xavier, dead and without life, part and not whole, obeyed with such generosity and fineness that, being in this state only half of himself, he consented that from even this half they cut such a principal part. It was as if he had said: Provided obedience remains whole, render the body in pieces and cut as much as you wish. So heroic was the last part of these three acts of obedience with which the perfection of the image was completed, as well as the depiction and illumination of the true and exact exemplar of obedience of the Society.

IX

As for the second aim of Divine Providence in such a gloriously tragic case, we said that it was God's wish to grant Xavier after death the martyrdom

---

74. "At a single word from the Lord, Lazarus came out alive and whole from where he had not been whole." This passage, attributed to Augustine in late medieval and early modern editions, actually comes from a sermon by Chromatius of Aquileia called *De Lazaro Svscitato.* See Sermon 27 in his *Opera,* ed. R. Étaix and J. Lemarié (Turnhout, Belgium: Brepols, 1974), p. 124.

that he had so desired in life. And to understand how continuous and ardent these desires were in the great Apostle, it would suffice to consider the many and manifest occasions that there were for him to have his life taken for the Faith that he preached. Always and everywhere he intrepidly ventured, condemning the false Sects of the Brahmans, of the Bonzes, of the Mohammedans, and all kinds of Heathens, in the presence of the same Priests and Kings who defended them, abominating and calling diabolical the Divinity of the *Camis* and *Fotoques*, and the other monsters that they adored as gods, smashing their idols, and knocking down their Temples.[75] He always lived by miracle, with the one and true God in his mouth and the Standard of Christ publicly in his hands, amid so many Nations, some so tenacious in their superstitions, others so presumptuous in their science, and all of them so barbarous and brutish. This that I say would be enough to understand how ardent Xavier's desires for martyrdom were. But the Saint himself declared it after he was dead, when he pulled Father Marcello Mastrilli from the throat of death in Naples, in the words of the vow that he dictated to him, and that all those present heard, promising to go to Japan and to suffer martyrdom for the Faith, adding: As I have always wished and never could attain.[76] From here follows that what Xavier suffered in his dead body was not involuntary, but truly by his will, like the thrust of the lance into Christ dead on the Cross was by prediction and prior acceptance.

What kind of martyrdom was it, then, of Xavier's dead body? I say the most perfect. In the three Martyrs that the Church celebrates in the three days following the Birth of the Redeemer, Saint Bernard distinguishes with skillful insight three kinds of martyrdom: In Saint Stephen, martyrdom with desire and with blood; in Saint John, martyrdom without blood and with desire; in the Holy Innocents, martyrdom without desire but

---

75. Vieira refers to Xavier's confrontations with representatives of Hinduism, Islam, Buddhism, and Shinto. His *Camis* and *Fotoques* are *kami* and *hotoke*, Shinto and Buddhist deities, respectively.

76. The miraculous healing of Marcello Mastrilli (1603–1637) at Naples in January 1634 was recounted in several contemporary publications. According to the story, Xavier appeared to the moribund young man and dictated his missionary vows to him. While these stories tell how Mastrilli mentioned Xavier's name at the end of the formula and how Mastrilli vowed to spill his blood for the faith in India, they only contain Vieira's phrase in spirit. See Garcia, *Vida y Milagros*, pp. 449–451, and, for example, Ignatius Stafford, *Historia da la Celestial Vocacion, Missiones apostolicas, y Gloriosa Muerte del Padre Marcelo Francisco Mastrili* (Lisbon: António Álvares, 1639), pp. 5–12.

with blood.[77] The martyrdom of Xavier was not like that of the Innocents, because he had a prior desire that they could not have had. Nor was it like that of Saint John, because it had the blood that he lacked. It was therefore like that of Saint Stephen, in which the blood perfected the desire, and the desire the blood. Was it in any other way perfect? Yes. Because in Saint Stephen's martyrdom out of hatred of the Faith, the martyrdom was enveloped in hatred and in the executors' sin. And in Xavier's martyrdom out of obedience, neither hatred nor sin intervened, only love and merit. Xavier's martyrdom resembled what would have been Isaac's, had it been accomplished. Isaac the Martyr, and the most beloved, the father the executor, or pious Tyrant, and the one who most loved him. Thus were all of those who were involved in Xavier's martyrdom. The Pontiff with love, the General with love, the Priests of India, like Abraham, with love, and Xavier, the sufferer like Isaac, not only loved, but because he was greatly loved. There was no more pure, nor more decanted martyrdom, even if that of Christ enters the count, Martyr of obedience though He was: *Factus obediens usque ad mortem*.[78] Because His Cup did not lack the dregs of hatred and of sin either: *Verum tamen fex ejus non est exinanita*.[79] For this, the Lord again repeated the same Sacrifice, and consecrated the same blood in the Sacrament of the Altar, where the Prophet calls it, *Vindemia defecata*;[80] because the hatred of those who spilled it in the Cup of the Passion were the dregs, and these were decanted by the pure love with which the most loving Redeemer left Himself in the Cup of the Sacrament and which He gave us to drink.

It may appear, however, that God was not pleased with this martyrdom of Xavier's body, not only because of the prodigious tremors that preceded it, but because afterward something remarkable, and much remarked, happened: All of the six Priests who were involved in the execution died within six months. And the brother who was the most immediate and principal executor went blind and, although he lived many years, died blind.[81] These were therefore demonstrations that God did not approve the martyrdom. I respond that God wanted and ordered one thing and the other, both for

---

77. This distinction is made in Bernard of Clairvaux's *Sermo in Navitate SS. Innocentium*, section 1.

78. Philippians 2:8, "Becoming obedient unto death."

79. Psalm 74:9, "But the dregs thereof are not emptied."

80. Isaiah 25:6, "Wine purified from the lees."

81. These details come from Garcia, *Vida y Milagros*, p. 321.

the greater glory of Xavier, and I prove it not with one, but with infinite examples. What thing is more common and wondrous among almost all Martyrs than for God to free them from the claws of Lions and Tigers, and from the fury of the elements on the sea and in the fire? And nevertheless He did not free them from the blades of swords in the hands of men. And why? The first reason is, as Author of nature, so as to not violate the juris-diction of free will that is only found in men, and not in beasts or in the elements. The second is, as Author of grace, so as to honor the Saints with the miracles and their reverence, and with the execution by others not to cheat them of their crowns. This is how the most learned Théophile solidly resolves this so controverted question, and I say the same about our case.[82] Where obedience was not blame, the demonstrations of God, even if they were rigorous, could not be punishment. But Divine Providence did not refrain from making them, and so publicly and notoriously, for two aims. The first for the greater honor and glory of Xavier, and example of the respect and veneration with which He wants his relics to be revered. The second to satisfy the desires for martyrdom with which the Saint burned in life; and after death to crown him with these new laurels or to dress him with this new stole, as we read was given to the Martyrs in Heaven who asked for a new satisfaction for their blood. Finally, as a last and miracu-lous confirmation of all that I have philosophized about the separation of Xavier's arm, pay very, very close attention to the mighty Angel, the figure of the same saint who, having two feet that served as the bases for the two columns, is described with no more than one arm: *Et in manu ejus libellum apertum.*[83]

X

Here ends the part of the prodigious tragedy of Xavier's dead body and severed arm that was played out on land. Now let us look briefly, since time does not permit more, at the second part, which had the sea for its stage. The holy arm was embarked at Goa and for a second time ripped from the Holy body, a separation in which I cannot help imagining it with great

---

82. Vieira invokes Théophile Raynaud (1583–1663), a French Jesuit who wrote extensively on theological questions, who is cited by Garcia. This particular argument appears to be derived from Raynaud's *De Martyrio per Pestem ad martyrium improprium, & proprium vulgare comparato, Disquitio Theologica* (Lyon: Jacques Cardon, 1630), pp. 160–161. See also Garcia, *Vida y Milagros*, p. 421.

83. Revelation 10:2, "And in his hand a little book open."

longing and as if speaking mutely, *Non aliter dolui, quam si mea membra relinquam.*[84] The embarkation and escort for such an inestimable treasure should have been the greatest and most powerful Armada that ever left India, yet since it went better defended on its own, the government of Heaven allowed (how the government of earth allowed it, I do not know) that it should be embarked on a caravel. By that time we were no longer such lords of those seas as in Xavier's time. And a few days into the journey, the Sailors, not the Soldiers since there were none, saw that a Dutch Corsair was following in their tracks.[85] Would that I could interject here how it was thanks to me that our caravels turned into such powerful and well-armed carracks as the ones which today compose our fleets. It so happened that when King Dom João IV of ever glorious memory was at Alcantara on the eve of the feast of Saint John, I offered to his Majesty an opinion about how to celebrate his Saint that night. The opinion was that thirty-nine bonfires be made out of that same number of caravels that could be counted in the river at Lisbon, because caravels, Lord, do not serve our sailors nor those who embark on them more than as schools for fleeing. This is what the ones on that caravel did, and after adding sail upon sail, and tossing into the sea all that could make it lighter, they recognized that the Corsair was approaching and was already so close that it would take the caravel without remedy. At that moment, Father Sebastião Gonçalves, Rector of the Goa Novitiate, remembered to attend to the Sacred relic in his charge. As soon as the powerful arm, the worker of so many marvels, appeared on deck, the Pirate ship with its sails full stopped that very moment, as if it had run aground. And as if all ropes had converted into mooring lines and all the nails into anchors, it moved not one step forward.

I do not remark upon the weakness of the wind and its impulses, with the sails full, and both they and the ship stopped, because all of the winds and even their king, Typhoon, either in blowing or in calming down were used to obeying the gestures of that arm. What I ponder is how the ravenous greed of the Pirate stayed there bound and stuck. Twice Saint Francis Xavier made the Sun stop, once by the prayers of Father Sebastião Vieira

---

84. "I suffered not otherwise than as if I were leaving my limbs behind." Vieira adapts line 73 from Ovid's *Tristia*, Book 1, Part 3; translation based on his *Tristia, Ex Ponto*, trans. A. L. Wheeler, ed. G. P. Goold (Cambridge, Mass.: Harvard University Press, 1924), p. 25.

85. This episode is recounted in Garcia, *Vida y Milagros*, pp. 321–322. Vieira himself claimed to have performed a similar feat in 1662 with a relic of Saint Boniface when a ship upon which he was returning from Brazil was chased by a pirate. See J. L. de Azevedo, *História de António Vieira*, 2 vols. (Lisbon: Livraria Clássica, 1918–1921), vol. 1, pp. 351–352.

while he sailed to Japan, where he died burned alive for the Faith; the other when he was invoked with tears by other sailors in extreme danger due to lack of light.[86] And in both cases repeating the two miracles of the same Sun that are mentioned in Sacred history. The first, as in the time of Hezekiah, with the Sun turning back, because, after setting, it again rose and climbed, persevering above the Horizon as long as was necessary for the ship to reach safety.[87] The second, as in the time of Joshua, when the Sun obeyed his voice, because when it was already racing to hide itself in the West, it was still and immobile while the sailors needed it to conquer the wind and seas, more powerful enemies than the Amorrhites.[88] Now I ask: Which was the greater miracle, that of the voice of Joshua in stalling and stopping the Sun, or that of the mute arm of Xavier in stalling and stopping the Pirate? This question has already been settled, decided by no less than the great Doctor of the Church Saint Ambrose. To understand the verdict it is necessary to posit that when Joshua entered the Promised Land, before conquering the first City, which was Jericho, he announced that no one was to take anything from the spoils of the City upon pain of death, because all of it was consecrated to God, in whose honor it was to be burned. Nevertheless the Sacred Text says that a Soldier named Achan stole some part of the spoils: *Tulit aliquid de anathemate.*[89] This theft was the reason why Joshua's army suffered a defeat in the conquest of the second City called Hai. Considering this, Saint Ambrose now says: *Jesus Nave, qui potuit Solem sistere ne procederet, avaritiam hominum non potuit sistere ne serperet. Ad vocem ejus Sol stetit, avaritia non stetit. Sole itaque stante confecit Jesus triumphum, avaritia procedente pene amisit victoriam.*[90] Joshua was

---

86. These feats are mentioned in Garcia, *Vida y Milagros*, p. 438. While the second miracle is not described in detail by Garcia, that which occurred to Sebastião Vieira is. This Vieira (1574–1634) traveled from Asia to Europe and back on behalf of the Japan mission between 1623 and 1629. Garcia reports that this miracle occurred during Sebastião Vieira's travels in the *Mar de la India*, likely on one of these voyages. He would die a martyr at Edo in 1634.

87. This episode is recounted in Isaiah 38:8, "Behold I will bring again the shadow of the lines, by which it is now gone down in the sun dial of Achaz with the sun, ten lines backward. And the sun returned then lines by the degrees by which it was gone down."

88. And this one is recounted in Joshua 10:12–13, "And he said before them: Move not, O sun, toward Gabaon, nor thou, O moon, toward the valley of Ajalon. And the sun and the moon stood still, till the people revenged themselves of their enemies."

89. Joshua 7:1, "took something of the anathema."

90. "So Joshua the son of Nun, who could stay the sun from setting, could not stay the love of money in man from creeping on. At the sound of his voice, the sun stood still, but the love of money stayed not. When the sun stood still Joshua completed his triumph, but when the

able to stop the Sun, but not to stop the thief's greed. He stopped the Sun, but he did not stop greed. In such a way that, once he stopped the Sun, he perfected the triumph; and not stopping greed, he almost missed victory. And since it is a greater miracle to stop the thief's greed than to stop the Sun's course, for Joshua was able to stop the Sun's course and was not able to stop and hold the thief, a much greater miracle was that of Xavier's arm in stopping this time the thief, his greed, and his ship, than that of stopping the Sun twice.

When the Emperor Caius was sailing in a Fleet of galleys, suddenly the flagship stopped, and the four hundred stout rowers with five rows of oars were of no use to make it move. The cause sought, it was found that the ship was held back by a remora stuck to the rudder. Once it was ripped off and taken aboard, Pliny says that what was most admired about this case was that outside of the vessel the remora had so much strength and virtue, but aboard it had none: *Peculiariter miratum, quomodo adhærens tenuisset, nec idem polleret in navigium receptus.*[91] Let us now compare Xavier's arm, which was the remora of the Corsair, with the remora of Caius, which also came like a pirate.[92] The living remora, the dead arm of Xavier; the remora attached to the rudder, Xavier's arm not touching anything; the remora prevailing over the impulse of so many oars and rowers, Xavier's arm over the sails and the winds. The remora pulled out of the sea lost all of its strength because they took it out of its element, Xavier's arm had the same strength everywhere, because it dominated all of the elements. The remora at last aboard the galley was not able from where it was to hold back that same galley, and Xavier's arm inside the vessel was able from where it was to stop the other ship where it was not.

But this is well worth noting: That arm of Xavier traveled in that same ship before the Pirate sighted or followed it; why then did it not perform this miracle until after the box in which it was enclosed appeared on deck? For that very fact. The Ark of the Covenant appeared in the Jordan, and at

---

love of money went on, he almost lost his victory." In Ambrose, *On the Duties of the Clergy*, Book 2, chapter 26, translated in *A Select Library of Nicene and Post-Nicene Fathers of the Christian Church*, 2nd ser., ed. Philip Schaff and Henry Wace, 14 vols. (New York: Christian Literature Company, 1890–1900), vol. 10, p. 63.

91. "That what astonished him in particular was how the fish had stopped him by sticking to the outside, yet when inside the ship it had not the same power." In Pliny's *Natural History*, Book 32, chapter 1, lines 5–6; in his *Natural History*, trans. W. H. S. Jones et al., 10 vols. (Cambridge, Mass.: Harvard University Press, 1963), vol. 8, p. 467.

92. Vieira says *vinha de corso*, an expression that has its roots in the term *corsair*.

the same spot the upper part of the River stopped and the lower part fled to the sea. David now asks it: *Quid est tibi mare quod fugisti, & tu Jordanis quia conversus es retrorsum?*[93] What reason did you have, Jordan, to stop, and you, sea, to flee? Here we have already one stopped, another fleeing, as in our case. And were I to ask it the same question, the response would also be the same: *A facie Domini à facie Dei Jacob.*[94] There one stopped, and the other fled, upon the appearance of the Ark in which God was. And here one stopped and the other fled, upon the appearance of the box in which Xavier's arm was.

Fleeing this way (which is the first time that fleeing was valor, and flight triumph), the fortunate wood that carried the Sacred deposit navigated happily for the rest of the voyage; and making port first in the Tagus, and later in the Tiber, it was received and celebrated by Rome with the solemnity and applause that such a desired expectation promised. And so the two arms of Xavier reached, while still in this world, that glory which the most proud ambition of Alexander the Great did not come to imagine or crave. The Ambassadors of the Scythians said to him, as Curtius mentions: *Si Dij habitum corporis tui aviditati animi parem esse voluissent orbis te non caperet: altera manu Orientem, altera Occidentem contingeres.*[95] If the gods, o King, wanted to give you a body equal to your spirit, you would not fit in the world; because with one arm your hand would reach the Orient, and with the other the Occident. And is this not what with immense extension Xavier's two arms embrace today? One in the Orient at Goa, head of Christendom in Asia, and the other in the Occident at Rome, head of Christendom and of the world. So it is, and we do not yet know what will be. I only know that a small relic of this arm, taken to the City of Mechelen in Flanders, worked so many and such continual miracles that they no longer fit in books.[96] And if this is what a small piece of that arm can do, there may come a time when Rome and the world will see what it can do whole.

---

93. Psalm 113:5, "What ailed thee, O thou sea, that thou didst flee: and thou, O Jordan, that thou wast turned back?"

94. Psalm 113:7, "At the presence of the Lord . . . at the presence of the God of Jacob."

95. "If the gods had willed that your bodily stature should be equal to your greed, the world would not contain you; with the one hand you would touch the rising, with the other the setting sun." In Quintus Curtius, *History of Alexander*, Book 7, lines 12–13; in his *History of Alexander*, trans. John C. Rolfe, 2 vols. (Cambridge, Mass.: Harvard University Press, 1946), vol. 2, p. 201.

96. So claims Garcia, *Vida y Milagros*, p. 467.

XI

With these hopes I have finished our Novena, and I promise that they are very firm and certain, that Saint Francis Xavier will not be ungrateful to those who serve and venerate him with so much devotion, pomp, solemnity, and expense. And although it is all done with such noble and disinterested liberality, the Saint is so excellent and his responses so punctual that he will not allow anything to be lost on him. When his dead body arrived in Malacca, there was a devotee who, instead of a candle, lit a taper in front of the ark of the Sacred deposit. This taper, which at best could last twenty-four hours, lasted always lit for eighteen days and eighteen nights, and afterward weighed more than it weighed before.[97] The only thing that I remark upon is that the days and nights were eighteen, which makes two Novenas; so that it be understood that whatever is used in Xavier's Novenas, if it is fire, it does not burn, if it is wax, it does not melt, and if it is value, it does not diminish but augments itself.

---

97. This story is found ibid., p. 314.

Index

CPSIA information can be obtained
at www.ICGtesting.com
Printed in the USA
BVHW032239070122
625767BV00002B/2